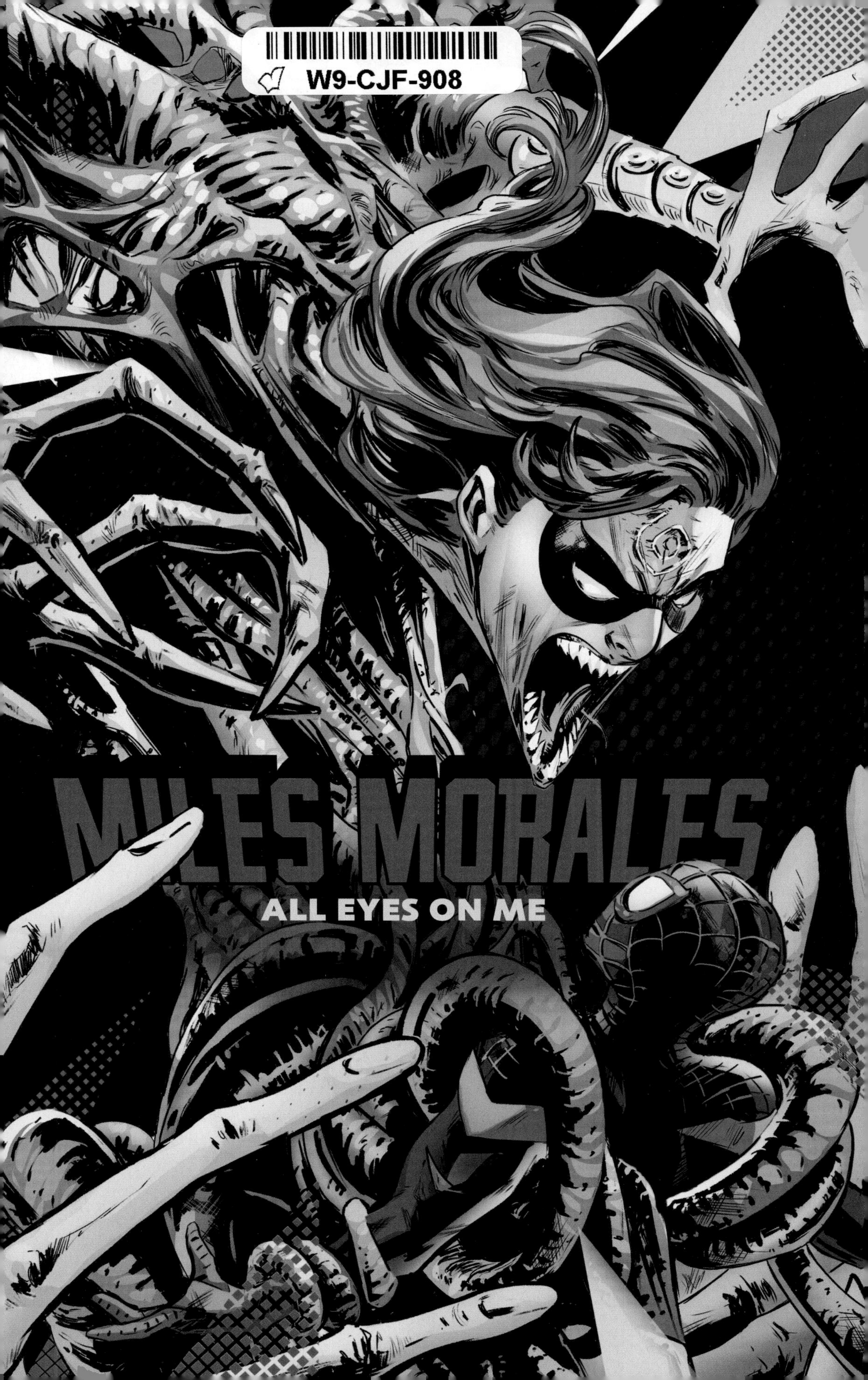
MILES MORALES
ALL EYES ON ME

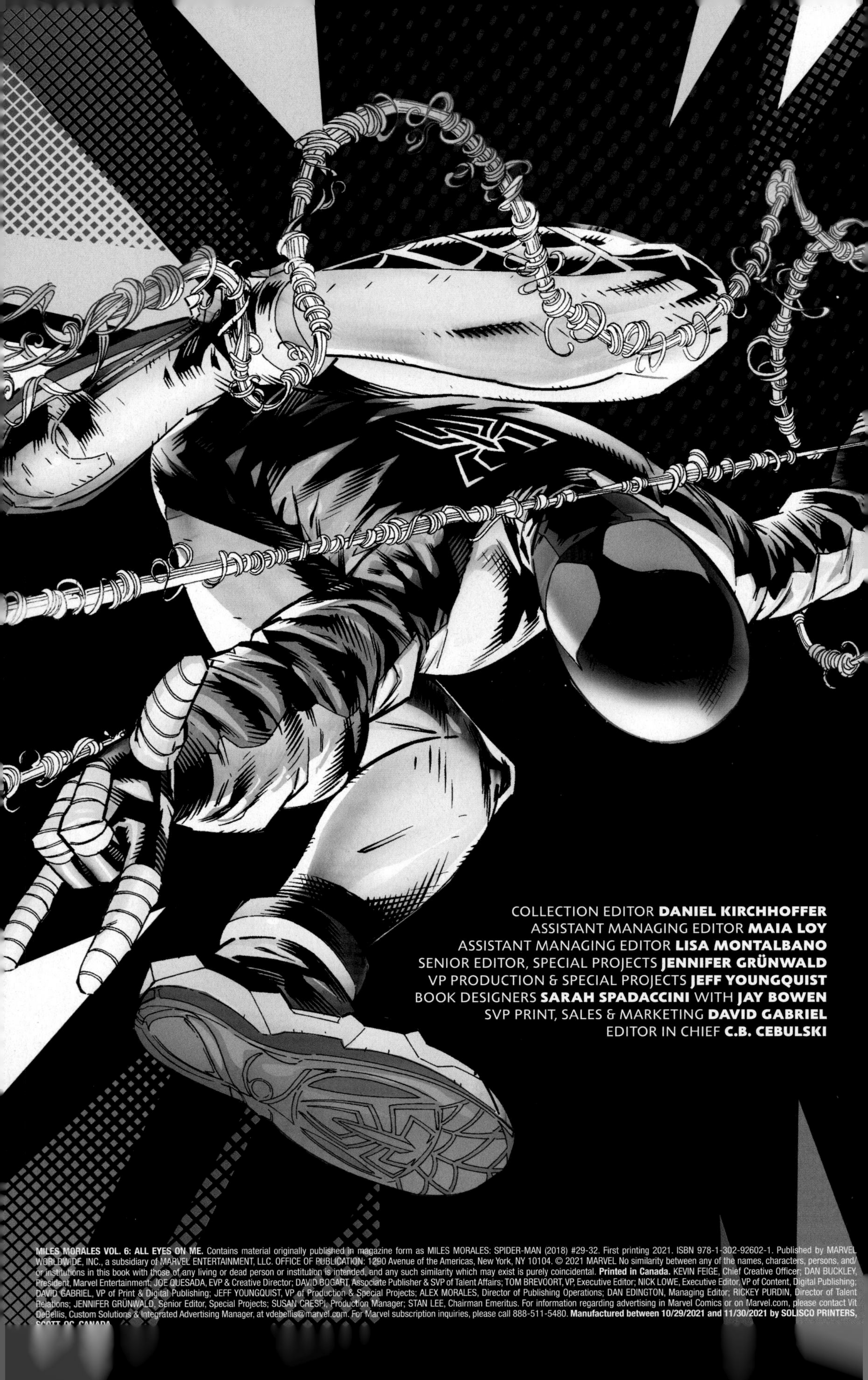

COLLECTION EDITOR **DANIEL KIRCHHOFFER**
ASSISTANT MANAGING EDITOR **MAIA LOY**
ASSISTANT MANAGING EDITOR **LISA MONTALBANO**
SENIOR EDITOR, SPECIAL PROJECTS **JENNIFER GRÜNWALD**
VP PRODUCTION & SPECIAL PROJECTS **JEFF YOUNGQUIST**
BOOK DESIGNERS **SARAH SPADACCINI** WITH **JAY BOWEN**
SVP PRINT, SALES & MARKETING **DAVID GABRIEL**
EDITOR IN CHIEF **C.B. CEBULSKI**

MILES MORALES VOL. 6: ALL EYES ON ME. Contains material originally published in magazine form as MILES MORALES: SPIDER-MAN (2018) #29-32. First printing 2021. ISBN 978-1-302-92602-1. Published by MARVEL WORLDWIDE, INC., a subsidiary of MARVEL ENTERTAINMENT, LLC. OFFICE OF PUBLICATION: 1290 Avenue of the Americas, New York, NY 10104.

Printed in Canada. KEVIN FEIGE, Chief Creative Officer; DAN BUCKLEY, President, Marvel Entertainment; JOE QUESADA, EVP & Creative Director; DAVID BOGART, Associate Publisher & SVP of Talent Affairs; TOM BREVOORT, VP, Executive Editor; NICK LOWE, Executive Editor, VP of Content, Digital Publishing; DAVID GABRIEL, VP of Print & Digital Publishing; JEFF YOUNGQUIST, VP of Production & Special Projects; ALEX MORALES, Director of Publishing Operations; DAN EDINGTON, Managing Editor; RICKEY PURDIN, Director of Talent Relations; JENNIFER GRÜNWALD, Senior Editor, Special Projects; SUSAN CRESPI, Production Manager; STAN LEE, Chairman Emeritus. For information regarding advertising in Marvel Comics or on Marvel.com, please contact Vit DeBellis, Custom Solutions & Integrated Advertising Manager, at vdebellis@marvel.com. For Marvel subscription inquiries, please call 888-511-5480. **Manufactured between 10/29/2021 and 11/30/2021 by SOLISCO PRINTERS, SCOTT, QC, CANADA.**

MILES MORALES

ALL EYES ON ME

Saladin Ahmed
WRITER

Christopher Allen (#29, #31-32)
& Carmen Carnero (#30)
ARTISTS

David Curiel (#29), Erick Arciniega (#30)
& Guru-eFX (#31-32)
COLOR ARTISTS

"THE BEST PART"

| Phil Lord, Christopher Miller, Kemp Powers & Jeff Loveness WRITERS | Sara Pichelli ARTIST | Rachelle Rosenberg COLOR ARTIST |

"DON'T RUN JUX"

| Cody Ziglar WRITER | Anthony Piper ARTIST |

VC's Cory Petit
LETTERER

Taurin Clarke
COVER ART

Shannon Andrews Ballesteros
& Tom Groneman
ASSISTANT EDITORS

Nick Lowe
EDITOR

SPIDER-MAN CREATED BY Stan Lee & Steve Ditko

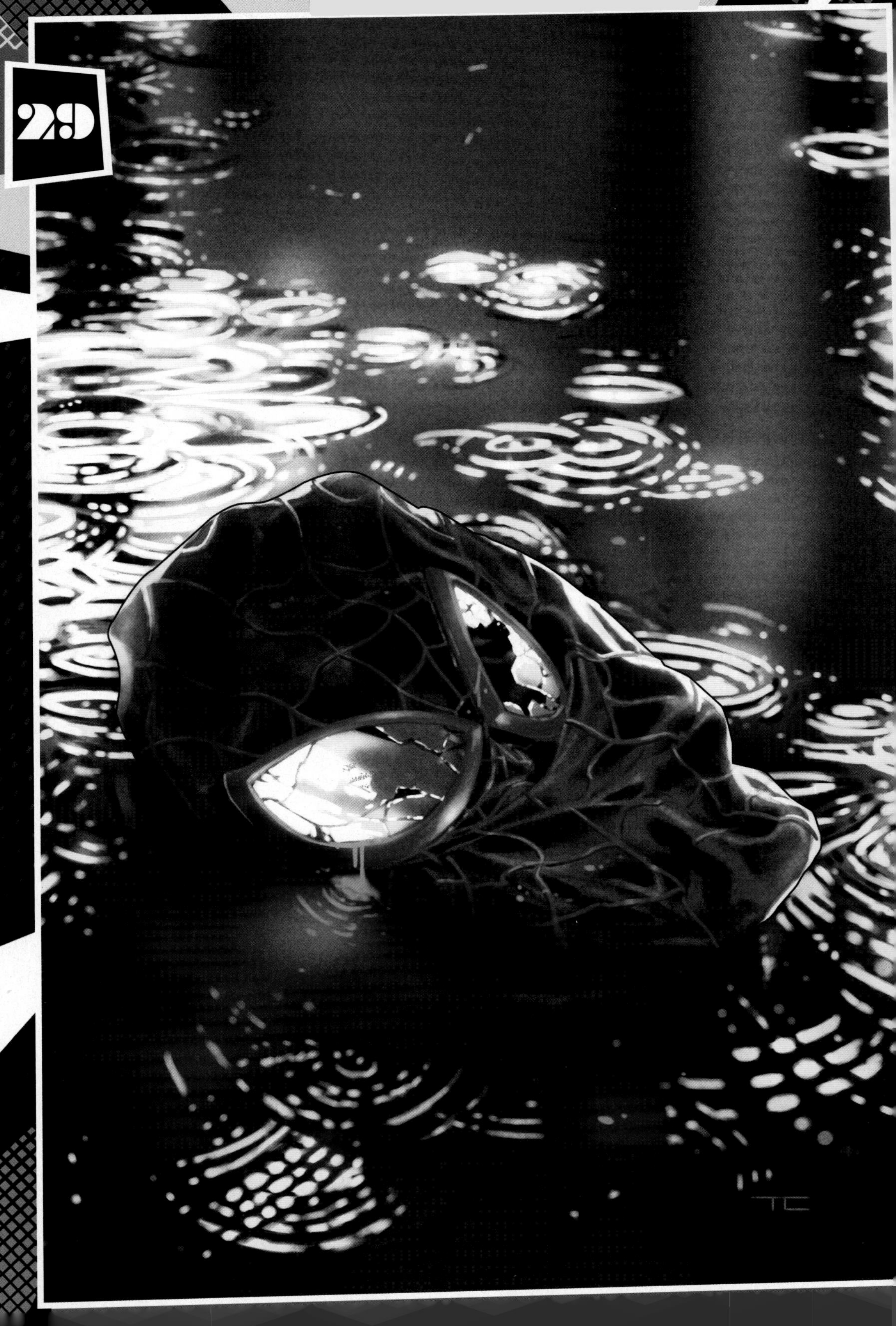
29

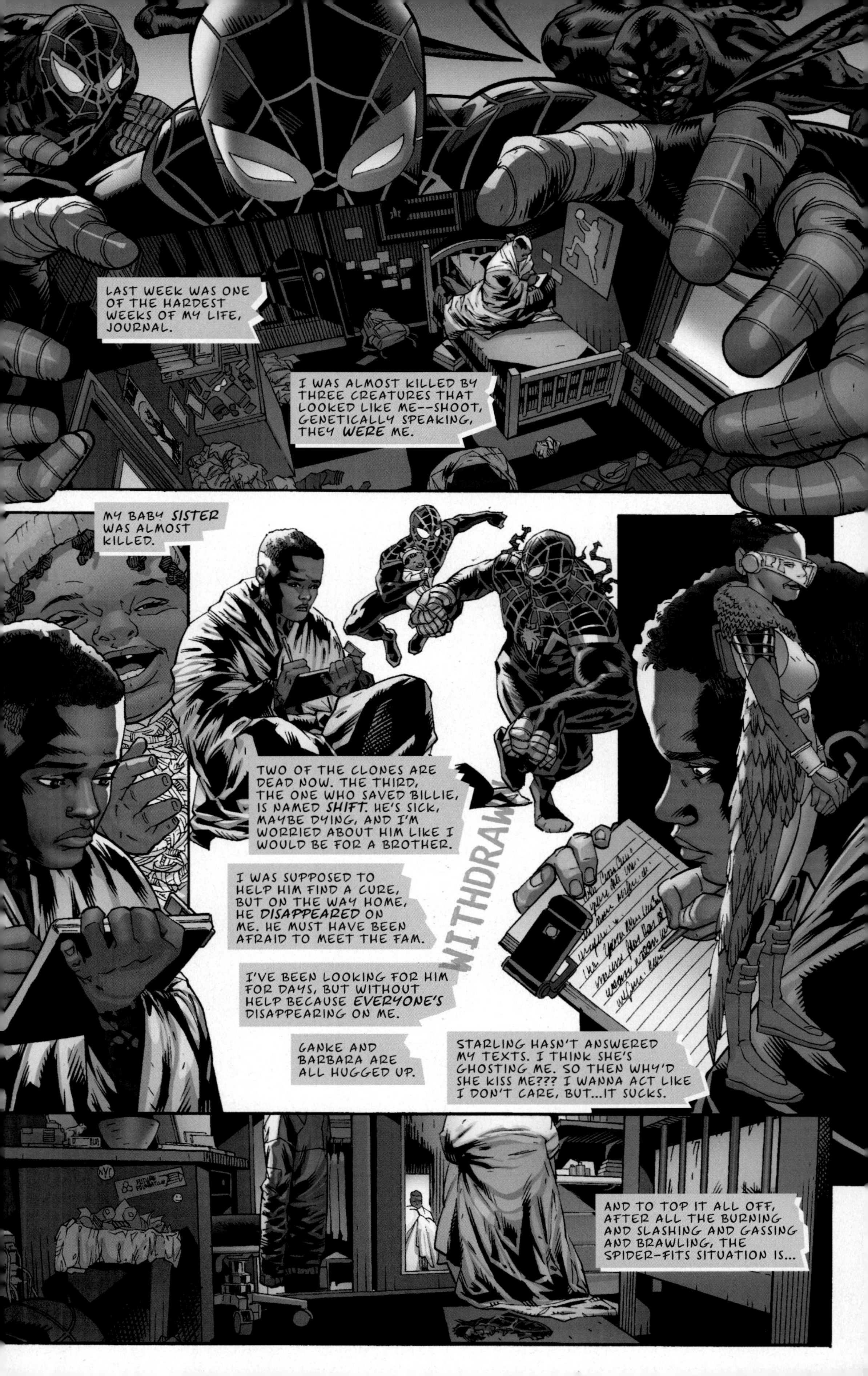
LAST WEEK WAS ONE OF THE HARDEST WEEKS OF MY LIFE, JOURNAL.
I WAS ALMOST KILLED BY THREE CREATURES THAT LOOKED LIKE ME--SHOOT, GENETICALLY SPEAKING, THEY WERE ME.
MY BABY SISTER WAS ALMOST KILLED.
TWO OF THE CLONES ARE DEAD NOW. THE THIRD, THE ONE WHO SAVED BILLIE, IS NAMED SHIFT. HE'S SICK, MAYBE DYING, AND I'M WORRIED ABOUT HIM LIKE I WOULD BE FOR A BROTHER.
I WAS SUPPOSED TO HELP HIM FIND A CURE, BUT ON THE WAY HOME, HE DISAPPEARED ON ME. HE MUST HAVE BEEN AFRAID TO MEET THE FAM.
I'VE BEEN LOOKING FOR HIM FOR DAYS, BUT WITHOUT HELP BECAUSE EVERYONE'S DISAPPEARING ON ME.
GANKE AND BARBARA ARE ALL HUGGED UP.
STARLING HASN'T ANSWERED MY TEXTS. I THINK SHE'S GHOSTING ME. SO THEN WHY'D SHE KISS ME??? I WANNA ACT LIKE I DON'T CARE, BUT...IT SUCKS.
AND TO TOP IT ALL OFF, AFTER ALL THE BURNING AND SLASHING AND GASSING AND BRAWLING, THE SPIDER-FITS SITUATION IS...

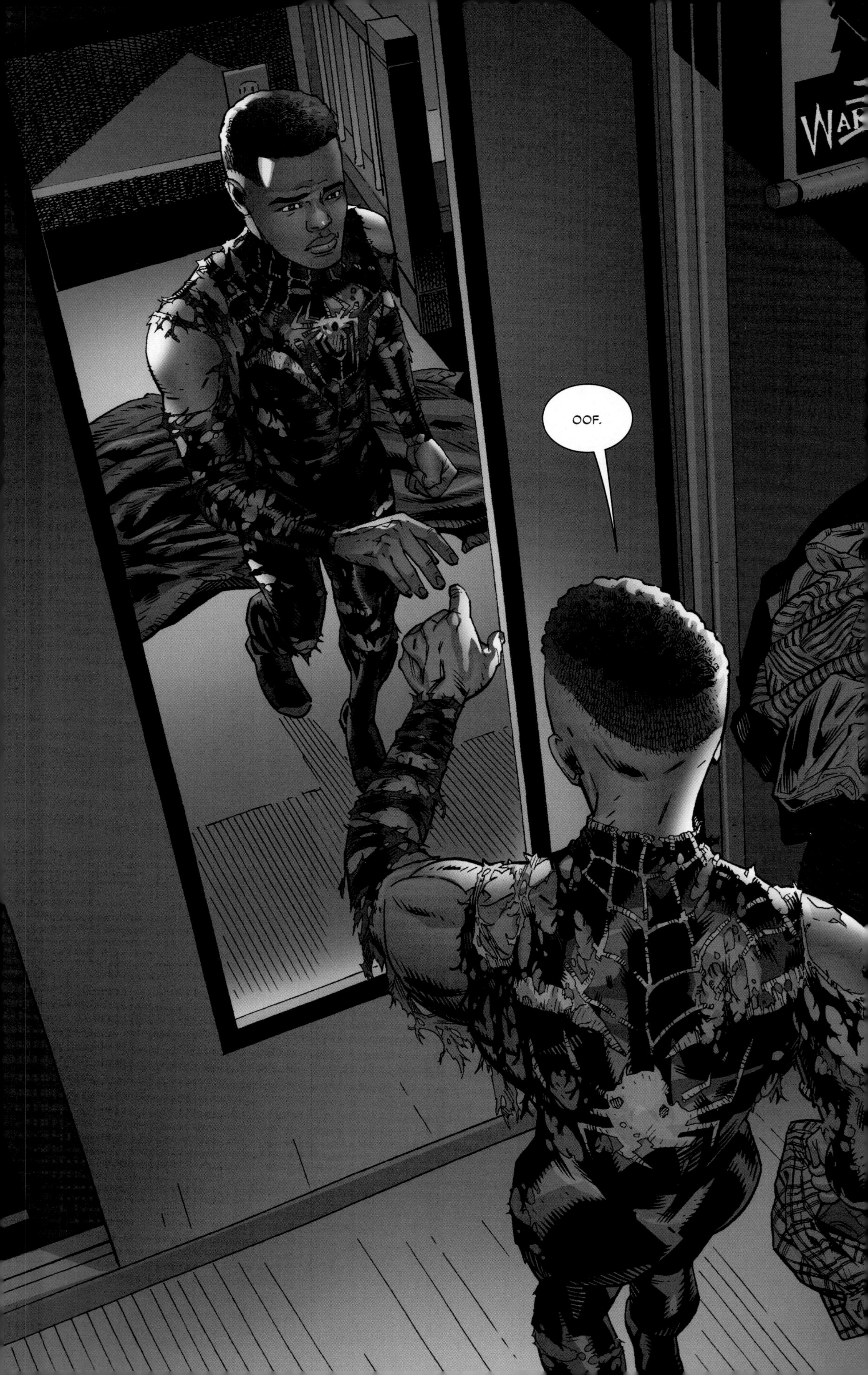
OOF.

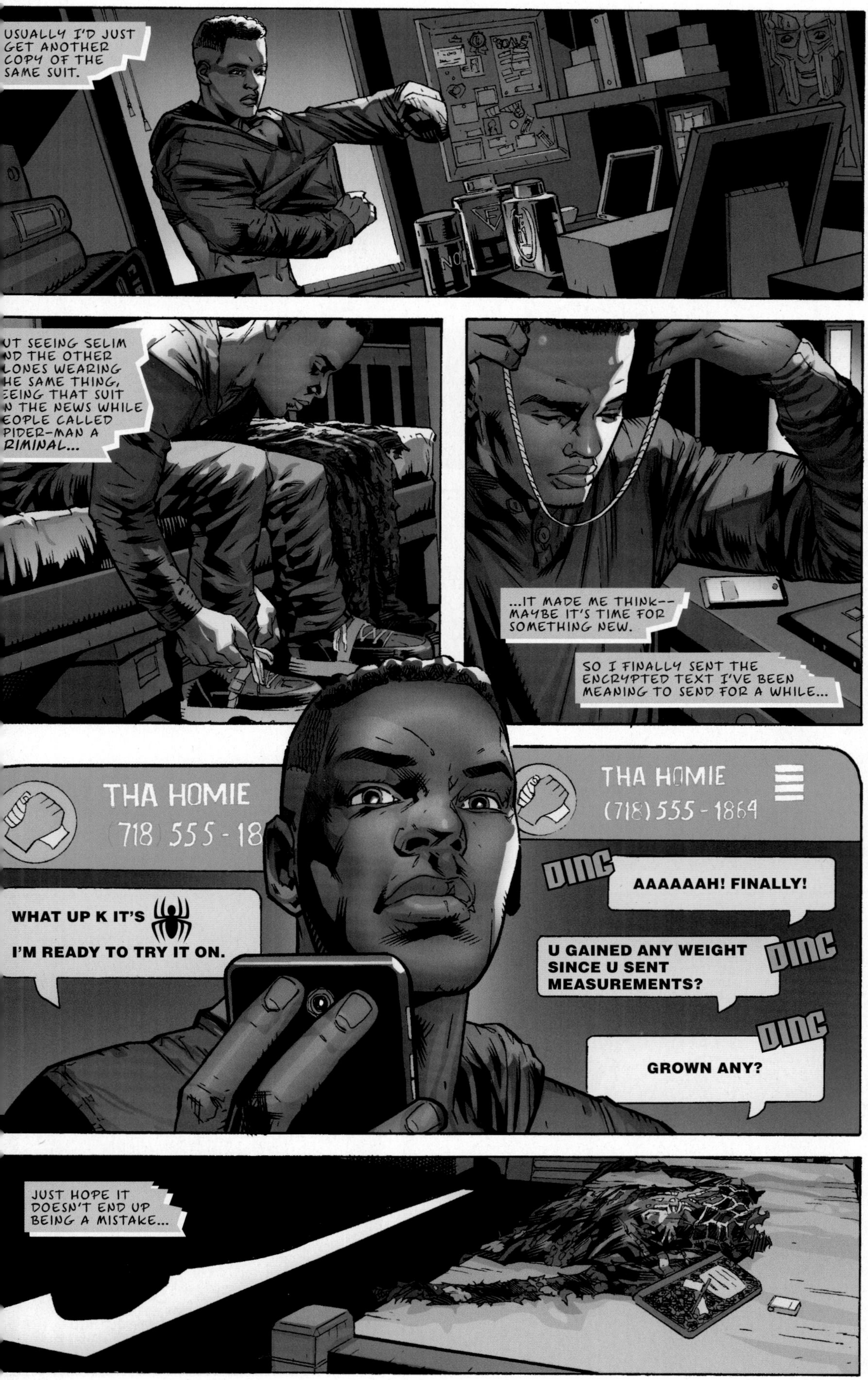

USUALLY I'D JUST GET ANOTHER COPY OF THE SAME SUIT.
UT SEEING SELIM ND THE OTHER LONES WEARING HE SAME THING, EEING THAT SUIT N THE NEWS WHILE EOPLE CALLED PIDER-MAN A RIMINAL...
...IT MADE ME THINK-- MAYBE IT'S TIME FOR SOMETHING NEW.
SO I FINALLY SENT THE ENCRYPTED TEXT I'VE BEEN MEANING TO SEND FOR A WHILE...
THA HOMIE
718 555 - 18
WHAT UP K IT'S
I'M READY TO TRY IT ON.
THA HOMIE
(718) 555 - 1864
DING
AAAAAAH! FINALLY!
U GAINED ANY WEIGHT SINCE U SENT MEASUREMENTS?
DING
DING
GROWN ANY?
JUST HOPE IT DOESN'T END UP BEING A MISTAKE...

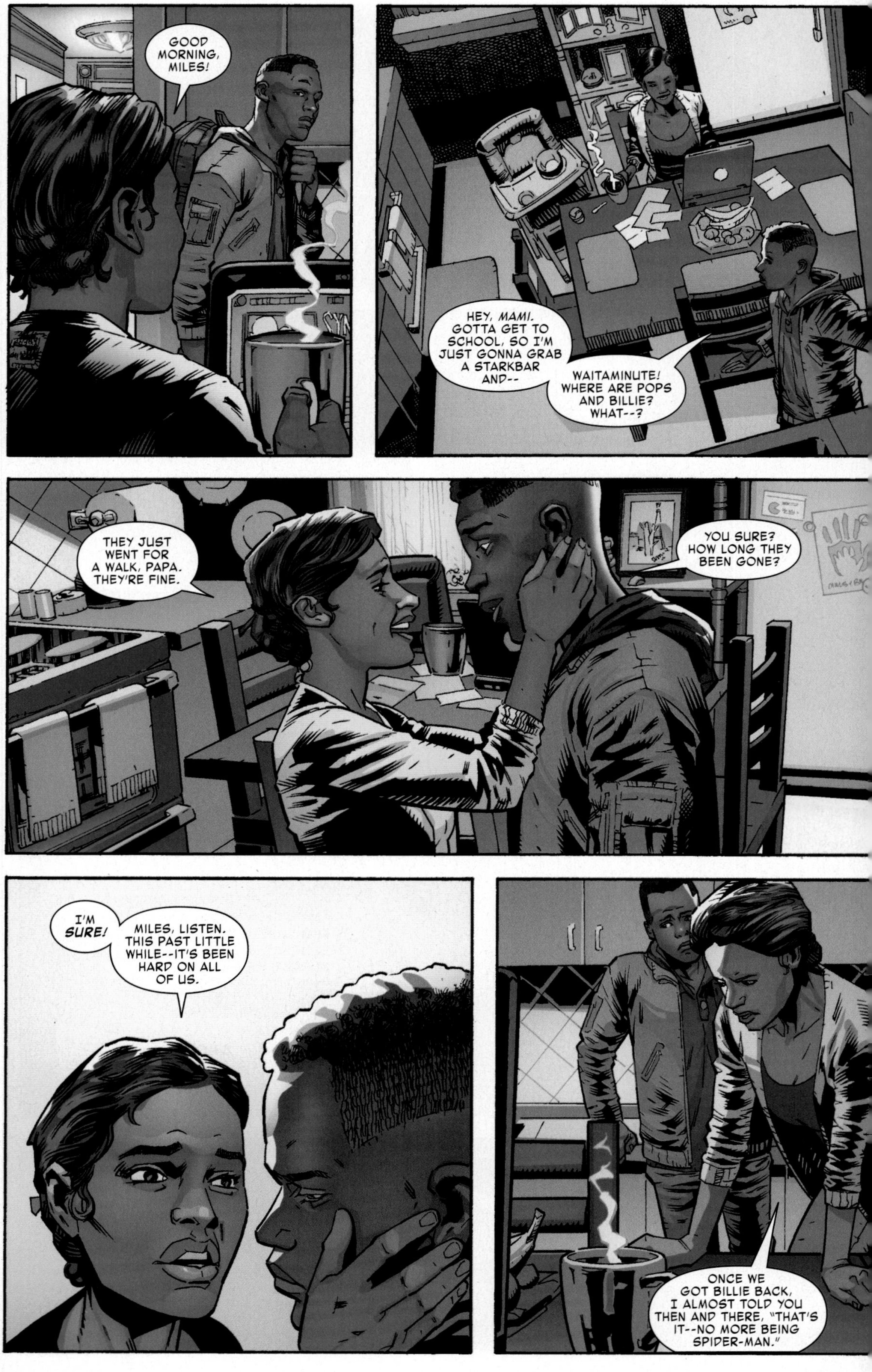
GOOD MORNING, MILES!
HEY, MAMI. GOTTA GET TO SCHOOL, SO I'M JUST GONNA GRAB A STARKBAR AND--
WAITAMINUTE! WHERE ARE POPS AND BILLIE? WHAT--?
THEY JUST WENT FOR A WALK, PAPA. THEY'RE FINE.
YOU SURE? HOW LONG THEY BEEN GONE?
I'M SURE!
MILES, LISTEN. THIS PAST LITTLE WHILE--IT'S BEEN HARD ON ALL OF US.
ONCE WE GOT BILLIE BACK, I ALMOST TOLD YOU THEN AND THERE, "THAT'S IT--NO MORE BEING SPIDER-MAN."

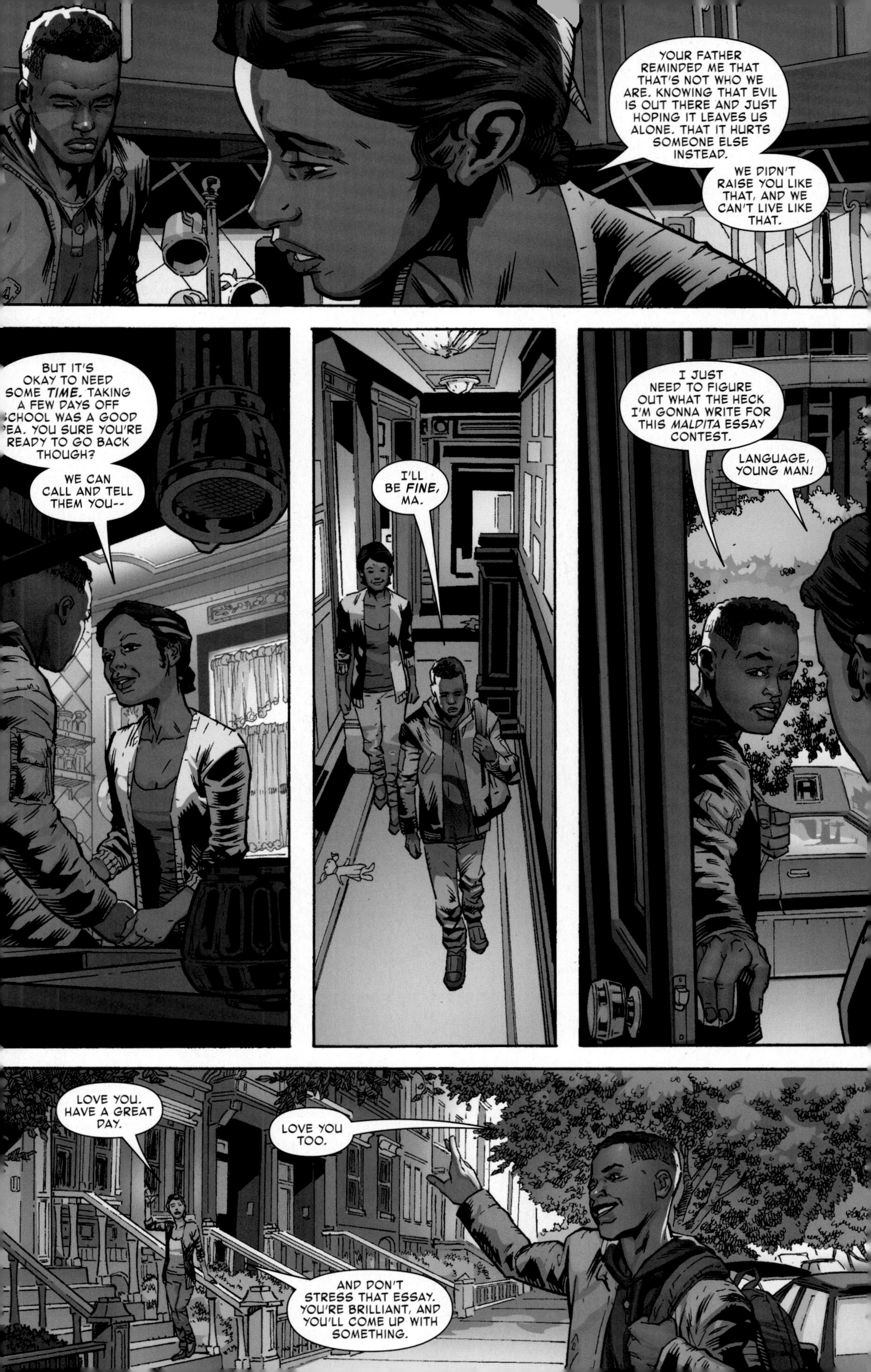

YOUR FATHER REMINDED ME THAT THAT'S NOT WHO WE ARE. KNOWING THAT EVIL IS OUT THERE AND JUST HOPING IT LEAVES US ALONE. THAT IT HURTS SOMEONE ELSE INSTEAD.
WE DIDN'T RAISE YOU LIKE THAT, AND WE CAN'T LIVE LIKE THAT.
BUT IT'S OKAY TO NEED SOME *TIME.* TAKING A FEW DAYS OFF SCHOOL WAS A GOOD IDEA. YOU SURE YOU'RE READY TO GO BACK THOUGH?
WE CAN CALL AND TELL THEM YOU--
I'LL BE *FINE,* MA.
I JUST NEED TO FIGURE OUT WHAT THE HECK I'M GONNA WRITE FOR THIS *MALDITA* ESSAY CONTEST.
LANGUAGE, YOUNG MAN!
LOVE YOU. HAVE A GREAT DAY.
LOVE YOU TOO.
AND DON'T STRESS THAT ESSAY. YOU'RE BRILLIANT, AND YOU'LL COME UP WITH SOMETHING.

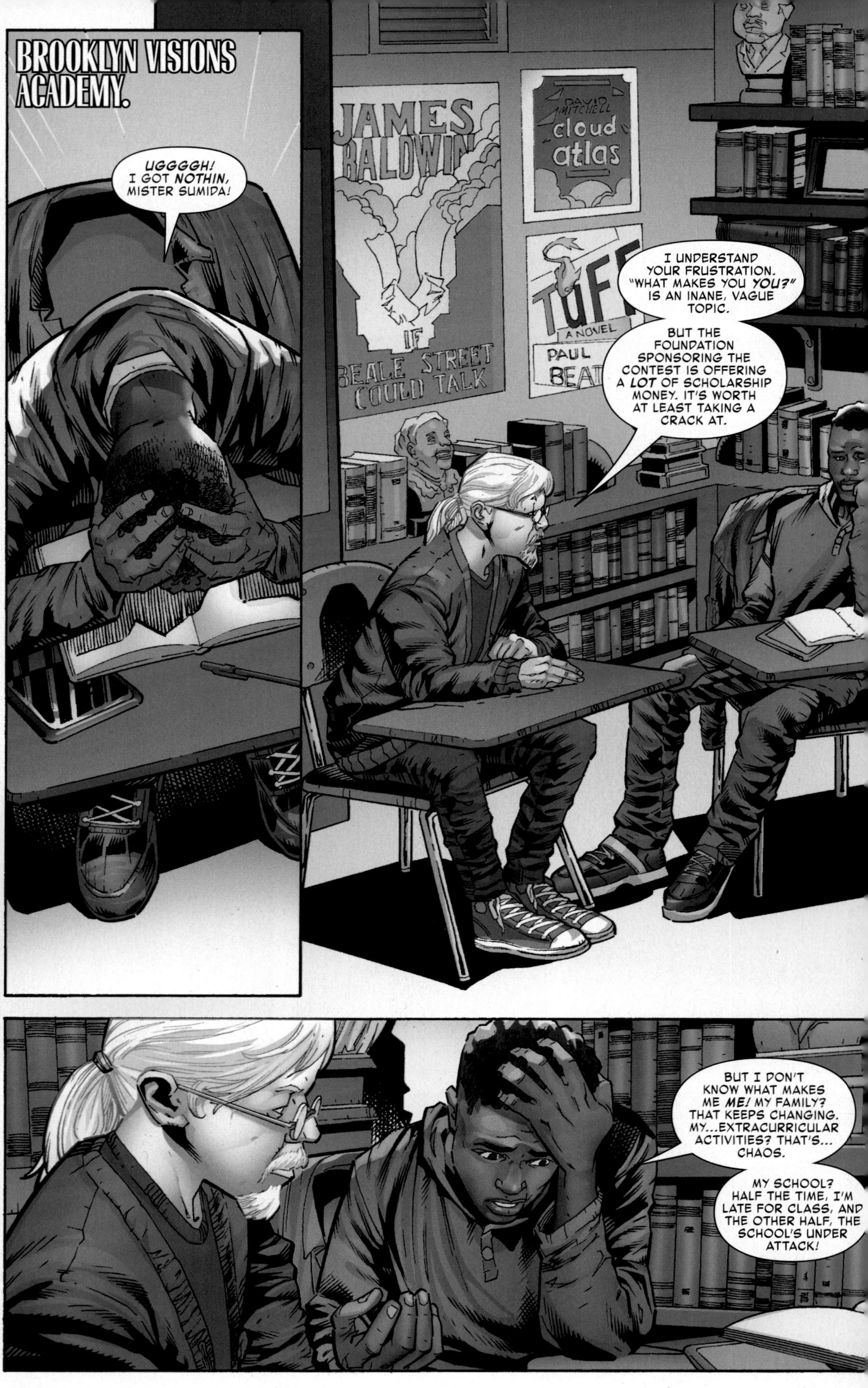
BROOKLYN VISIONS ACADEMY.
UGGGGH! I GOT NOTHIN, MISTER SUMIDA!
DAVID MITCHELL cloud atlas
IF BEALE STREET COULD TALK
A NOVEL
I UNDERSTAND YOUR FRUSTRATION. "WHAT MAKES YOU YOU?" IS AN INANE, VAGUE TOPIC.
BUT THE FOUNDATION SPONSORING THE CONTEST IS OFFERING A LOT OF SCHOLARSHIP MONEY. IT'S WORTH AT LEAST TAKING A CRACK AT.
BUT I DON'T KNOW WHAT MAKES ME ME! MY FAMILY? THAT KEEPS CHANGING. MY...EXTRACURRICULAR ACTIVITIES? THAT'S... CHAOS.
MY SCHOOL? HALF THE TIME, I'M LATE FOR CLASS, AND THE OTHER HALF, THE SCHOOL'S UNDER ATTACK!

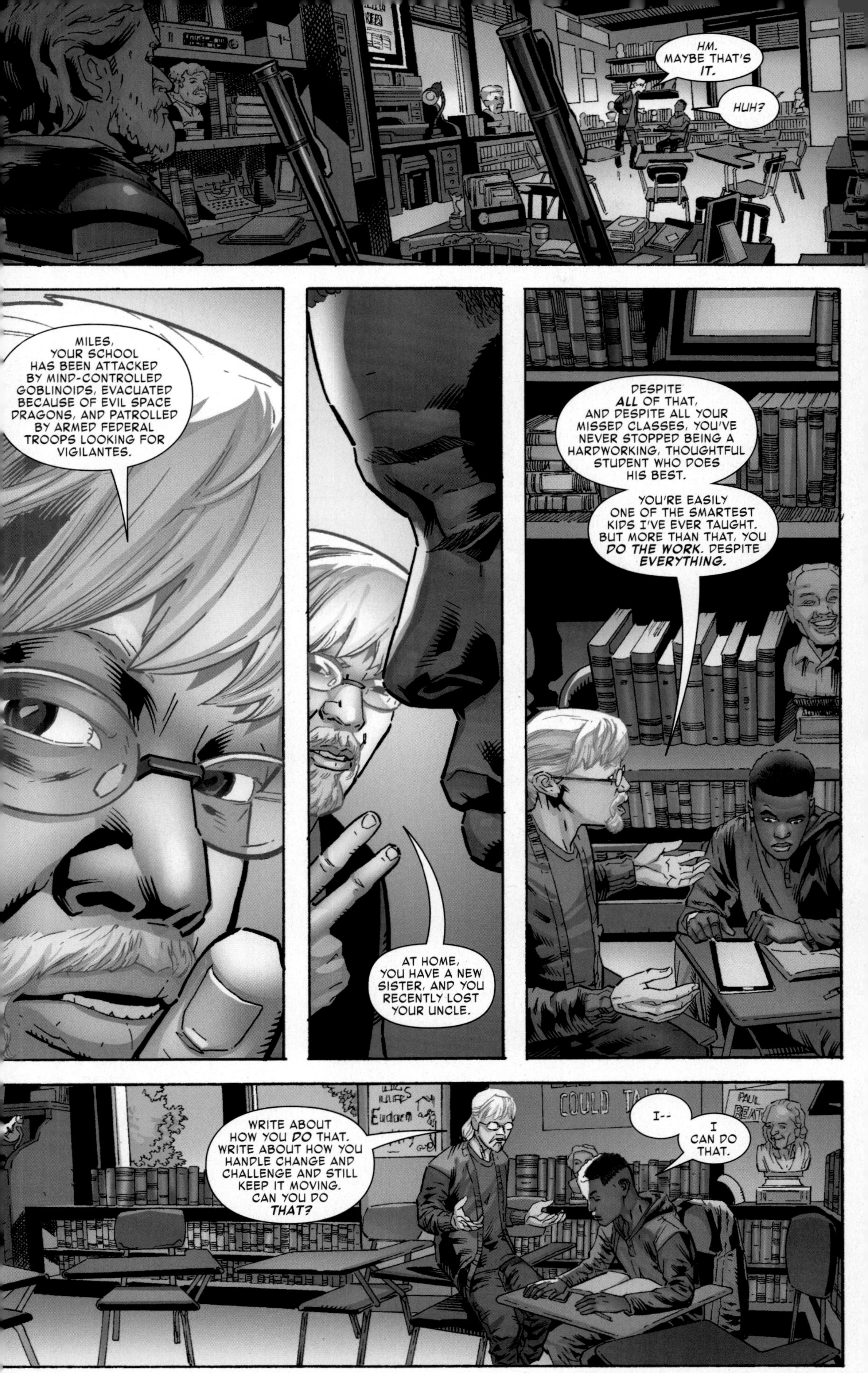
HM. MAYBE THAT'S *IT.*
HUH?
MILES, YOUR SCHOOL HAS BEEN ATTACKED BY MIND-CONTROLLED GOBLINOIDS, EVACUATED BECAUSE OF EVIL SPACE DRAGONS, AND PATROLLED BY ARMED FEDERAL TROOPS LOOKING FOR VIGILANTES.
AT HOME, YOU HAVE A NEW SISTER, AND YOU RECENTLY LOST YOUR UNCLE.
DESPITE *ALL* OF THAT, AND DESPITE ALL YOUR MISSED CLASSES, YOU'VE NEVER STOPPED BEING A HARDWORKING, THOUGHTFUL STUDENT WHO DOES HIS BEST.
YOU'RE EASILY ONE OF THE SMARTEST KIDS I'VE EVER TAUGHT. BUT MORE THAN THAT, YOU *DO THE WORK.* DESPITE *EVERYTHING.*
WRITE ABOUT HOW YOU *DO* THAT. WRITE ABOUT HOW YOU HANDLE CHANGE AND CHALLENGE AND STILL KEEP IT MOVING. CAN YOU DO *THAT?*
I--
I CAN DO THAT.

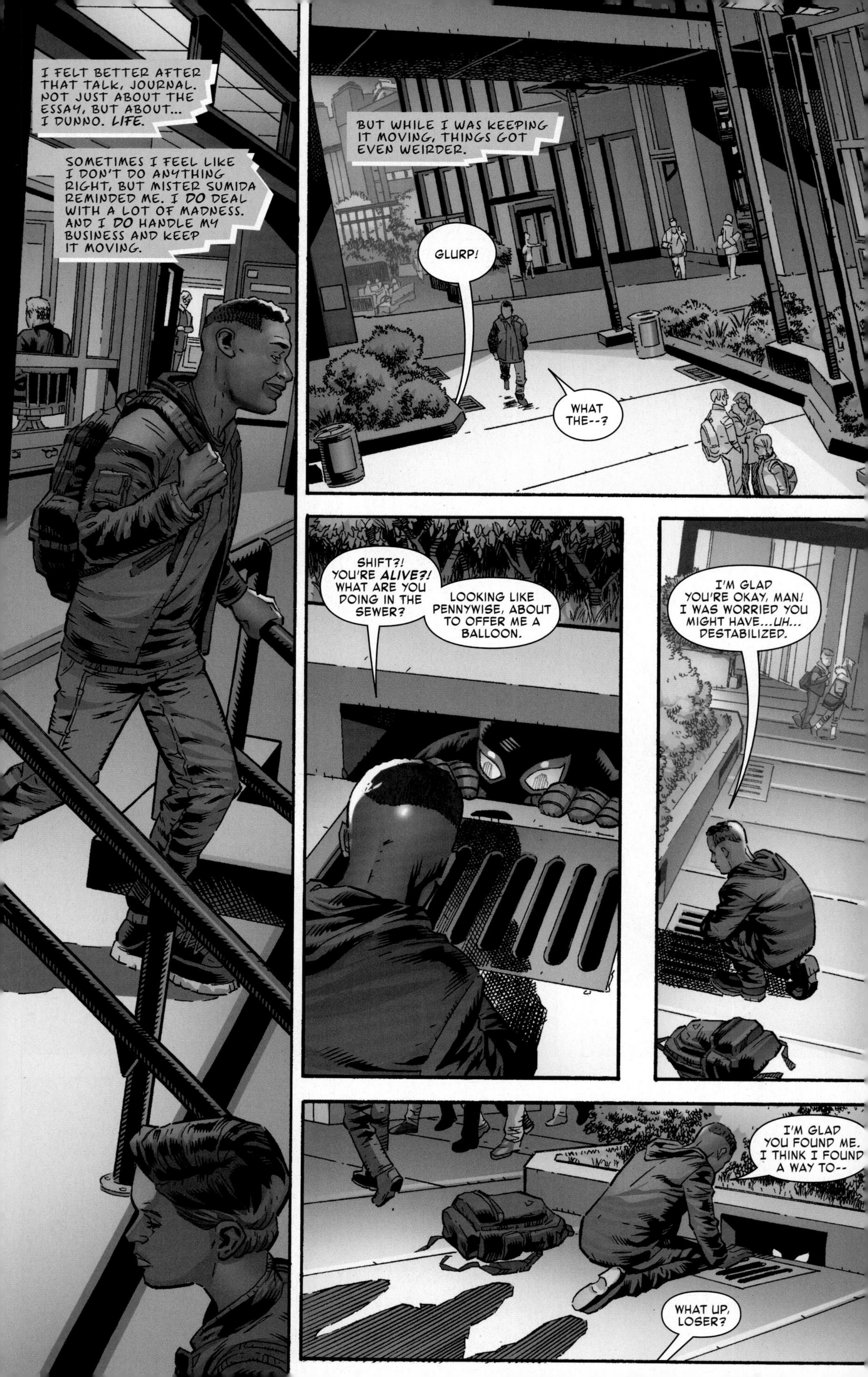
I FELT BETTER AFTER THAT TALK, JOURNAL. NOT JUST ABOUT THE ESSAY, BUT ABOUT... I DUNNO. LIFE.
SOMETIMES I FEEL LIKE I DON'T DO ANYTHING RIGHT, BUT MISTER SUMIDA REMINDED ME. I DO DEAL WITH A LOT OF MADNESS. AND I DO HANDLE MY BUSINESS AND KEEP IT MOVING.
BUT WHILE I WAS KEEPING IT MOVING, THINGS GOT EVEN WEIRDER.
GLURP!
WHAT THE--?
SHIFT?! YOU'RE ALIVE?! WHAT ARE YOU DOING IN THE SEWER?
LOOKING LIKE PENNYWISE, ABOUT TO OFFER ME A BALLOON.
I'M GLAD YOU'RE OKAY, MAN! I WAS WORRIED YOU MIGHT HAVE...UH... DESTABILIZED.
I'M GLAD YOU FOUND ME. I THINK I FOUND A WAY TO--
WHAT UP, LOSER?

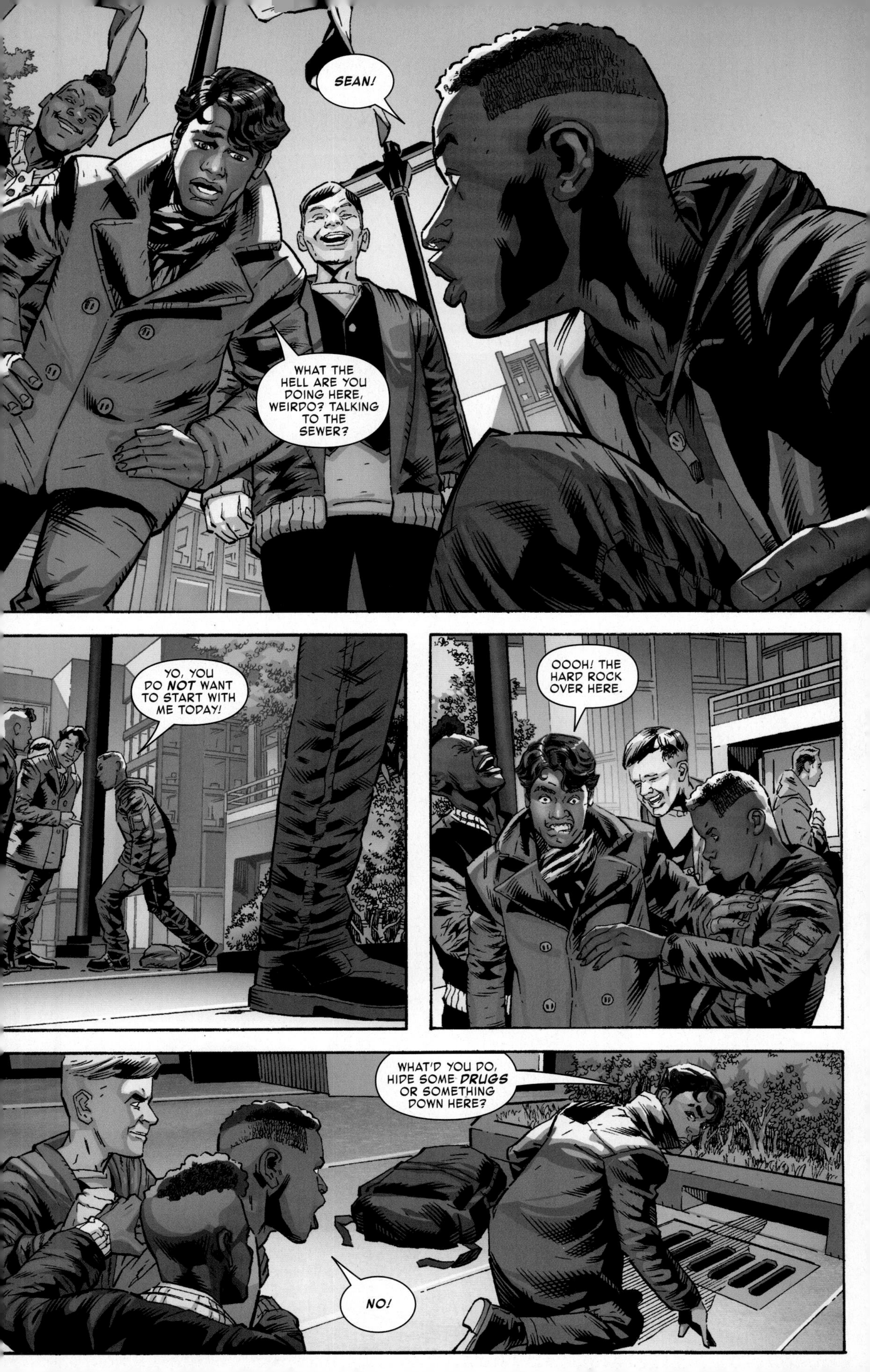
SEAN!
WHAT THE HELL ARE YOU DOING HERE, WEIRDO? TALKING TO THE SEWER?
YO, YOU DO NOT WANT TO START WITH ME TODAY!
OOOH! THE HARD ROCK OVER HERE.
WHAT'D YOU DO, HIDE SOME DRUGS OR SOMETHING DOWN HERE?
NO!

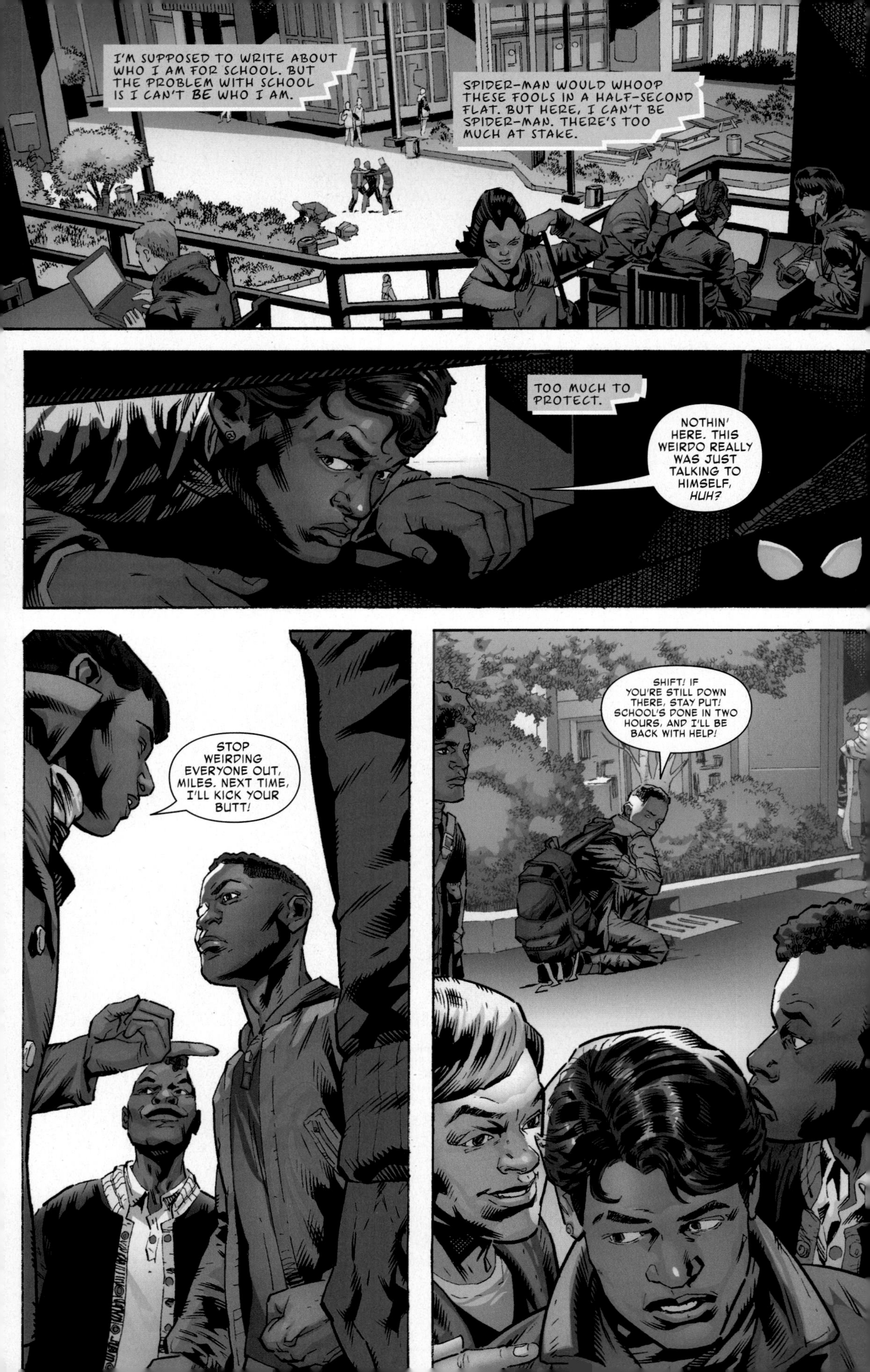
I'M SUPPOSED TO WRITE ABOUT WHO I AM FOR SCHOOL. BUT THE PROBLEM WITH SCHOOL IS I CAN'T BE WHO I AM.
SPIDER-MAN WOULD WHOOP THESE FOOLS IN A HALF-SECOND FLAT. BUT HERE, I CAN'T BE SPIDER-MAN. THERE'S TOO MUCH AT STAKE.
TOO MUCH TO PROTECT.
NOTHIN' HERE. THIS WEIRDO REALLY WAS JUST TALKING TO HIMSELF, HUH?
STOP WEIRDING EVERYONE OUT, MILES. NEXT TIME, I'LL KICK YOUR BUTT!
SHIFT! IF YOU'RE STILL DOWN THERE, STAY PUT! SCHOOL'S DONE IN TWO HOURS, AND I'LL BE BACK WITH HELP!

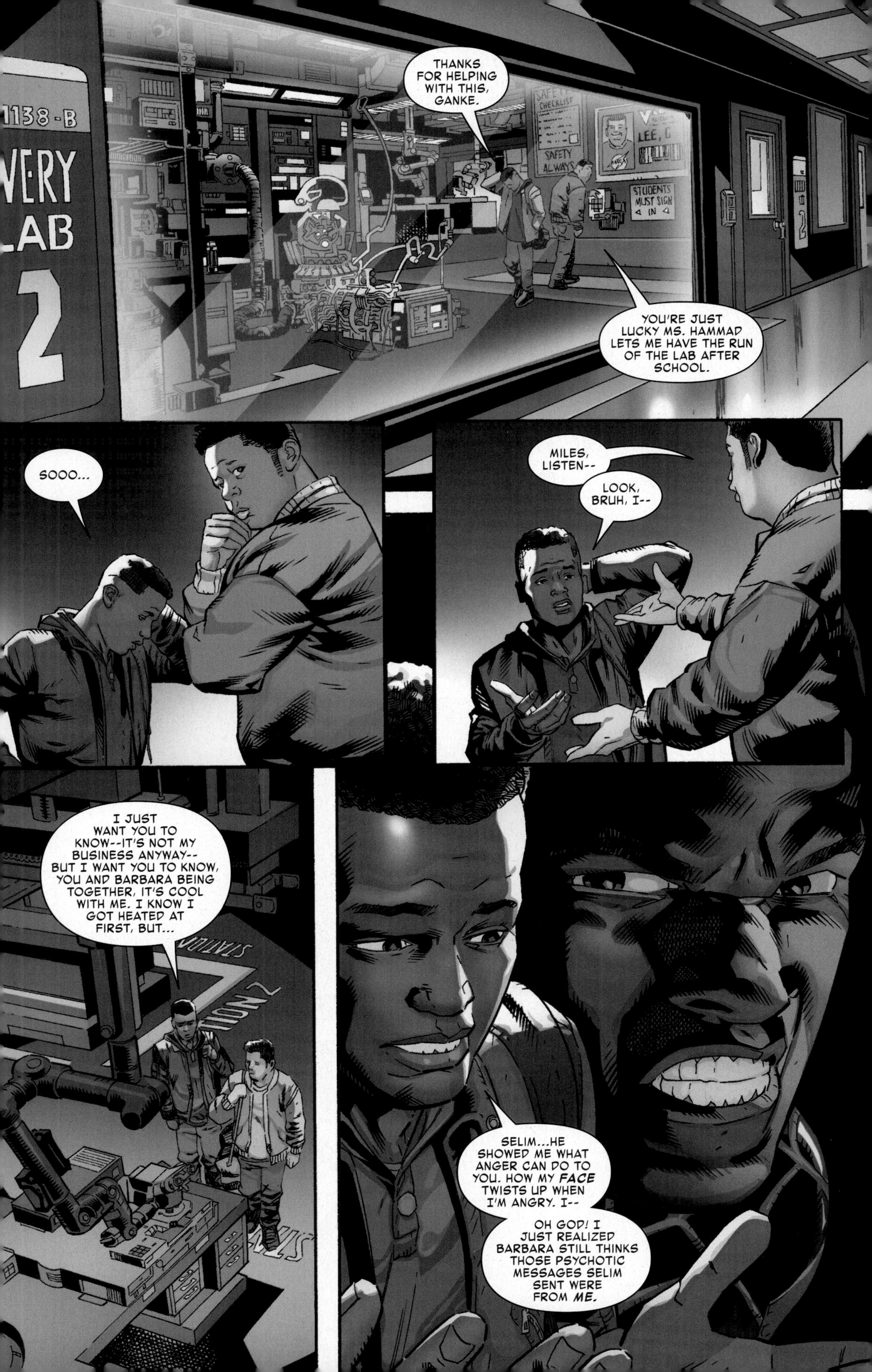
1138-B
VERY
LAB
2
THANKS FOR HELPING WITH THIS, GANKE.
SAFETY CHECKLIST
SAFETY ALWAYS
LEE, G
STUDENTS MUST SIGN IN
YOU'RE JUST LUCKY MS. HAMMAD LETS ME HAVE THE RUN OF THE LAB AFTER SCHOOL.
SOOO...
MILES, LISTEN--
LOOK, BRUH, I--
I JUST WANT YOU TO KNOW--IT'S NOT MY BUSINESS ANYWAY--BUT I WANT YOU TO KNOW, YOU AND BARBARA BEING TOGETHER, IT'S COOL WITH ME. I KNOW I GOT HEATED AT FIRST, BUT...
SELIM...HE SHOWED ME WHAT ANGER CAN DO TO YOU. HOW MY *FACE* TWISTS UP WHEN I'M ANGRY. I--
OH GOD! I JUST REALIZED BARBARA STILL THINKS THOSE PSYCHOTIC MESSAGES SELIM SENT WERE FROM *ME.*

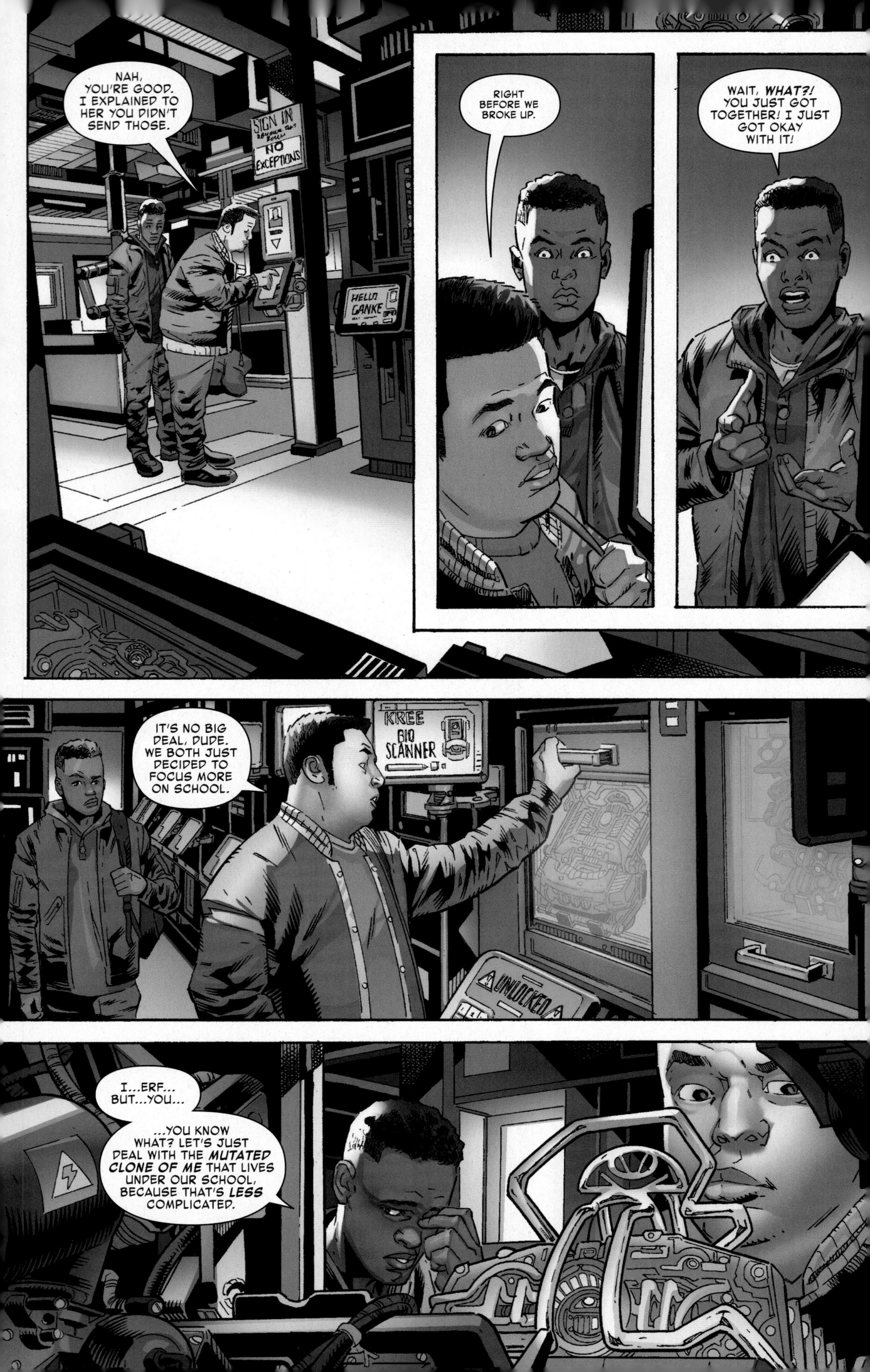
NAH, YOU'RE GOOD. I EXPLAINED TO HER YOU DIDN'T SEND THOSE.
SIGN IN
NO EXCEPTIONS
HELLO GANKE
RIGHT BEFORE WE BROKE UP.
WAIT, WHAT?! YOU JUST GOT TOGETHER! I JUST GOT OKAY WITH IT!
IT'S NO BIG DEAL, DUDE. WE BOTH JUST DECIDED TO FOCUS MORE ON SCHOOL.
KREE BIO SCANNER
UNLOCKED
I...ERF... BUT...YOU...
...YOU KNOW WHAT? LET'S JUST DEAL WITH THE MUTATED CLONE OF ME THAT LIVES UNDER OUR SCHOOL, BECAUSE THAT'S LESS COMPLICATED.

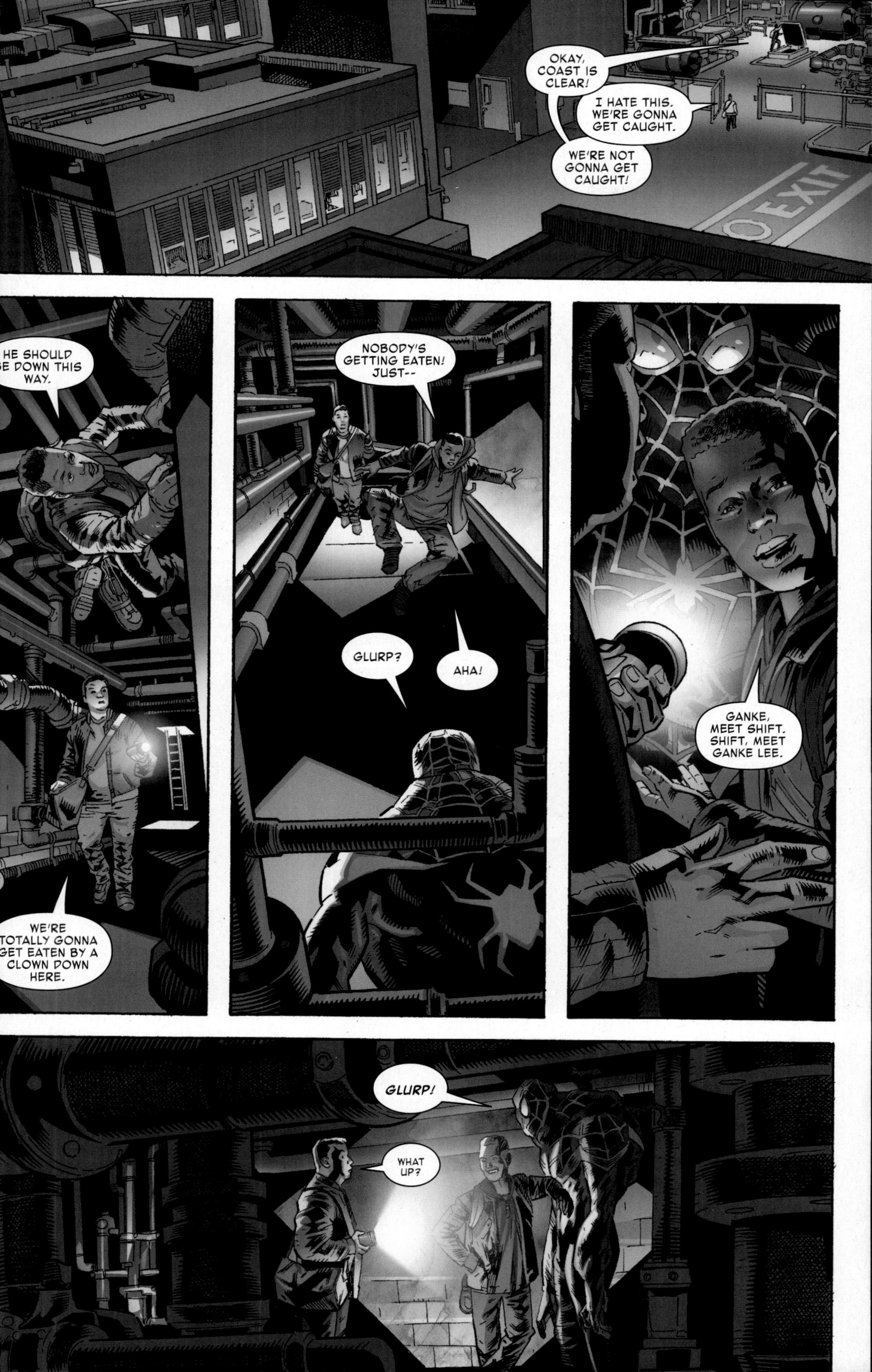
OKAY, COAST IS CLEAR!
I HATE THIS. WE'RE GONNA GET CAUGHT.
WE'RE NOT GONNA GET CAUGHT!
HE SHOULD BE DOWN THIS WAY.
WE'RE TOTALLY GONNA GET EATEN BY A CLOWN DOWN HERE.
NOBODY'S GETTING EATEN! JUST--
GLURP?
AHA!
GANKE, MEET SHIFT. SHIFT, MEET GANKE LEE.
GLURP!
WHAT UP?

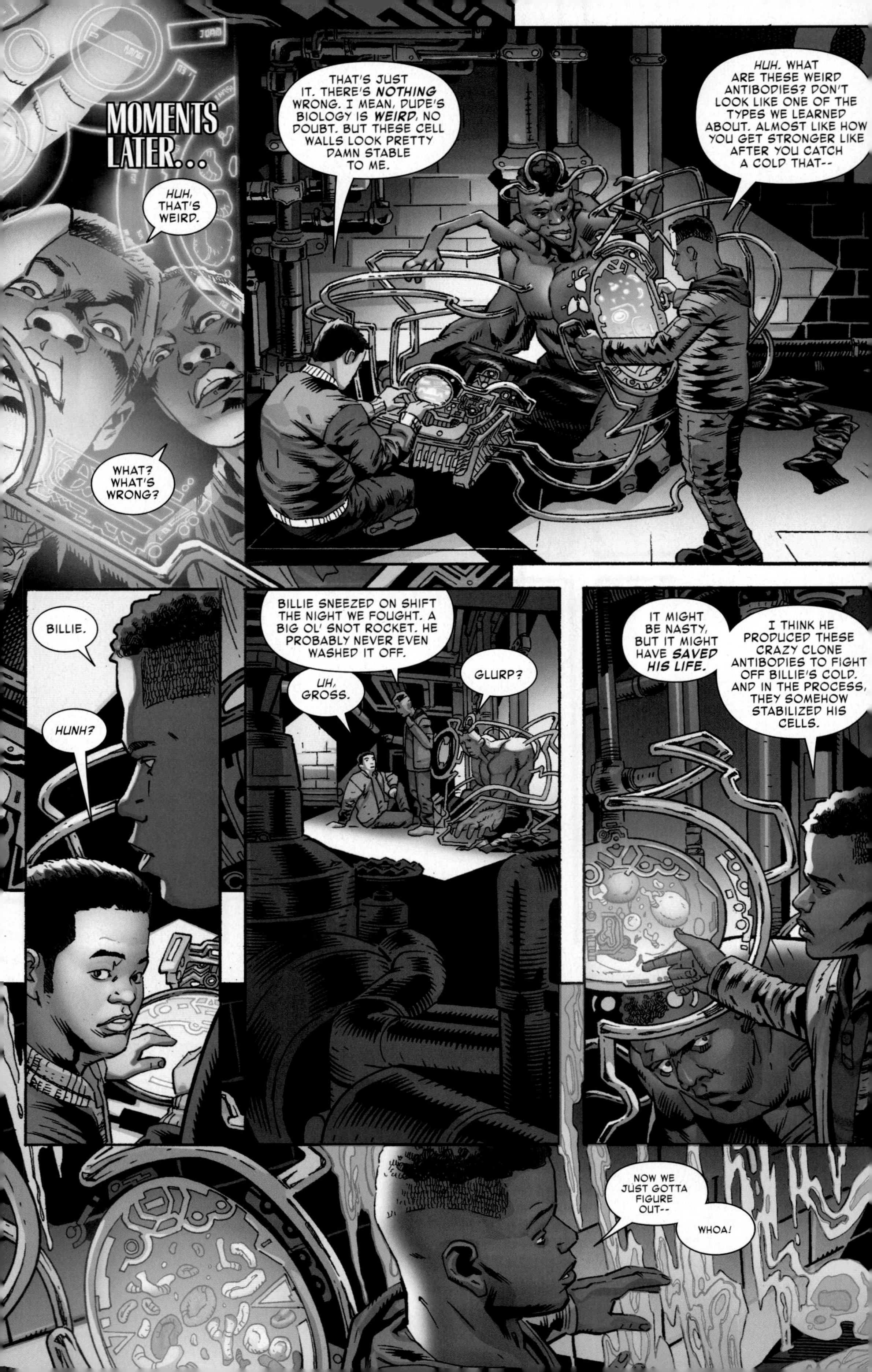

MOMENTS LATER...
HUH, THAT'S WEIRD.
WHAT? WHAT'S WRONG?
THAT'S JUST IT. THERE'S NOTHING WRONG. I MEAN, DUDE'S BIOLOGY IS WEIRD, NO DOUBT. BUT THESE CELL WALLS LOOK PRETTY DAMN STABLE TO ME.
HUH. WHAT ARE THESE WEIRD ANTIBODIES? DON'T LOOK LIKE ONE OF THE TYPES WE LEARNED ABOUT. ALMOST LIKE HOW YOU GET STRONGER LIKE AFTER YOU CATCH A COLD THAT--
BILLIE.
HUNH?
BILLIE SNEEZED ON SHIFT THE NIGHT WE FOUGHT. A BIG OL' SNOT ROCKET. HE PROBABLY NEVER EVEN WASHED IT OFF.
UH, GROSS.
GLURP?
IT MIGHT BE NASTY, BUT IT MIGHT HAVE SAVED HIS LIFE.
I THINK HE PRODUCED THESE CRAZY CLONE ANTIBODIES TO FIGHT OFF BILLIE'S COLD. AND IN THE PROCESS, THEY SOMEHOW STABILIZED HIS CELLS.
NOW WE JUST GOTTA FIGURE OUT--
WHOA!

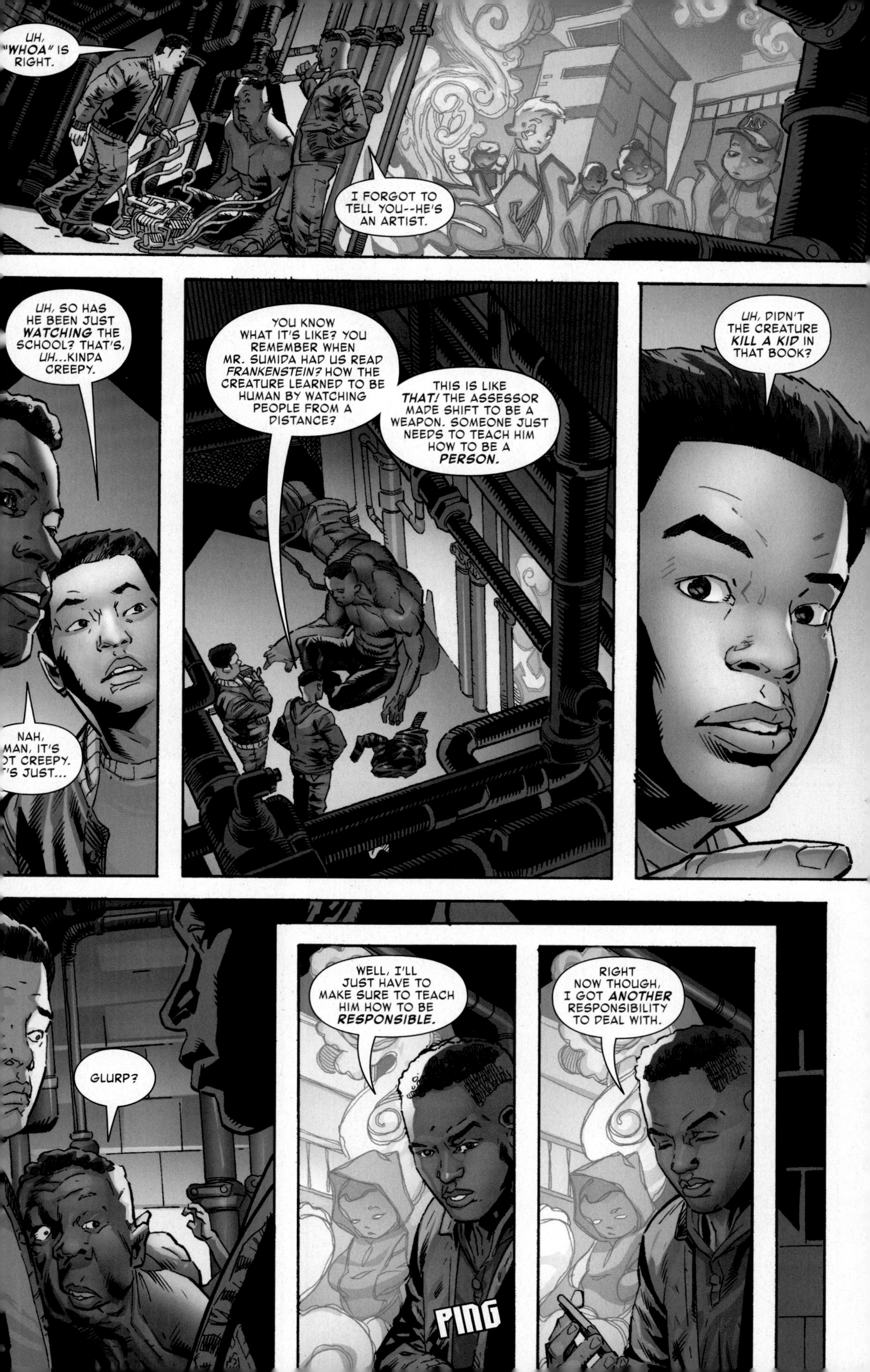
UH, "WHOA" IS RIGHT.
I FORGOT TO TELL YOU--HE'S AN ARTIST.
UH, SO HAS HE BEEN JUST WATCHING THE SCHOOL? THAT'S, UH...KINDA CREEPY.
NAH, MAN, IT'S OT CREEPY. T'S JUST...
YOU KNOW WHAT IT'S LIKE? YOU REMEMBER WHEN MR. SUMIDA HAD US READ FRANKENSTEIN? HOW THE CREATURE LEARNED TO BE HUMAN BY WATCHING PEOPLE FROM A DISTANCE?
THIS IS LIKE THAT! THE ASSESSOR MADE SHIFT TO BE A WEAPON. SOMEONE JUST NEEDS TO TEACH HIM HOW TO BE A PERSON.
UH, DIDN'T THE CREATURE KILL A KID IN THAT BOOK?
GLURP?
WELL, I'LL JUST HAVE TO MAKE SURE TO TEACH HIM HOW TO BE RESPONSIBLE.
PING
RIGHT NOW THOUGH, I GOT ANOTHER RESPONSIBILITY TO DEAL WITH.

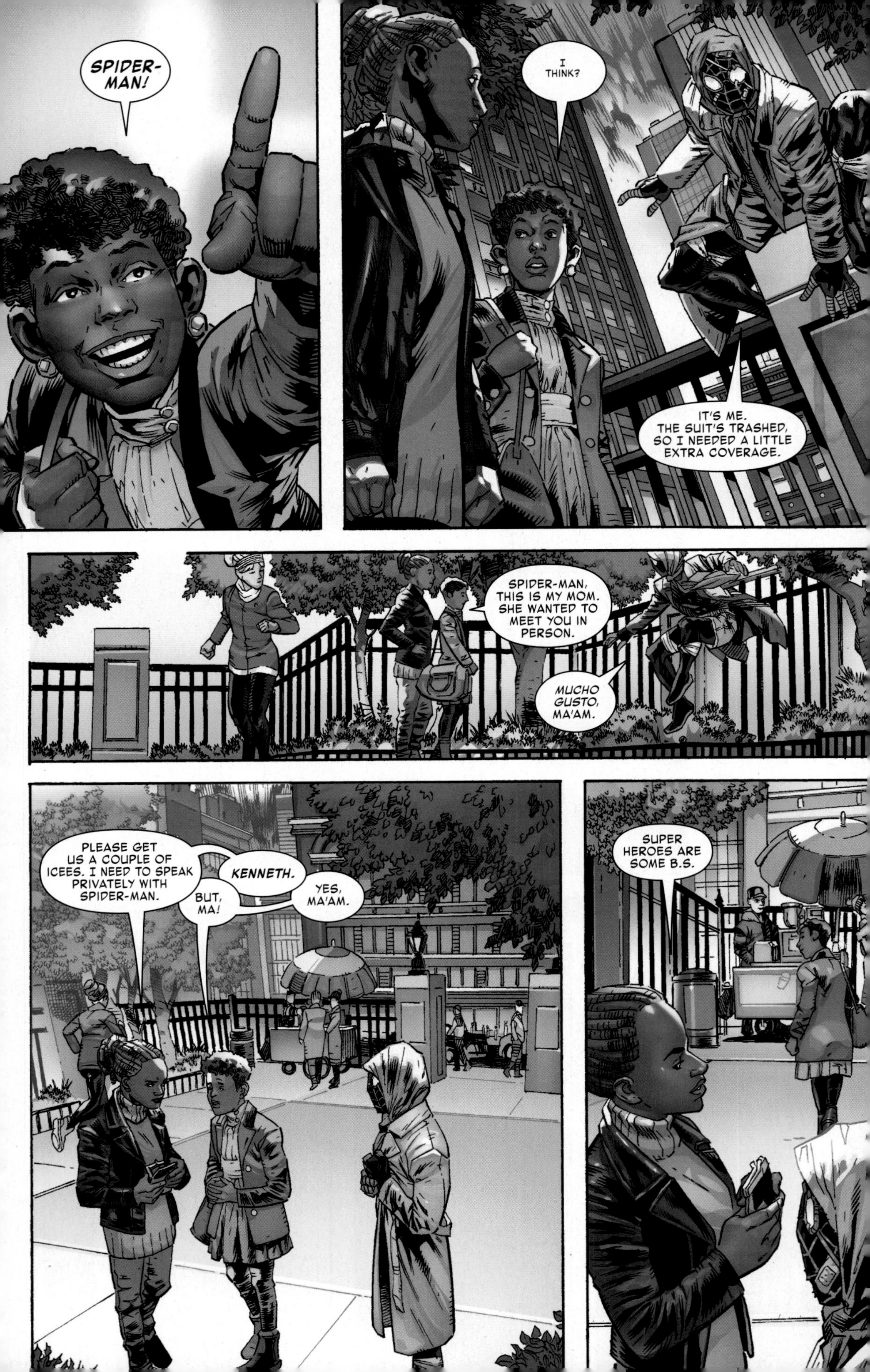
SPIDER-MAN!
I THINK?
IT'S ME. THE SUIT'S TRASHED, SO I NEEDED A LITTLE EXTRA COVERAGE.
SPIDER-MAN, THIS IS MY MOM. SHE WANTED TO MEET YOU IN PERSON.
MUCHO GUSTO, MA'AM.
PLEASE GET US A COUPLE OF ICEES. I NEED TO SPEAK PRIVATELY WITH SPIDER-MAN.
BUT, MA!
KENNETH.
YES, MA'AM.
SUPER HEROES ARE SOME B.S.

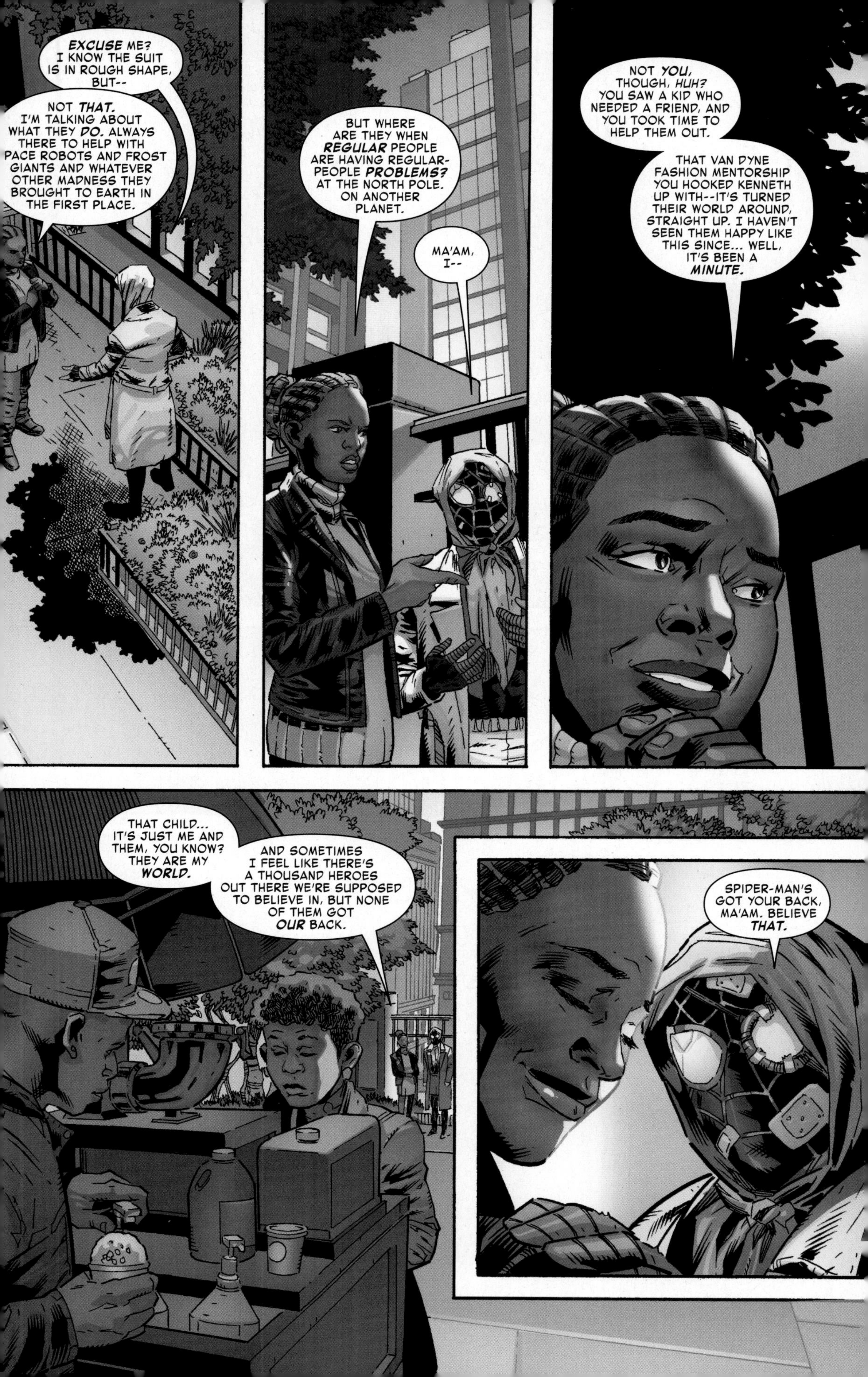
EXCUSE ME? I KNOW THE SUIT IS IN ROUGH SHAPE, BUT--
NOT THAT. I'M TALKING ABOUT WHAT THEY DO. ALWAYS THERE TO HELP WITH PACE ROBOTS AND FROST GIANTS AND WHATEVER OTHER MADNESS THEY BROUGHT TO EARTH IN THE FIRST PLACE.
BUT WHERE ARE THEY WHEN REGULAR PEOPLE ARE HAVING REGULAR-PEOPLE PROBLEMS? AT THE NORTH POLE. ON ANOTHER PLANET.
MA'AM, I--
NOT YOU, THOUGH, HUH? YOU SAW A KID WHO NEEDED A FRIEND, AND YOU TOOK TIME TO HELP THEM OUT.
THAT VAN DYNE FASHION MENTORSHIP YOU HOOKED KENNETH UP WITH--IT'S TURNED THEIR WORLD AROUND, STRAIGHT UP. I HAVEN'T SEEN THEM HAPPY LIKE THIS SINCE... WELL, IT'S BEEN A MINUTE.
THAT CHILD... IT'S JUST ME AND THEM, YOU KNOW? THEY ARE MY WORLD.
AND SOMETIMES I FEEL LIKE THERE'S A THOUSAND HEROES OUT THERE WE'RE SUPPOSED TO BELIEVE IN, BUT NONE OF THEM GOT OUR BACK.
SPIDER-MAN'S GOT YOUR BACK, MA'AM. BELIEVE THAT.

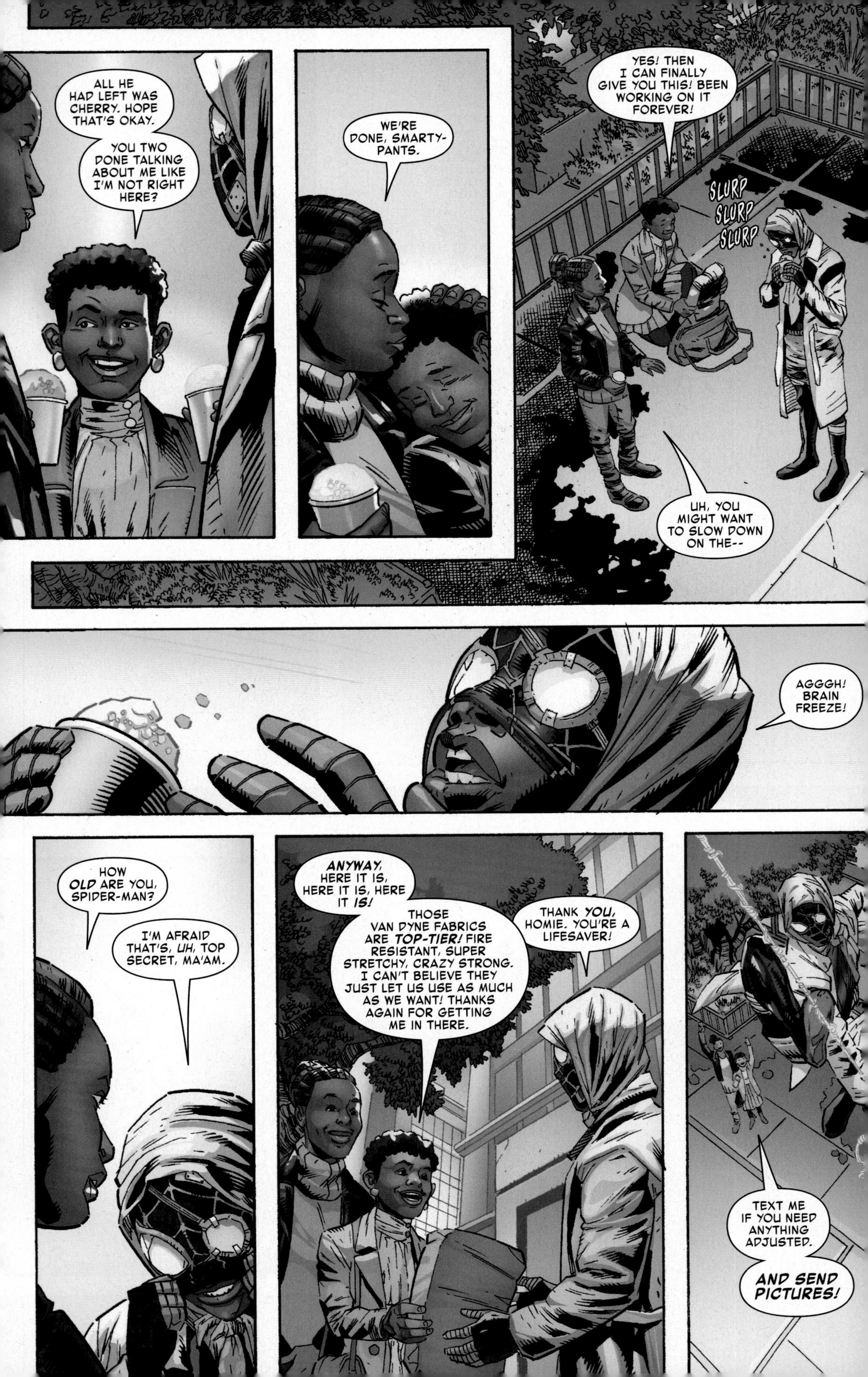
ALL HE HAD LEFT WAS CHERRY. HOPE THAT'S OKAY.
YOU TWO DONE TALKING ABOUT ME LIKE I'M NOT RIGHT HERE?
WE'RE DONE, SMARTY-PANTS.
YES! THEN I CAN FINALLY GIVE YOU THIS! BEEN WORKING ON IT FOREVER!
SLURP SLURP SLURP
UH, YOU MIGHT WANT TO SLOW DOWN ON THE--
AGGGH! BRAIN FREEZE!
HOW OLD ARE YOU, SPIDER-MAN?
I'M AFRAID THAT'S, UH, TOP SECRET, MA'AM.
ANYWAY, HERE IT IS, HERE IT IS, HERE IT IS!
THOSE VAN DYNE FABRICS ARE TOP-TIER! FIRE RESISTANT, SUPER STRETCHY, CRAZY STRONG. I CAN'T BELIEVE THEY JUST LET US USE AS MUCH AS WE WANT! THANKS AGAIN FOR GETTING ME IN THERE.
THANK YOU, HOMIE. YOU'RE A LIFESAVER!
TEXT ME IF YOU NEED ANYTHING ADJUSTED.
AND SEND PICTURES!

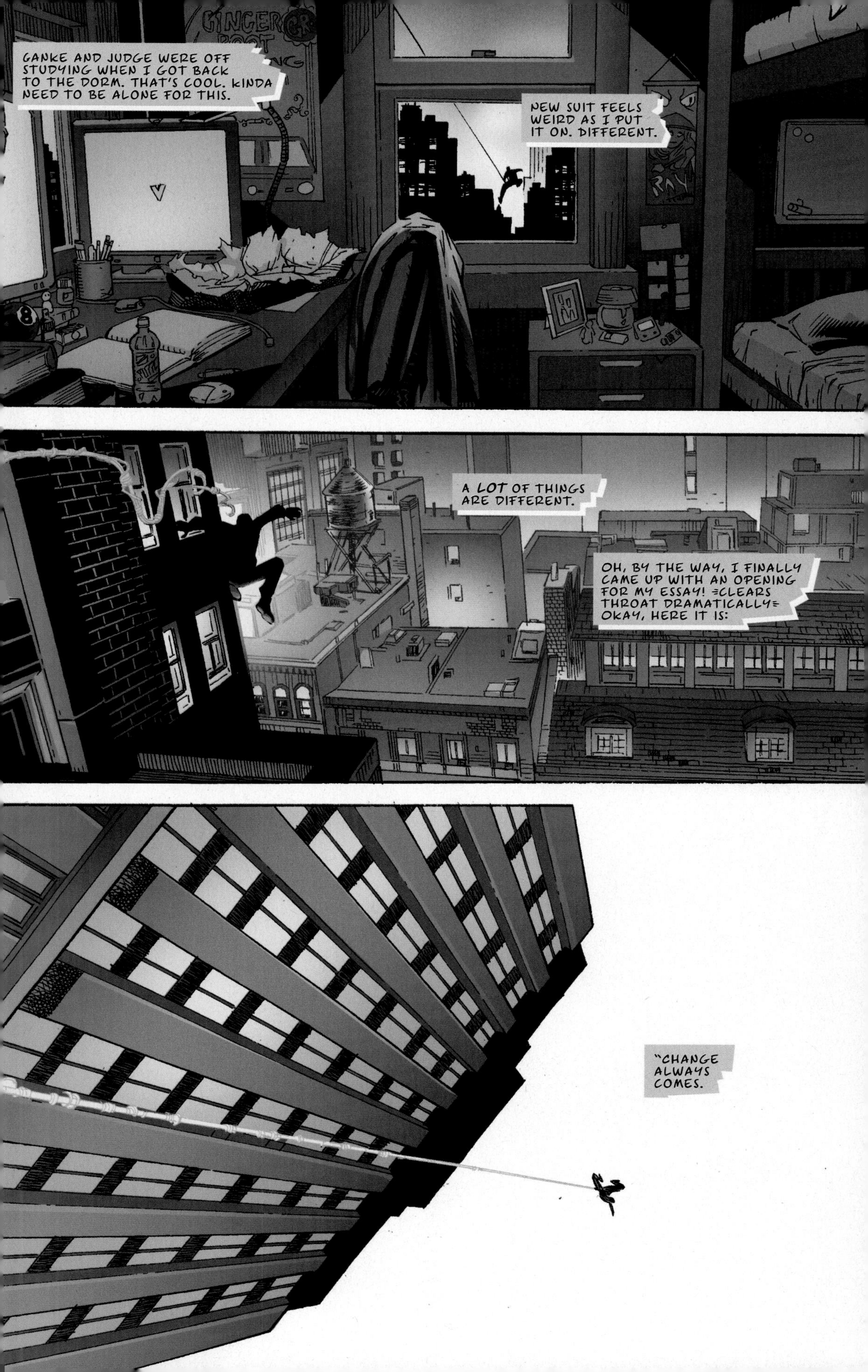
GINGER ROOT
GANKE AND JUDGE WERE OFF STUDYING WHEN I GOT BACK TO THE DORM. THAT'S COOL. KINDA NEED TO BE ALONE FOR THIS.
NEW SUIT FEELS WEIRD AS I PUT IT ON. DIFFERENT.
A LOT OF THINGS ARE DIFFERENT.
OH, BY THE WAY, I FINALLY CAME UP WITH AN OPENING FOR MY ESSAY! =CLEARS THROAT DRAMATICALLY= OKAY, HERE IT IS:
"CHANGE ALWAYS COMES.

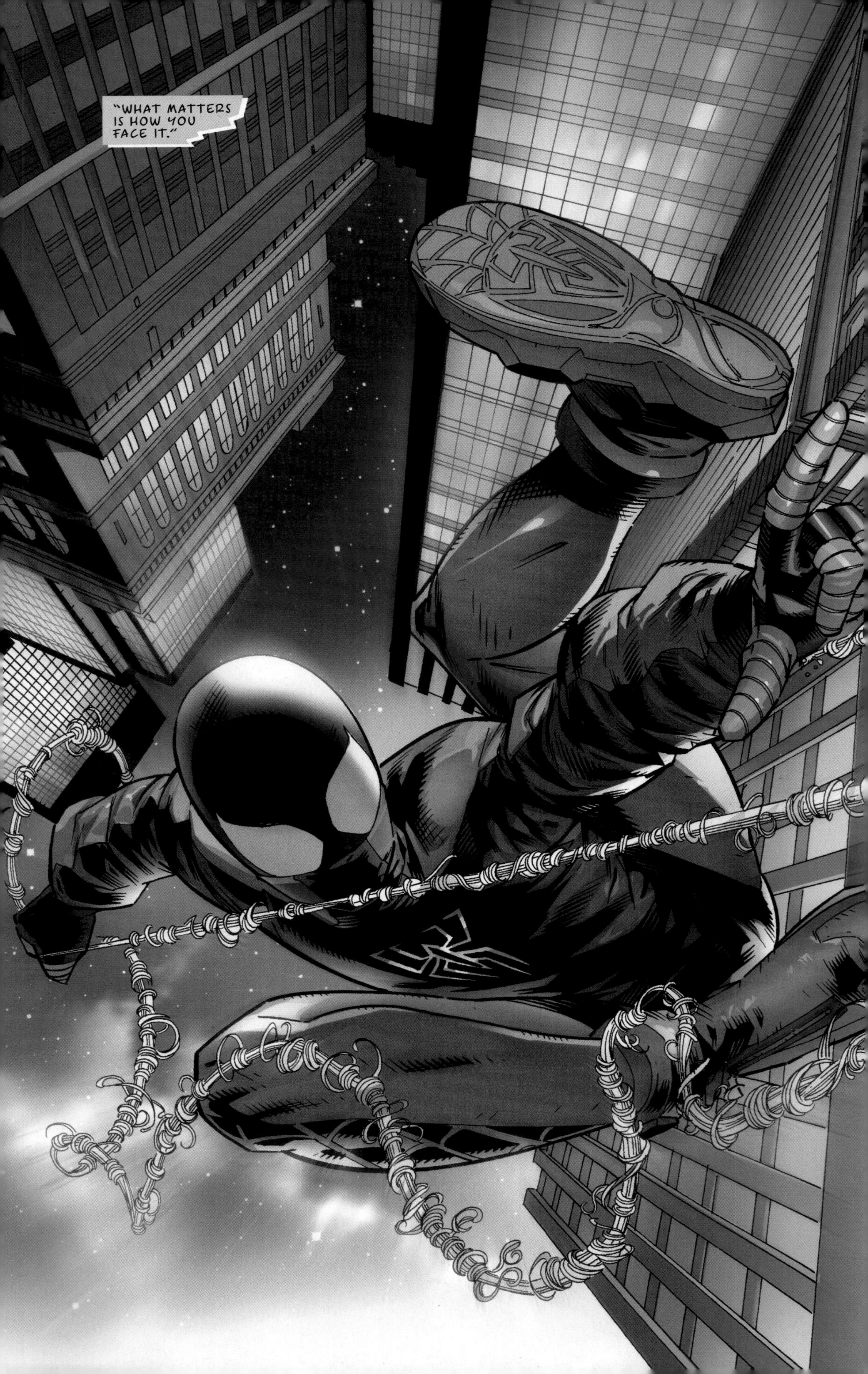
"WHAT MATTERS IS HOW YOU FACE IT."

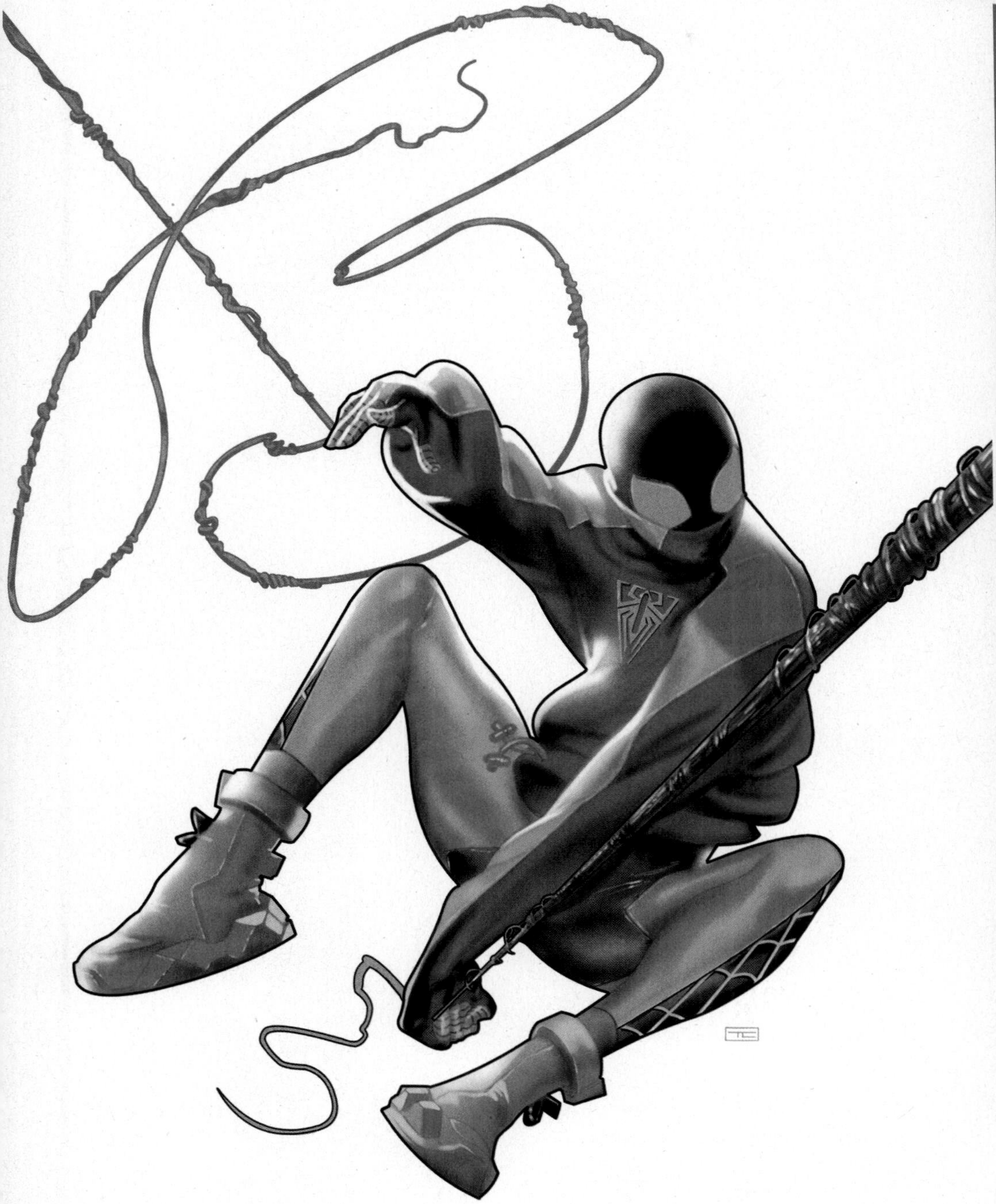

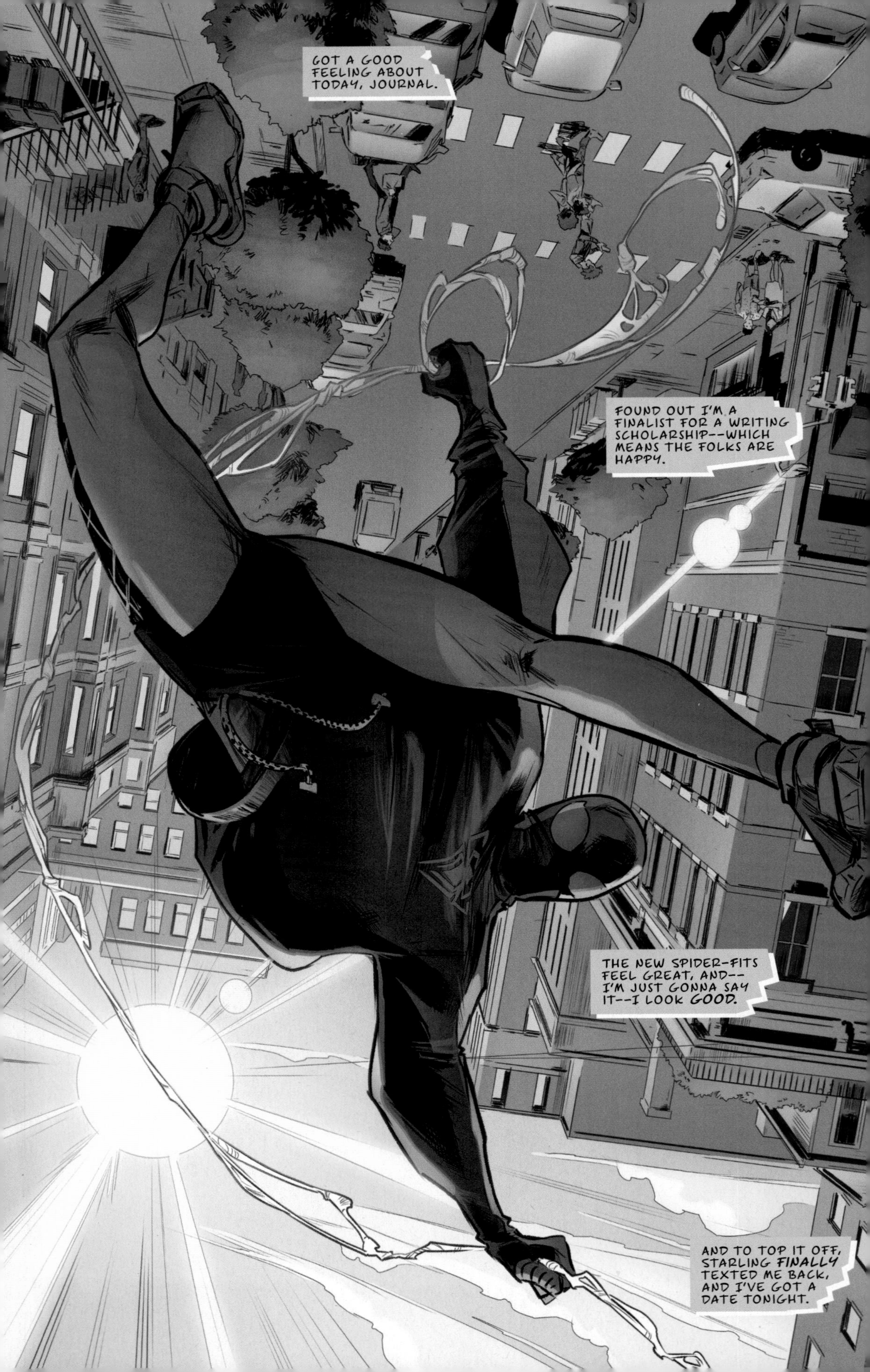
GOT A GOOD FEELING ABOUT TODAY, JOURNAL.
FOUND OUT I'M A FINALIST FOR A WRITING SCHOLARSHIP--WHICH MEANS THE FOLKS ARE HAPPY.
THE NEW SPIDER-FITS FEEL GREAT, AND--I'M JUST GONNA SAY IT--I LOOK GOOD.
AND TO TOP IT OFF, STARLING FINALLY TEXTED ME BACK, AND I'VE GOT A DATE TONIGHT.

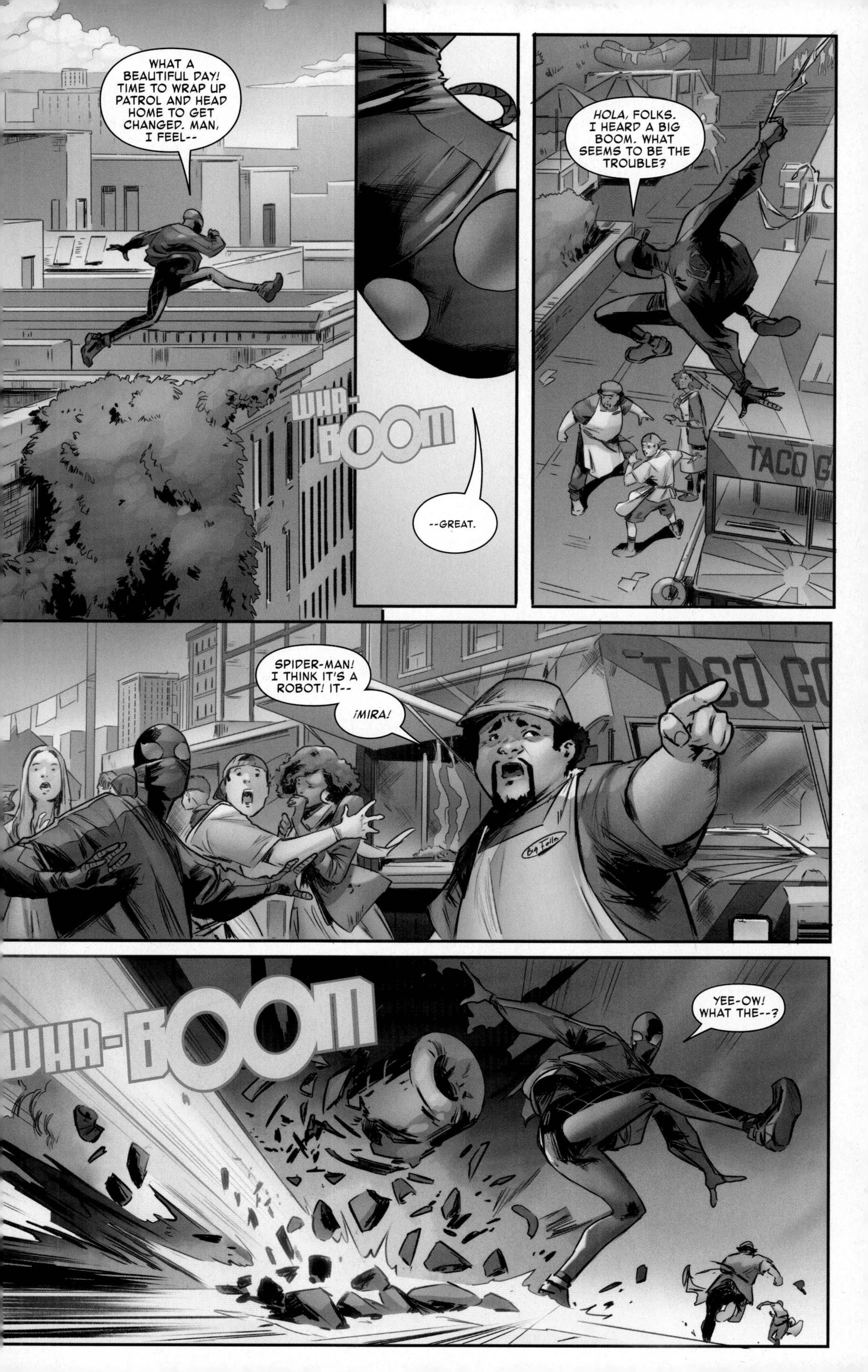
WHAT A BEAUTIFUL DAY! TIME TO WRAP UP PATROL AND HEAD HOME TO GET CHANGED. MAN, I FEEL--
WHA-BOOM
--GREAT.
HOLA, FOLKS. I HEARD A BIG BOOM. WHAT SEEMS TO BE THE TROUBLE?
TACO G
SPIDER-MAN! I THINK IT'S A ROBOT! IT--
¡MIRA!
TACO GO
WHA-BOOM
YEE-OW! WHAT THE--?

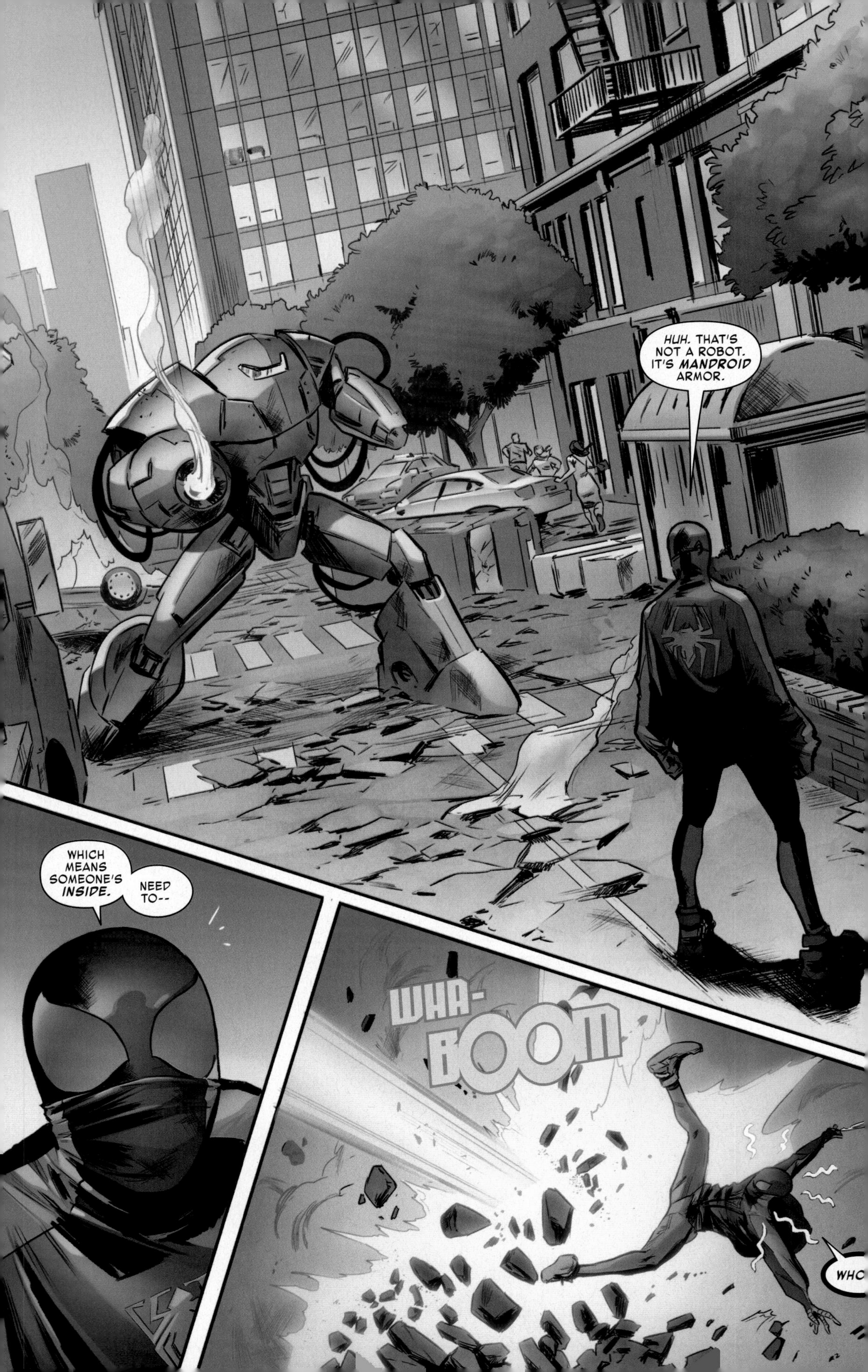
HUH. THAT'S NOT A ROBOT. IT'S MANDROID ARMOR.
WHICH MEANS SOMEONE'S INSIDE.
NEED TO--
WHA-BOOM
WHO

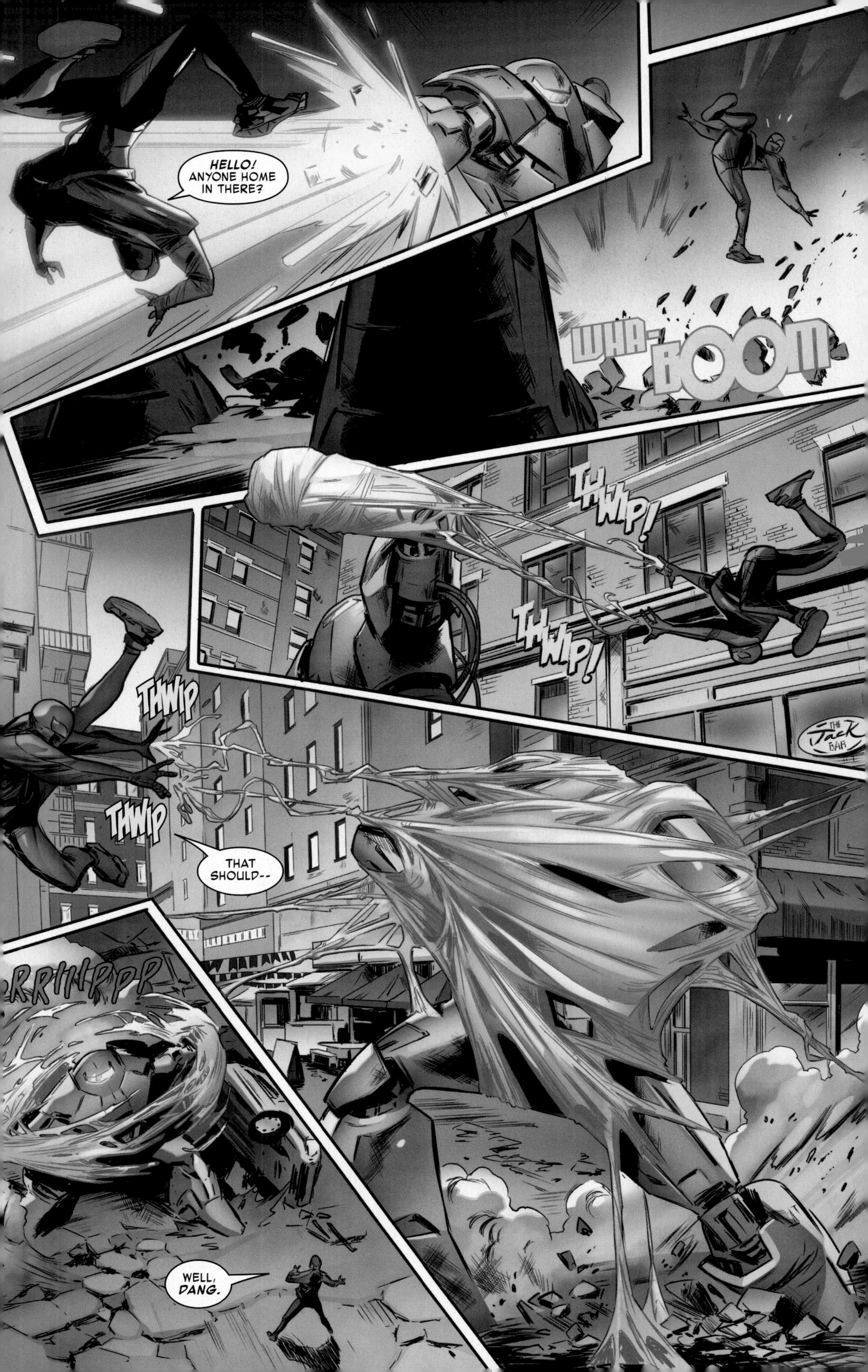
HELLO! ANYONE HOME IN THERE?
WHA-BOOM
THWIP!
THWIP!
THE JACK BAR
THWIP
THWIP
THAT SHOULD--
RRIIIPPP
WELL, DANG.

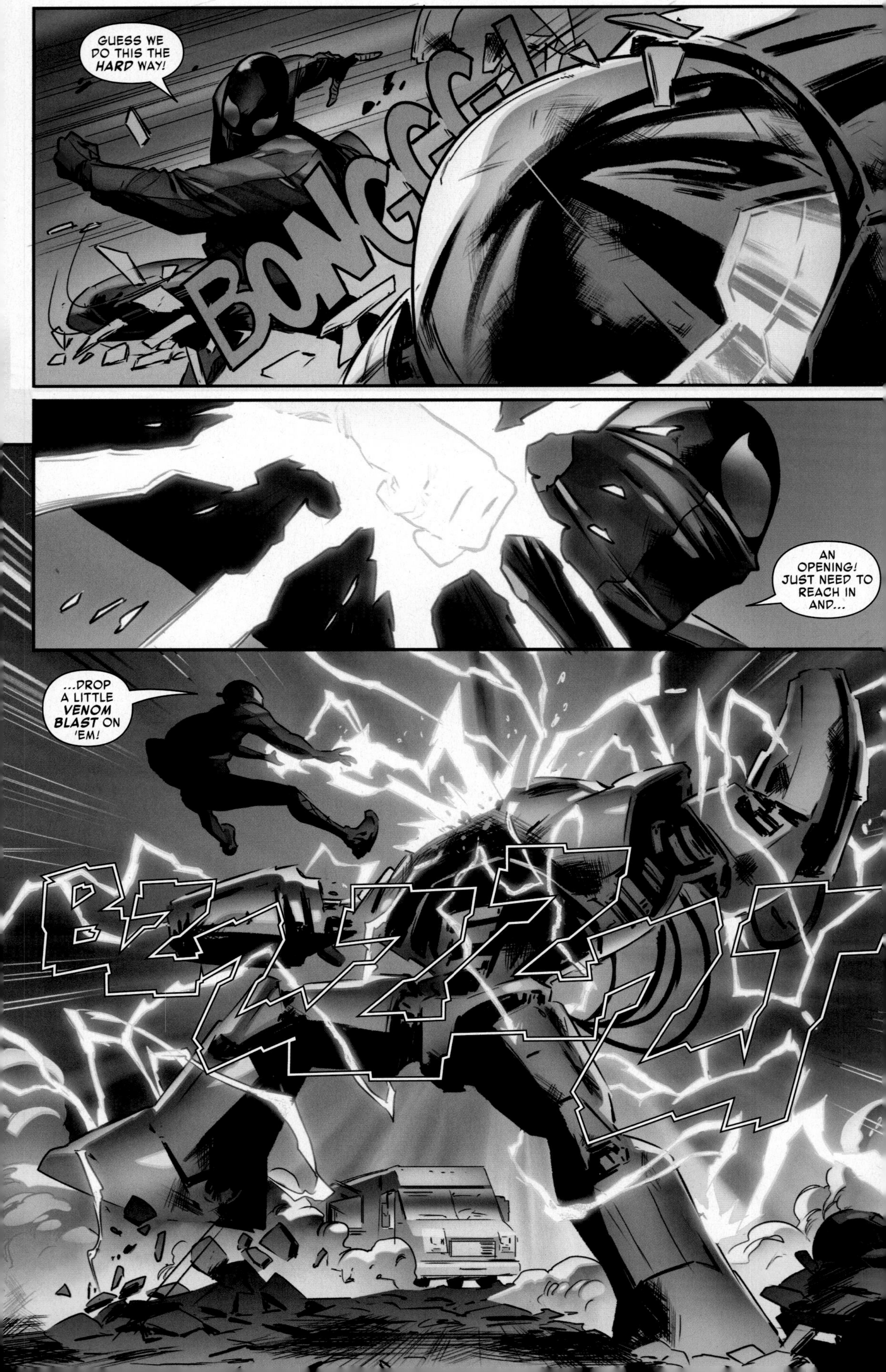

GUESS WE DO THIS THE HARD WAY!
BONGGG!
AN OPENING! JUST NEED TO REACH IN AND...
...DROP A LITTLE VENOM BLAST ON 'EM!
BZZZZAT

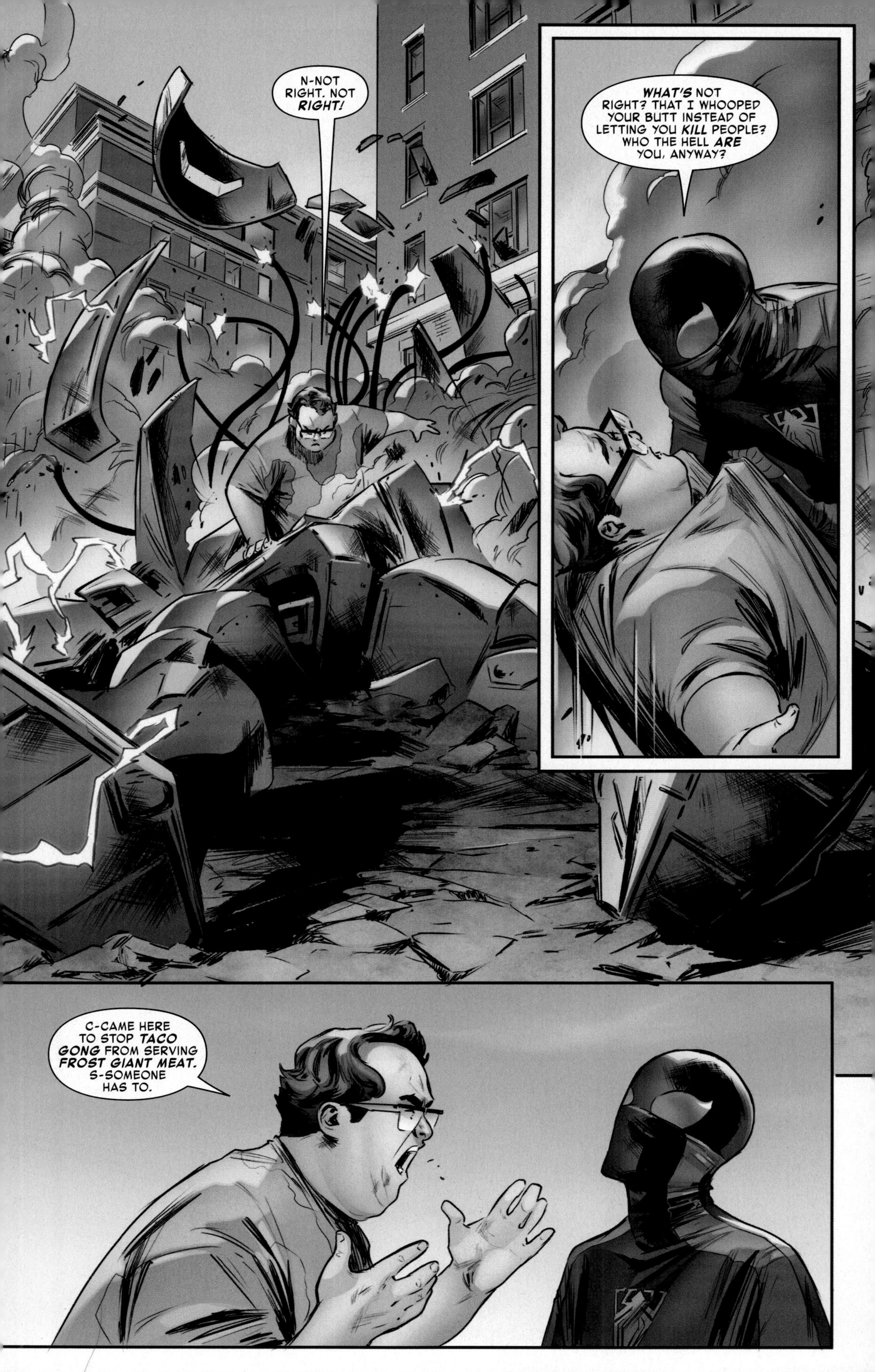
N-NOT RIGHT. NOT RIGHT!
WHAT'S NOT RIGHT? THAT I WHOOPED YOUR BUTT INSTEAD OF LETTING YOU KILL PEOPLE? WHO THE HELL ARE YOU, ANYWAY?
C-CAME HERE TO STOP TACO GONG FROM SERVING FROST GIANT MEAT. S-SOMEONE HAS TO.

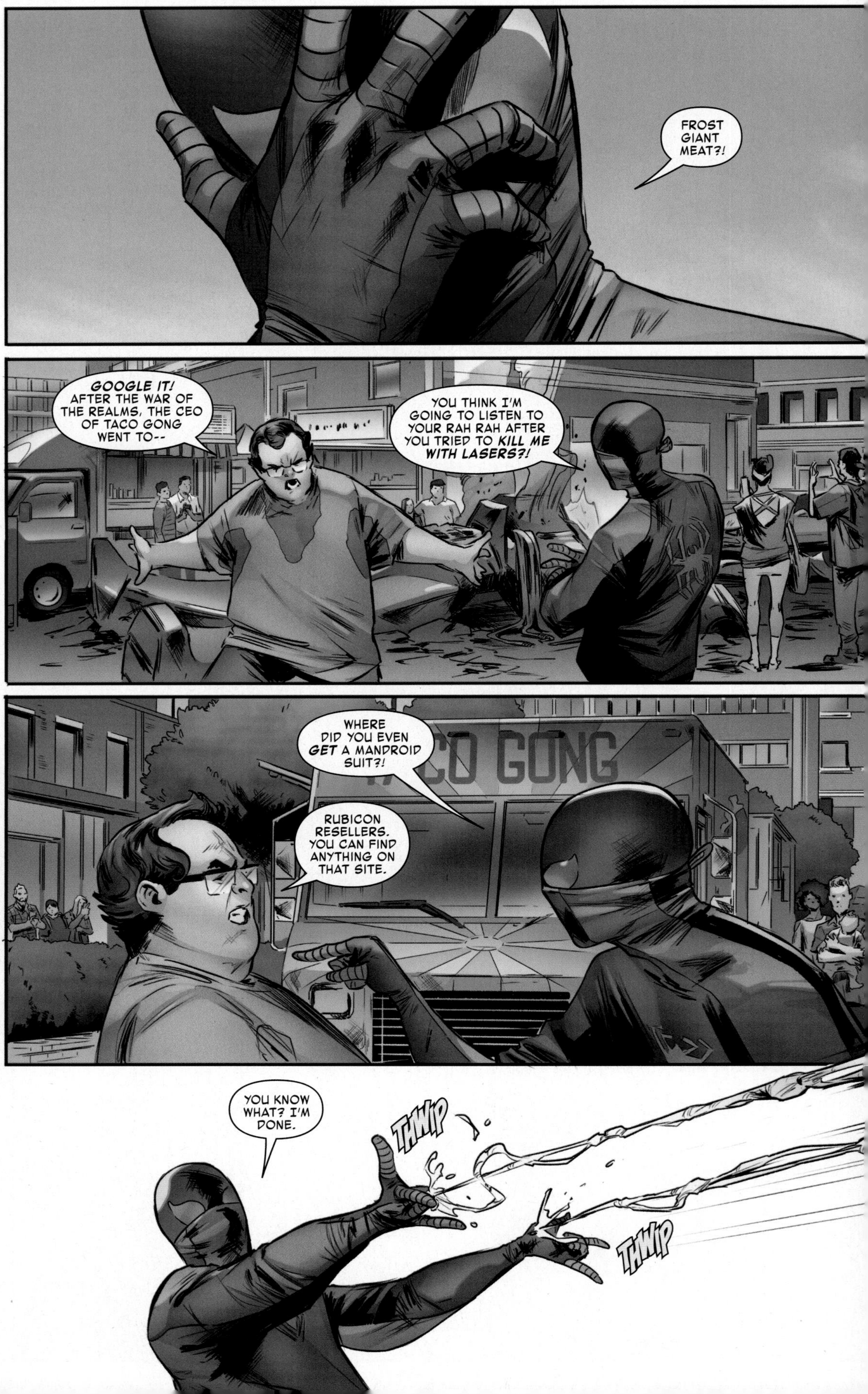
FROST GIANT MEAT?!
GOOGLE IT! AFTER THE WAR OF THE REALMS, THE CEO OF TACO GONG WENT TO--
YOU THINK I'M GOING TO LISTEN TO YOUR RAH RAH AFTER YOU TRIED TO KILL ME WITH LASERS?!
TACO GONG
WHERE DID YOU EVEN GET A MANDROID SUIT?!
RUBICON RESELLERS. YOU CAN FIND ANYTHING ON THAT SITE.
YOU KNOW WHAT? I'M DONE.
THWIP
THWIP

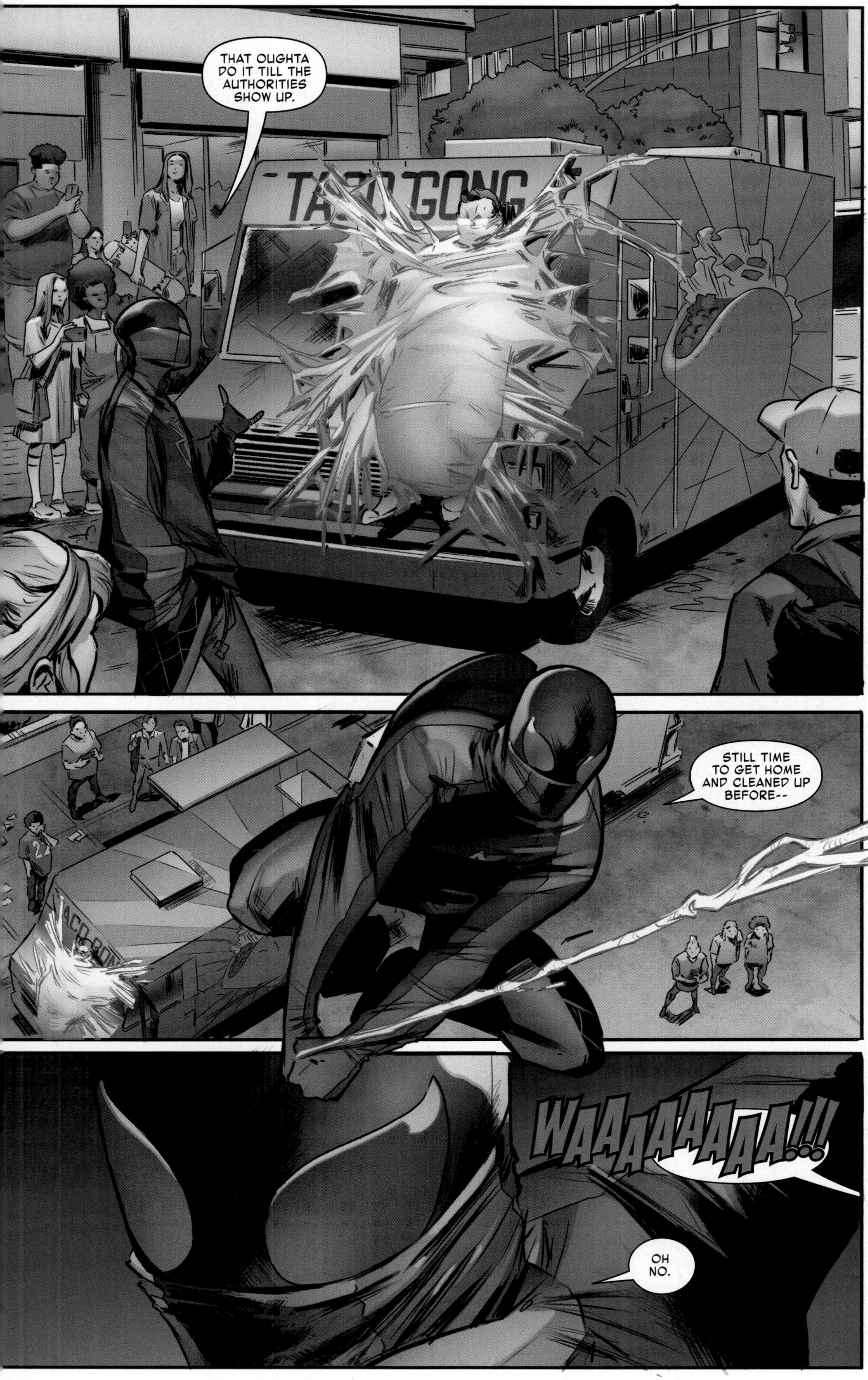
THAT OUGHTA DO IT TILL THE AUTHORITIES SHOW UP.
TACO GONG
STILL TIME TO GET HOME AND CLEANED UP BEFORE--
WAAAAAAAAA!!!
OH NO.

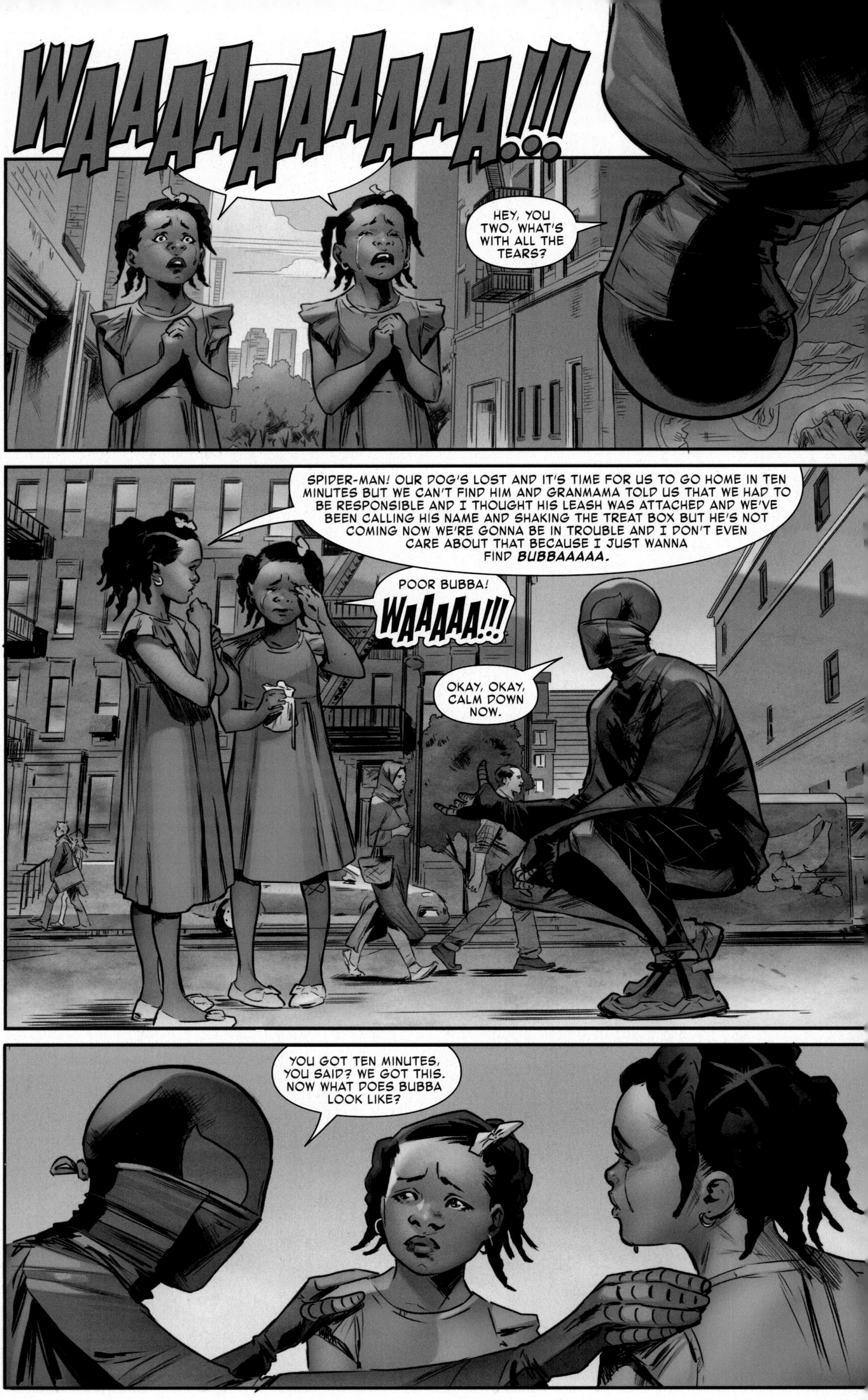
WAAAAAAAAAAA!!!
HEY, YOU TWO, WHAT'S WITH ALL THE TEARS?
SPIDER-MAN! OUR DOG'S LOST AND IT'S TIME FOR US TO GO HOME IN TEN MINUTES BUT WE CAN'T FIND HIM AND GRANMAMA TOLD US THAT WE HAD TO BE RESPONSIBLE AND I THOUGHT HIS LEASH WAS ATTACHED AND WE'VE BEEN CALLING HIS NAME AND SHAKING THE TREAT BOX BUT HE'S NOT COMING NOW WE'RE GONNA BE IN TROUBLE AND I DON'T EVEN CARE ABOUT THAT BECAUSE I JUST WANNA FIND **BUBBAAAAA.**
POOR BUBBA!
WAAAAA!!!
OKAY, OKAY, CALM DOWN NOW.
YOU GOT TEN MINUTES, YOU SAID? WE GOT THIS. NOW WHAT DOES BUBBA LOOK LIKE?

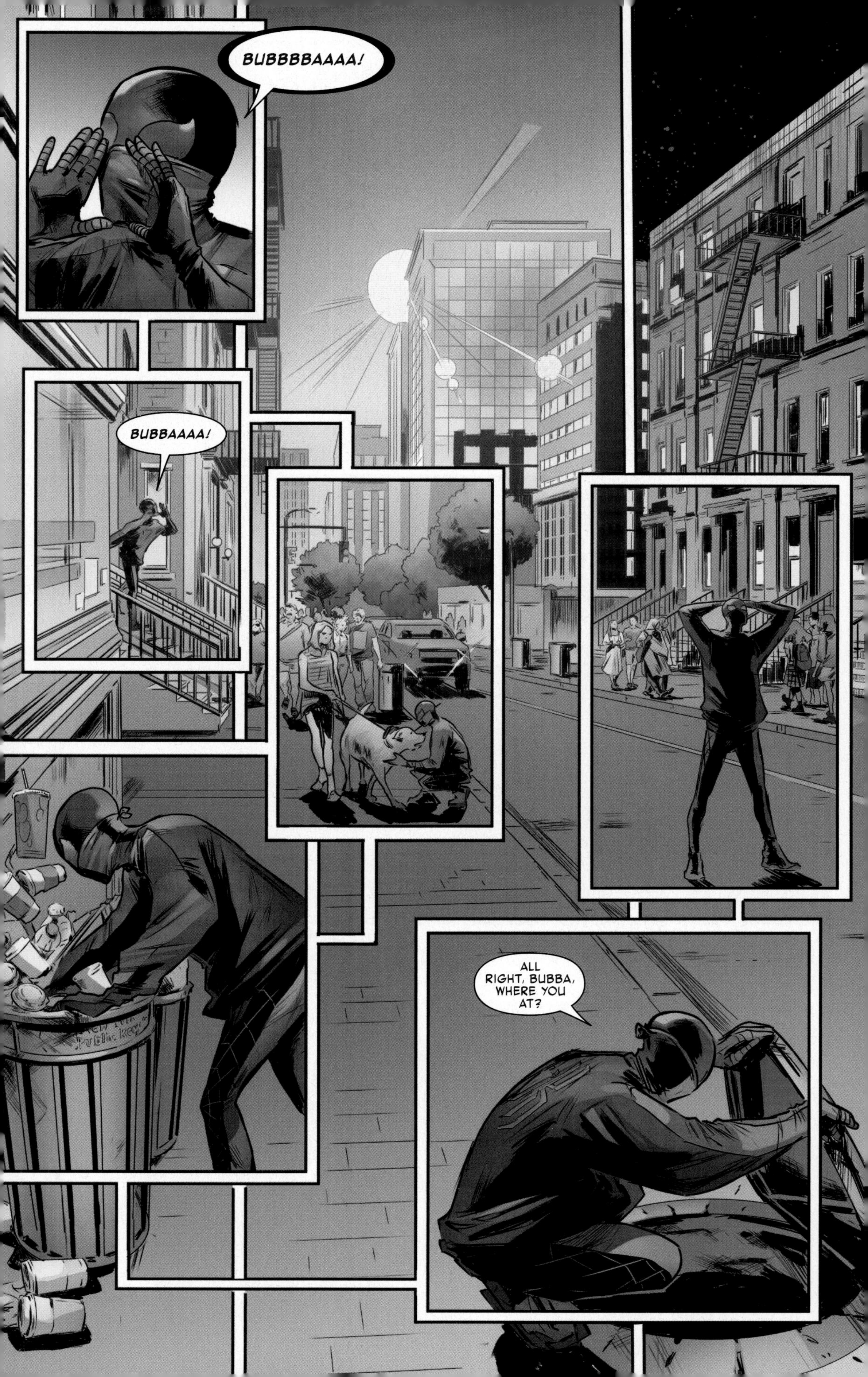
BUBBBBAAAA!
BUBBAAAA!
ALL RIGHT, BUBBA, WHERE YOU AT?

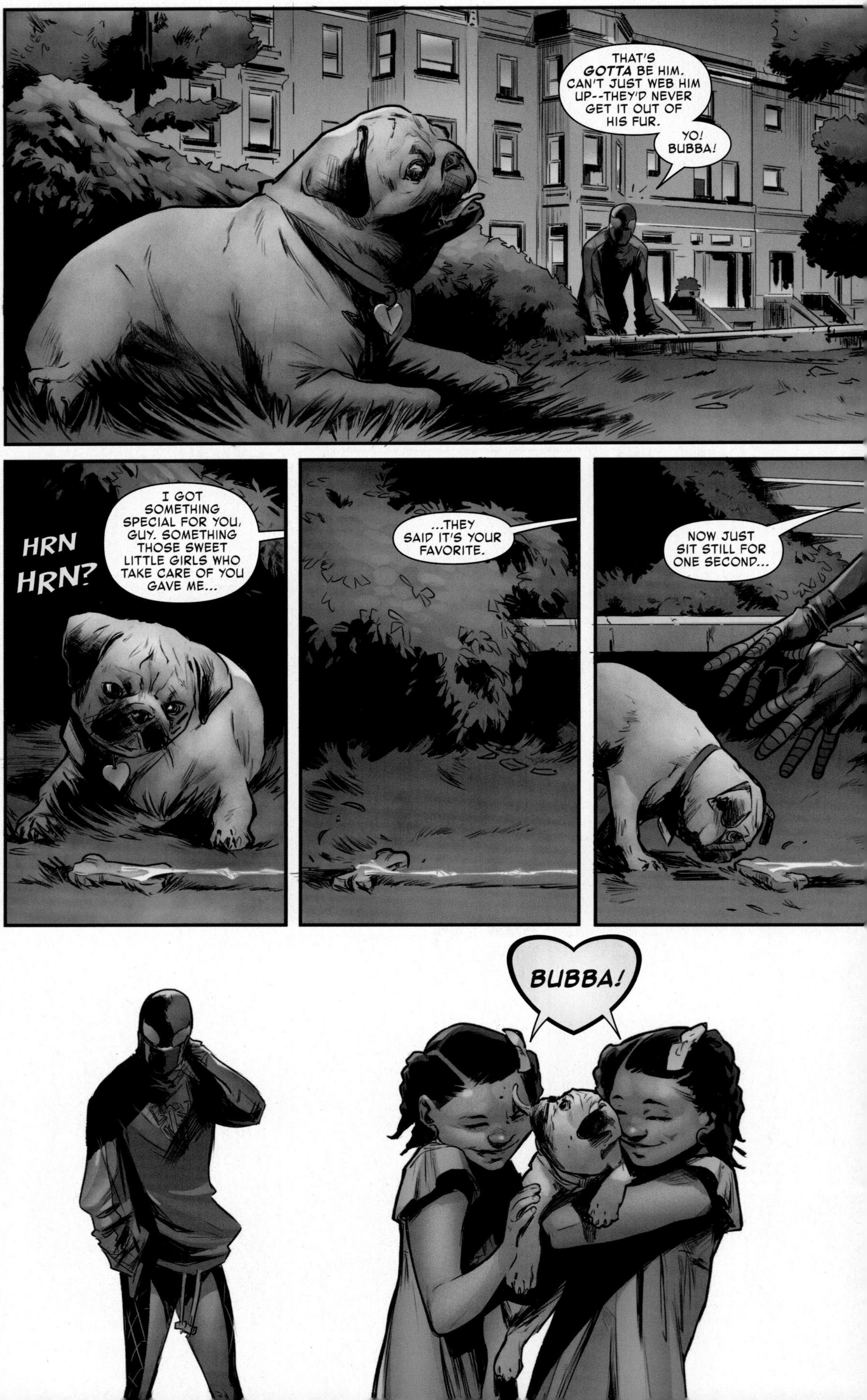
THAT'S GOTTA BE HIM. CAN'T JUST WEB HIM UP--THEY'D NEVER GET IT OUT OF HIS FUR.
YO! BUBBA!
HRN HRN?
I GOT SOMETHING SPECIAL FOR YOU, GUY. SOMETHING THOSE SWEET LITTLE GIRLS WHO TAKE CARE OF YOU GAVE ME...
...THEY SAID IT'S YOUR FAVORITE.
NOW JUST SIT STILL FOR ONE SECOND...
BUBBA!

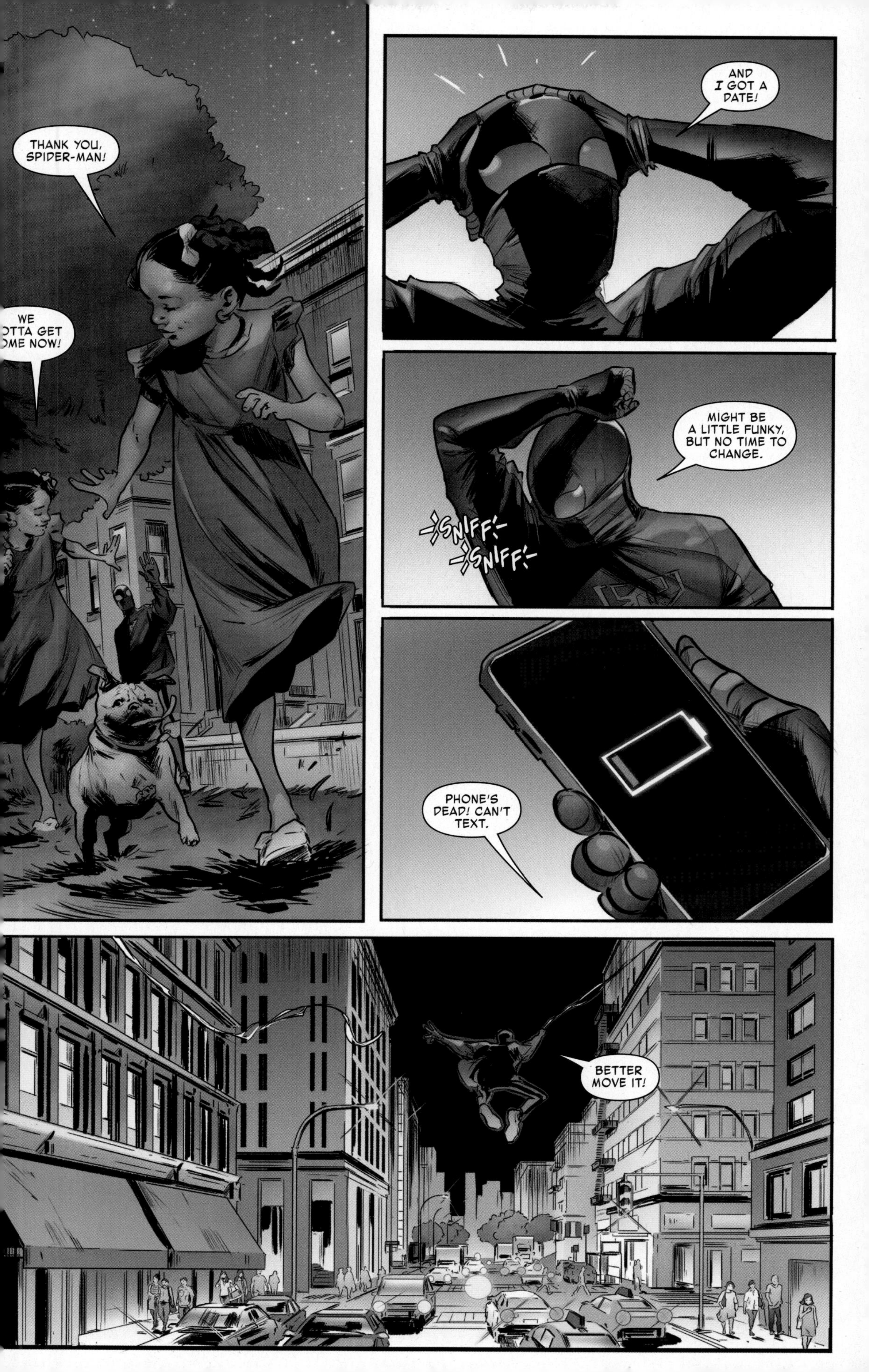
THANK YOU, SPIDER-MAN!
WE OTTA GET OME NOW!
AND I GOT A DATE!
MIGHT BE A LITTLE FUNKY, BUT NO TIME TO CHANGE.
SNIFF
SNIFF
PHONE'S DEAD! CAN'T TEXT.
BETTER MOVE IT!

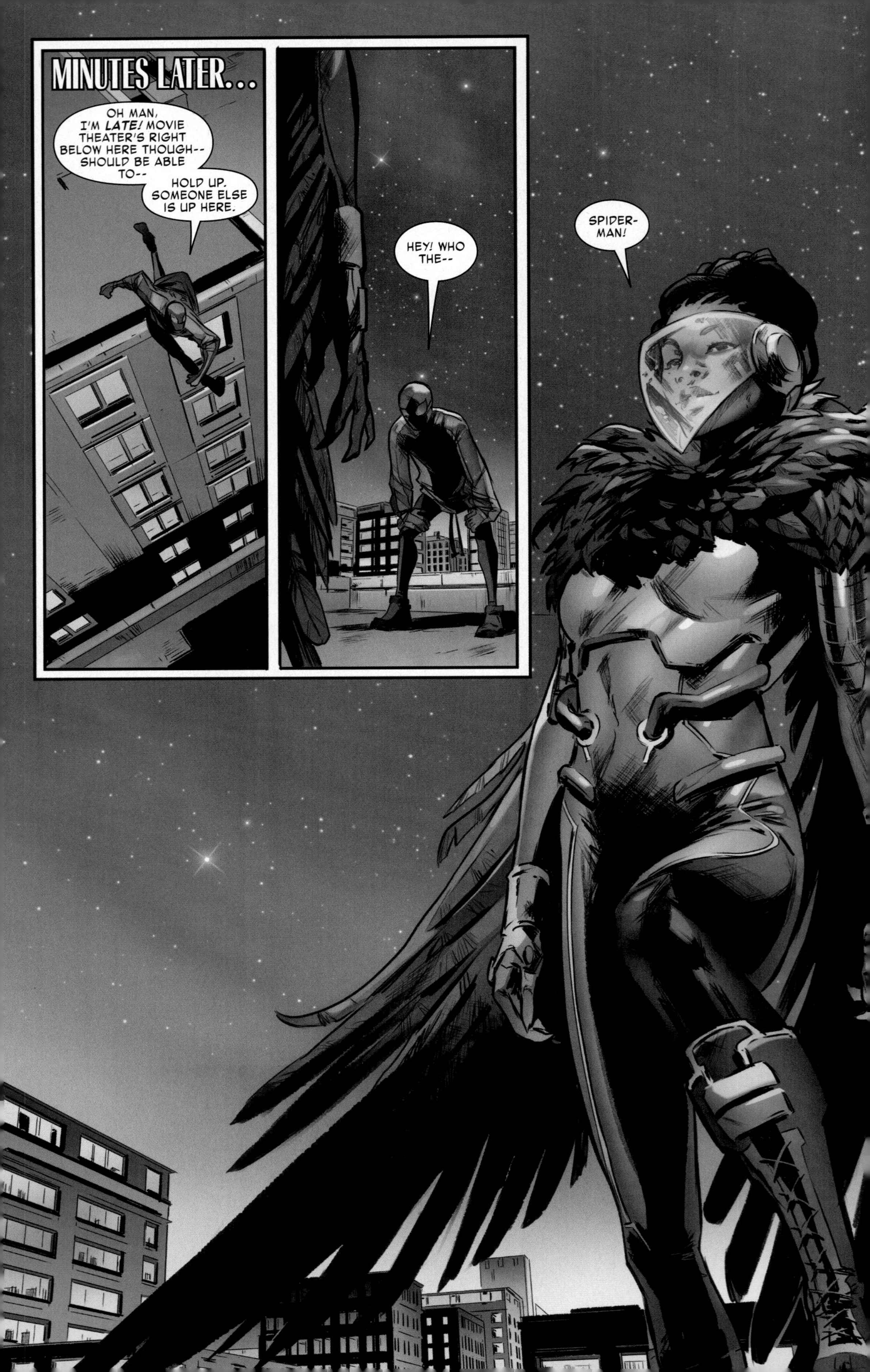
MINUTES LATER...
OH MAN, I'M LATE! MOVIE THEATER'S RIGHT BELOW HERE THOUGH-- SHOULD BE ABLE TO--
HOLD UP. SOMEONE ELSE IS UP HERE.
HEY! WHO THE--
SPIDER-MAN!

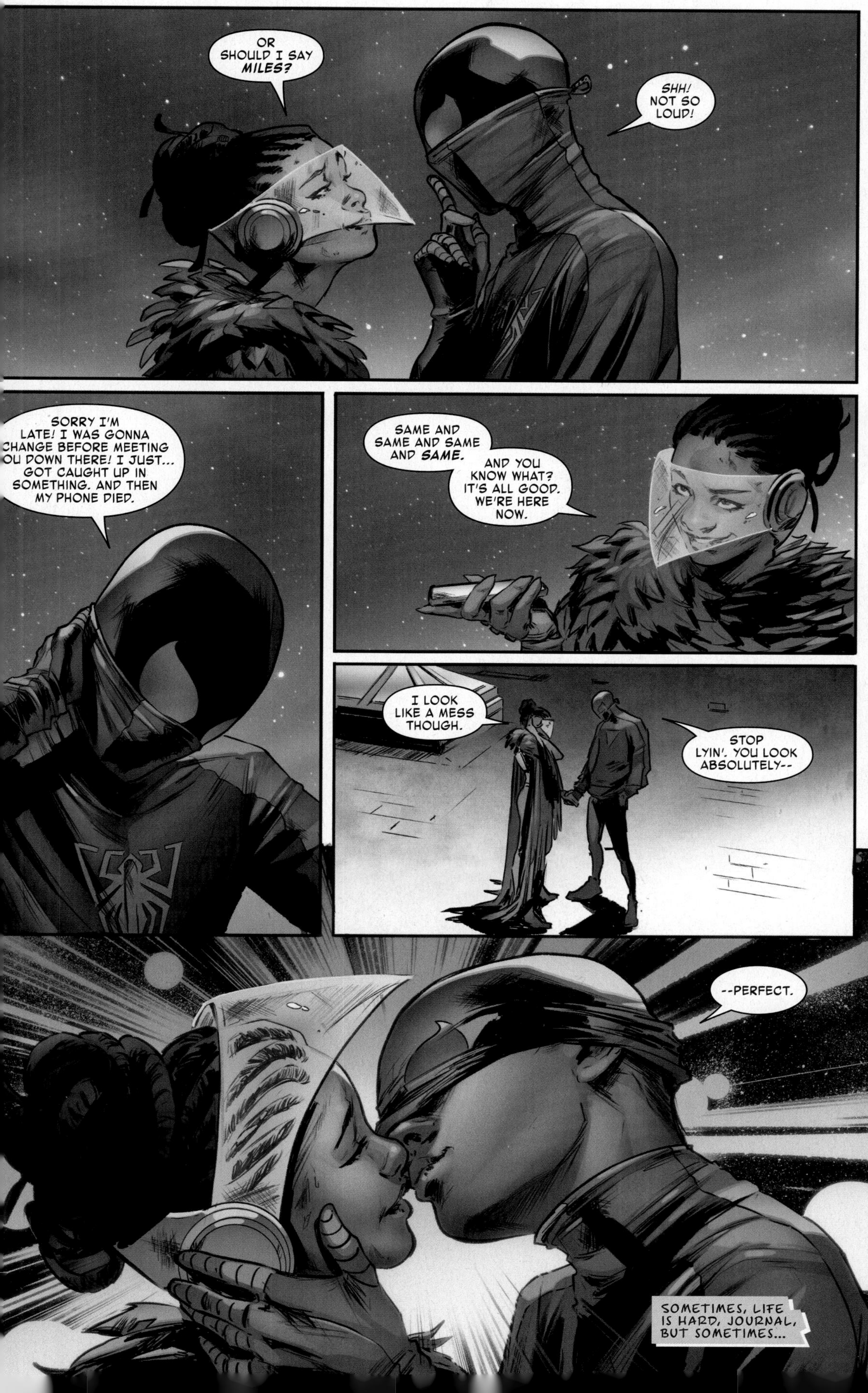
OR SHOULD I SAY MILES?
SHH! NOT SO LOUD!
SORRY I'M LATE! I WAS GONNA CHANGE BEFORE MEETING OU DOWN THERE! I JUST... GOT CAUGHT UP IN SOMETHING. AND THEN MY PHONE DIED.
SAME AND SAME AND SAME AND SAME.
AND YOU KNOW WHAT? IT'S ALL GOOD. WE'RE HERE NOW.
I LOOK LIKE A MESS THOUGH.
STOP LYIN'. YOU LOOK ABSOLUTELY--
--PERFECT.
SOMETIMES, LIFE IS HARD, JOURNAL, BUT SOMETIMES...

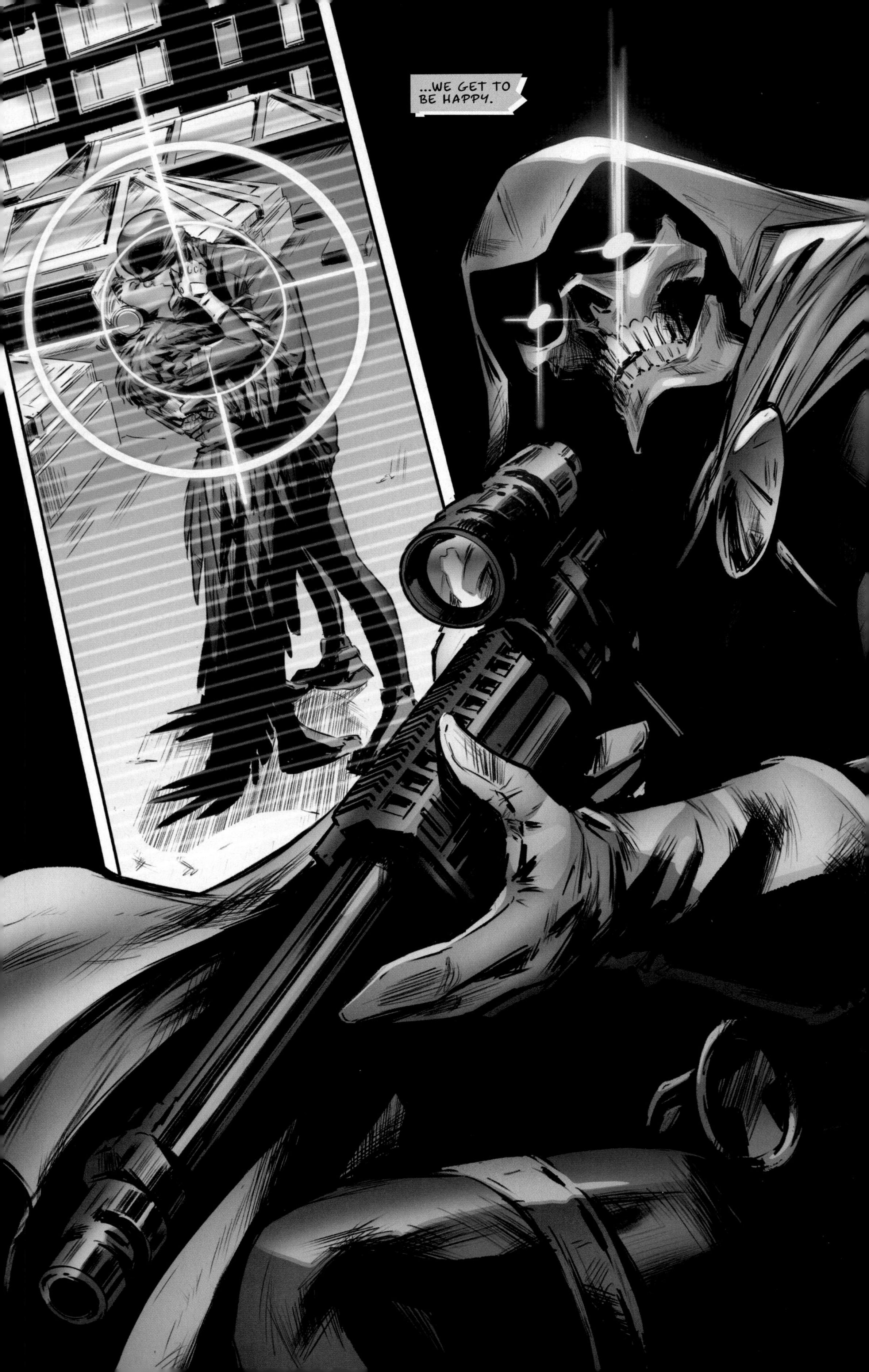
...WE GET TO BE HAPPY.

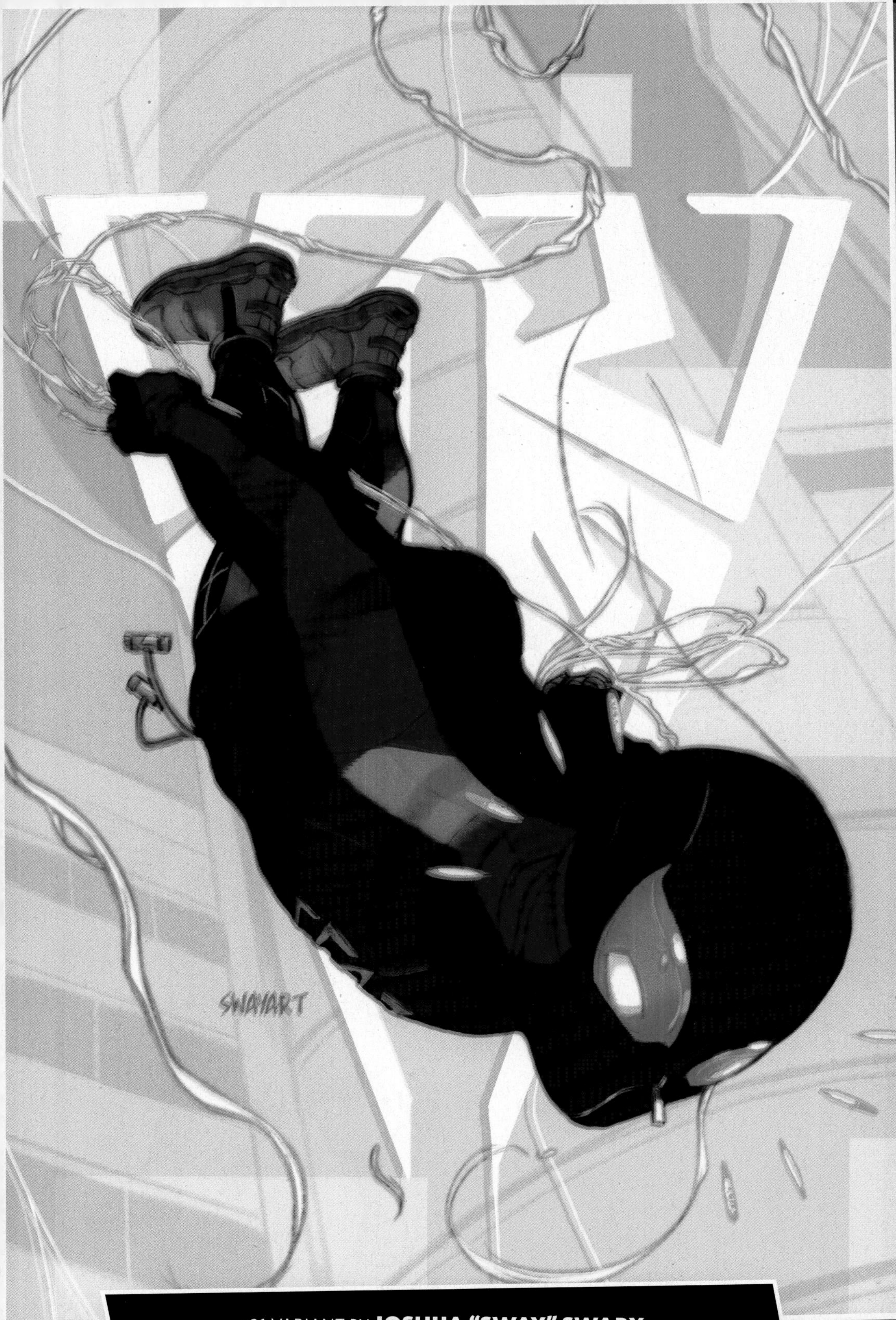
SWAYART

#31 VARIANT BY **JOSHUA "SWAY" SWABY**

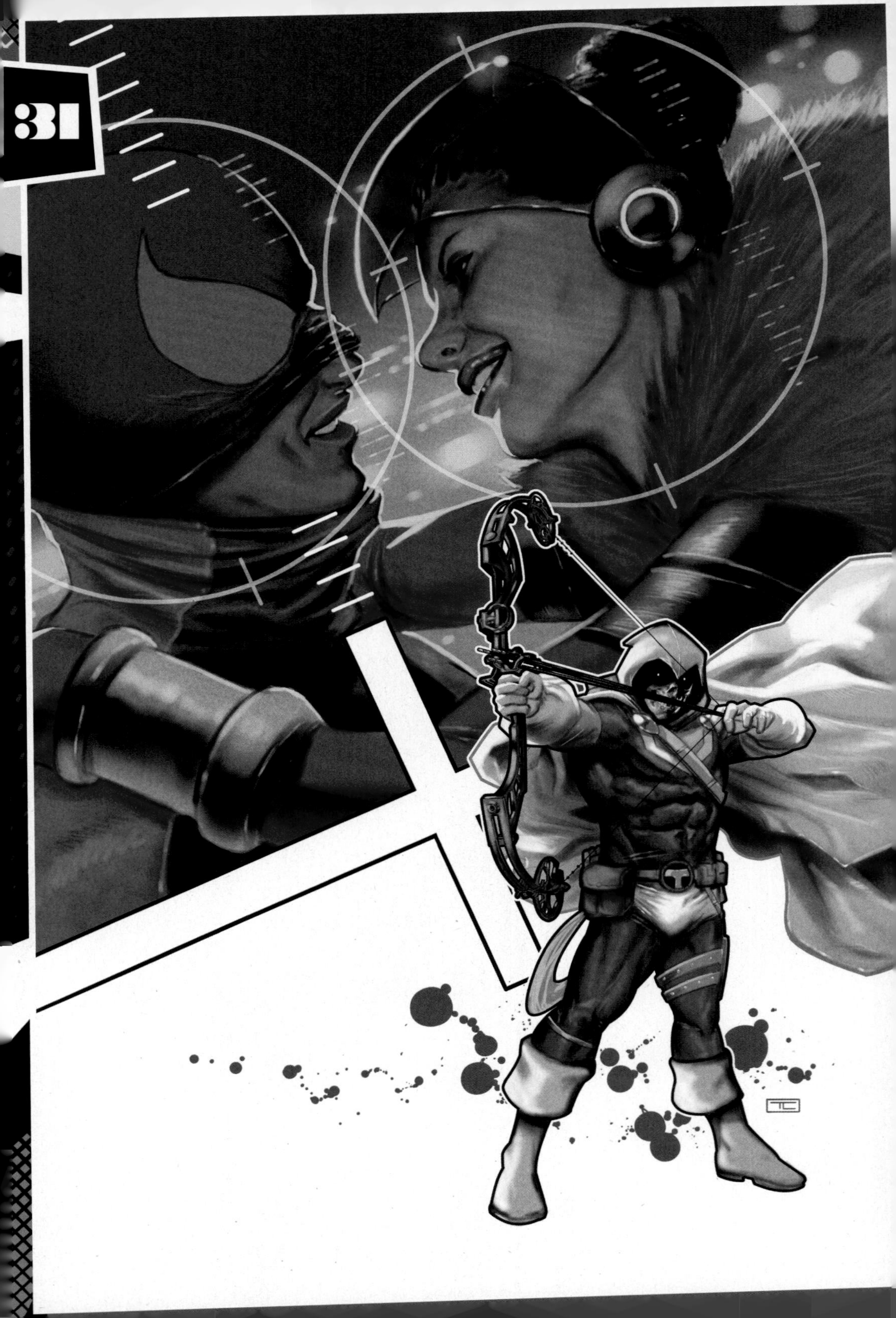
31

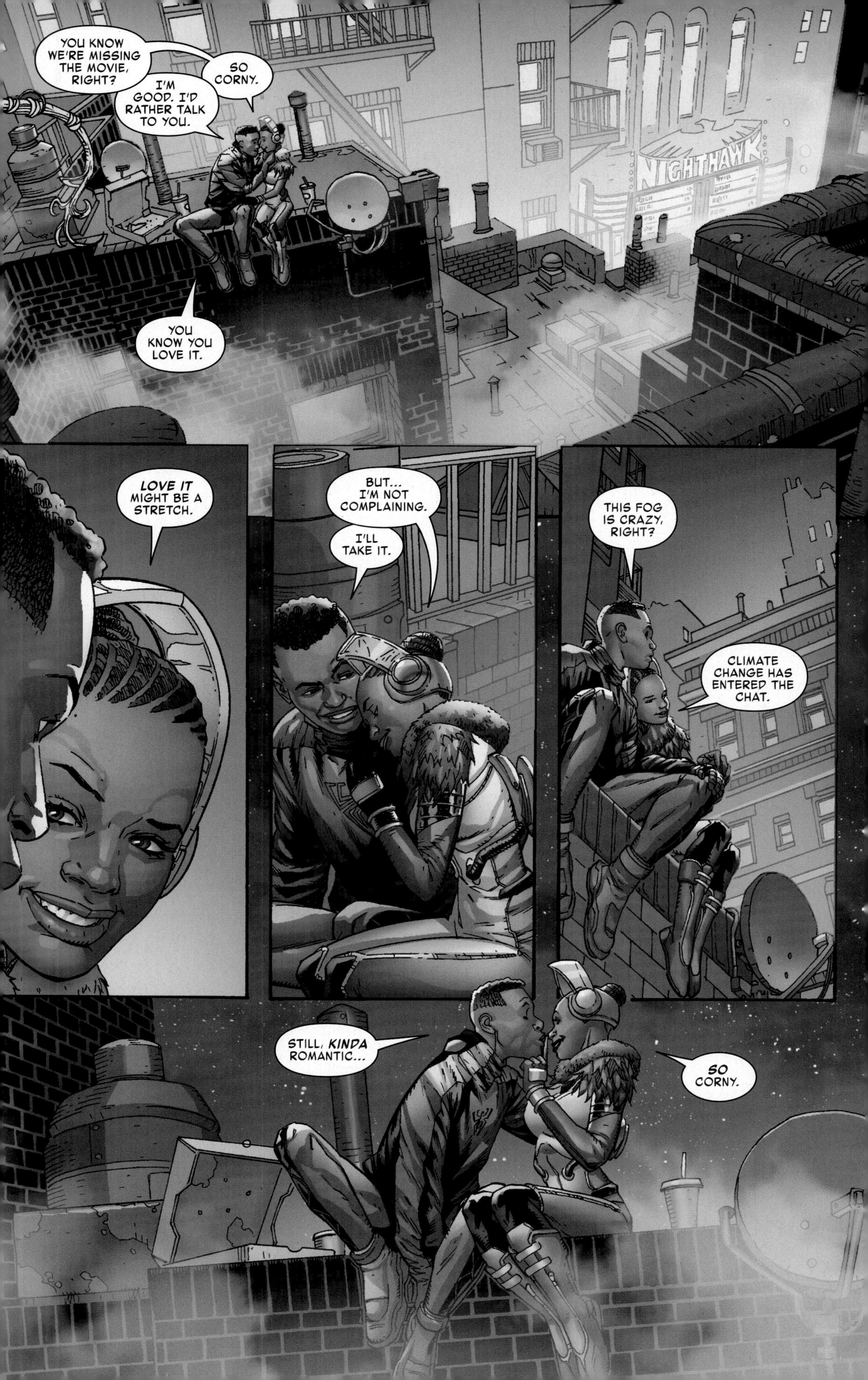
YOU KNOW WE'RE MISSING THE MOVIE, RIGHT?
I'M GOOD. I'D RATHER TALK TO YOU.
SO CORNY.
YOU KNOW YOU LOVE IT.
NIGHTHAWK
LOVE IT MIGHT BE A STRETCH.
BUT... I'M NOT COMPLAINING.
I'LL TAKE IT.
THIS FOG IS CRAZY, RIGHT?
CLIMATE CHANGE HAS ENTERED THE CHAT.
STILL, *KINDA* ROMANTIC...
SO CORNY.

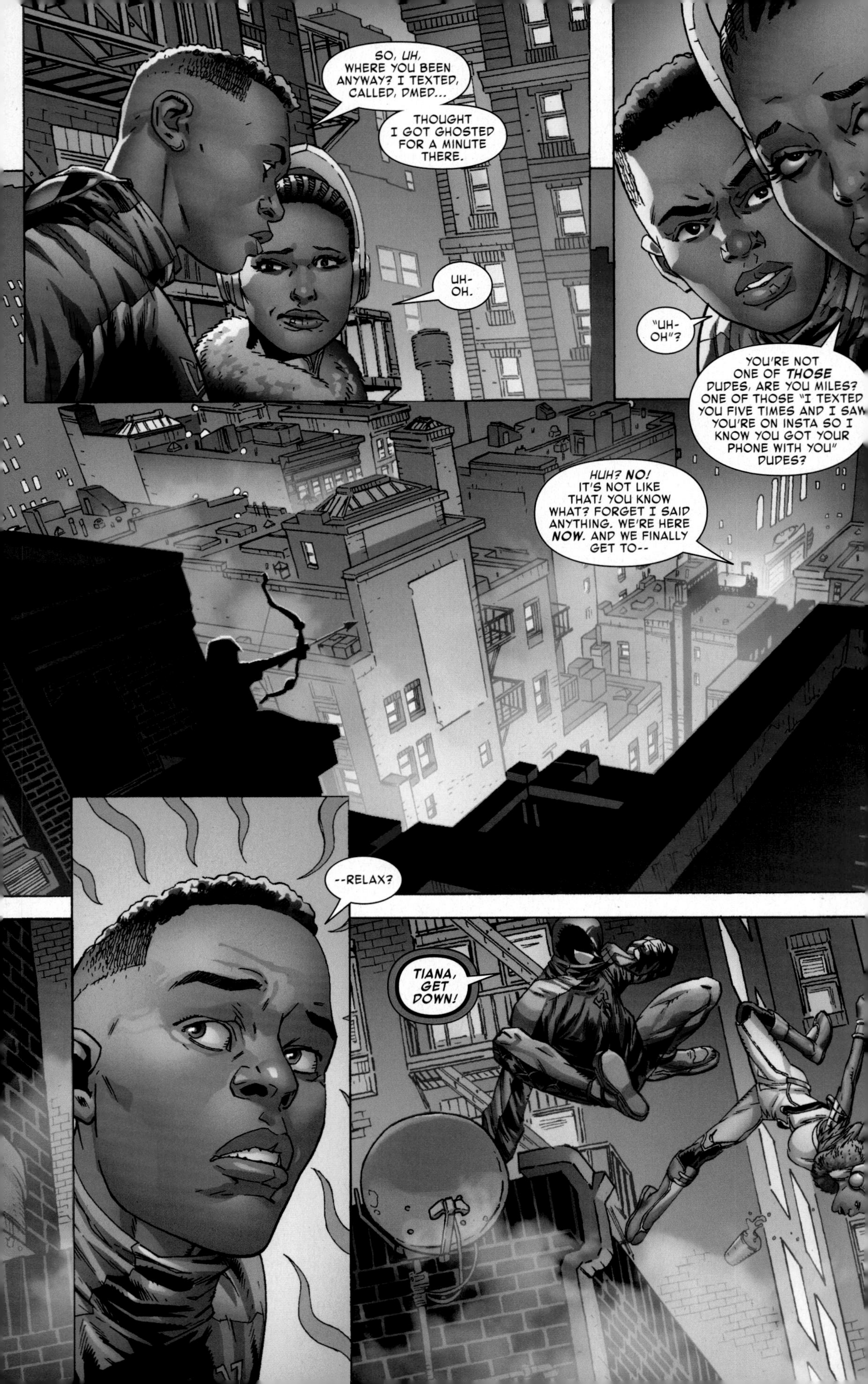
SO, UH, WHERE YOU BEEN ANYWAY? I TEXTED, CALLED, DMED...
THOUGHT I GOT GHOSTED FOR A MINUTE THERE.
UH-OH.
"UH-OH"?
YOU'RE NOT ONE OF THOSE DUDES, ARE YOU MILES? ONE OF THOSE "I TEXTED YOU FIVE TIMES AND I SAW YOU'RE ON INSTA SO I KNOW YOU GOT YOUR PHONE WITH YOU" DUDES?
HUH? NO! IT'S NOT LIKE THAT! YOU KNOW WHAT? FORGET I SAID ANYTHING. WE'RE HERE NOW. AND WE FINALLY GET TO--
--RELAX?
TIANA, GET DOWN!

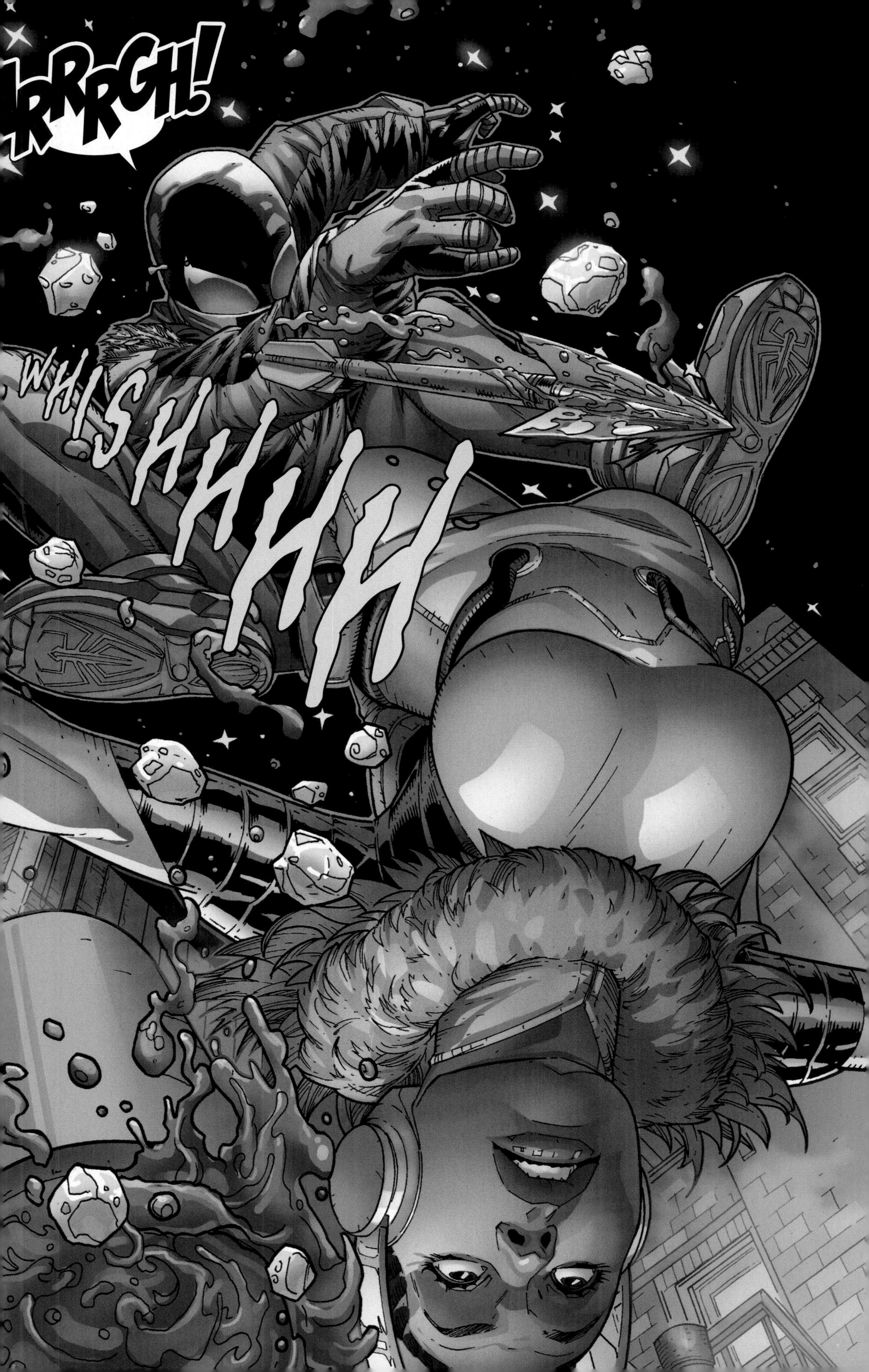
RRRGH!
WHISHHHH

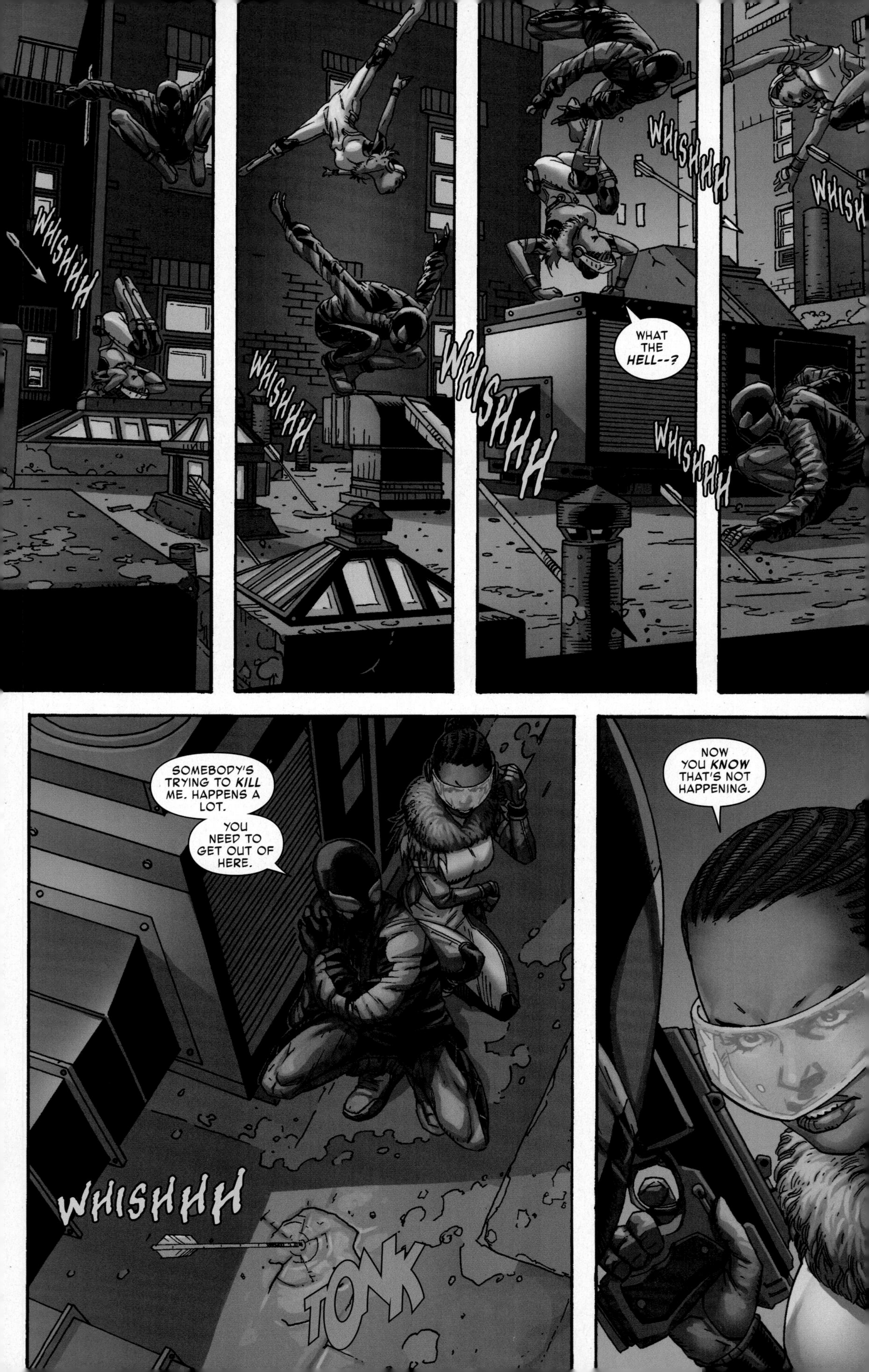
WHISHHH
WHISHHH
WHISHHH
WHISHHH
WHAT THE HELL--?
WHISHHH
WHISHHH
WHISHHH
SOMEBODY'S TRYING TO KILL ME. HAPPENS A LOT.
YOU NEED TO GET OUT OF HERE.
WHISHHH
TONK
NOW YOU KNOW THAT'S NOT HAPPENING.

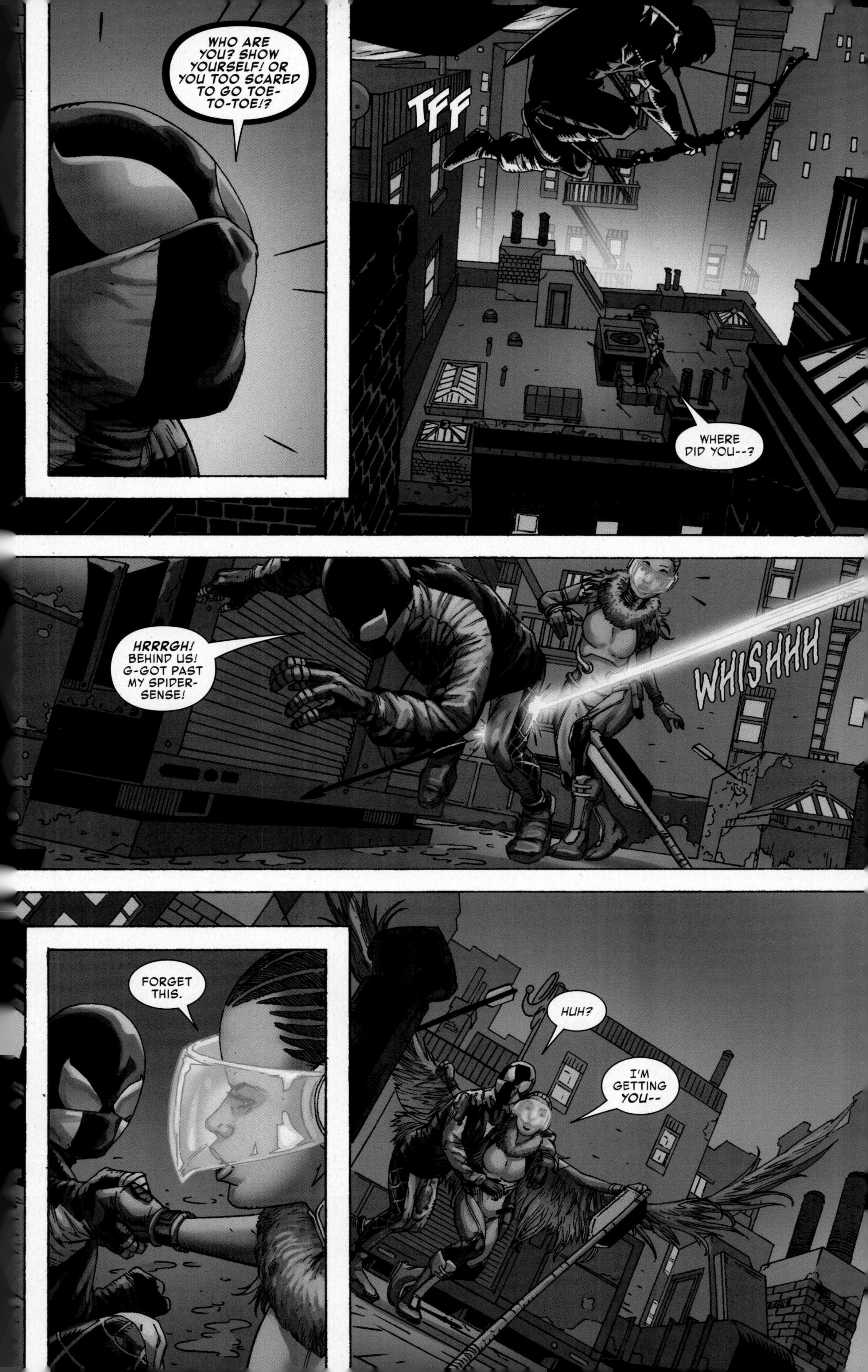
WHO ARE YOU? SHOW YOURSELF! OR YOU TOO SCARED TO GO TOE-TO-TOE!?
TFF
WHERE DID YOU--?
HRRRGH! BEHIND US! G-GOT PAST MY SPIDER-SENSE!
WHISHHH
FORGET THIS.
HUH?
I'M GETTING YOU--

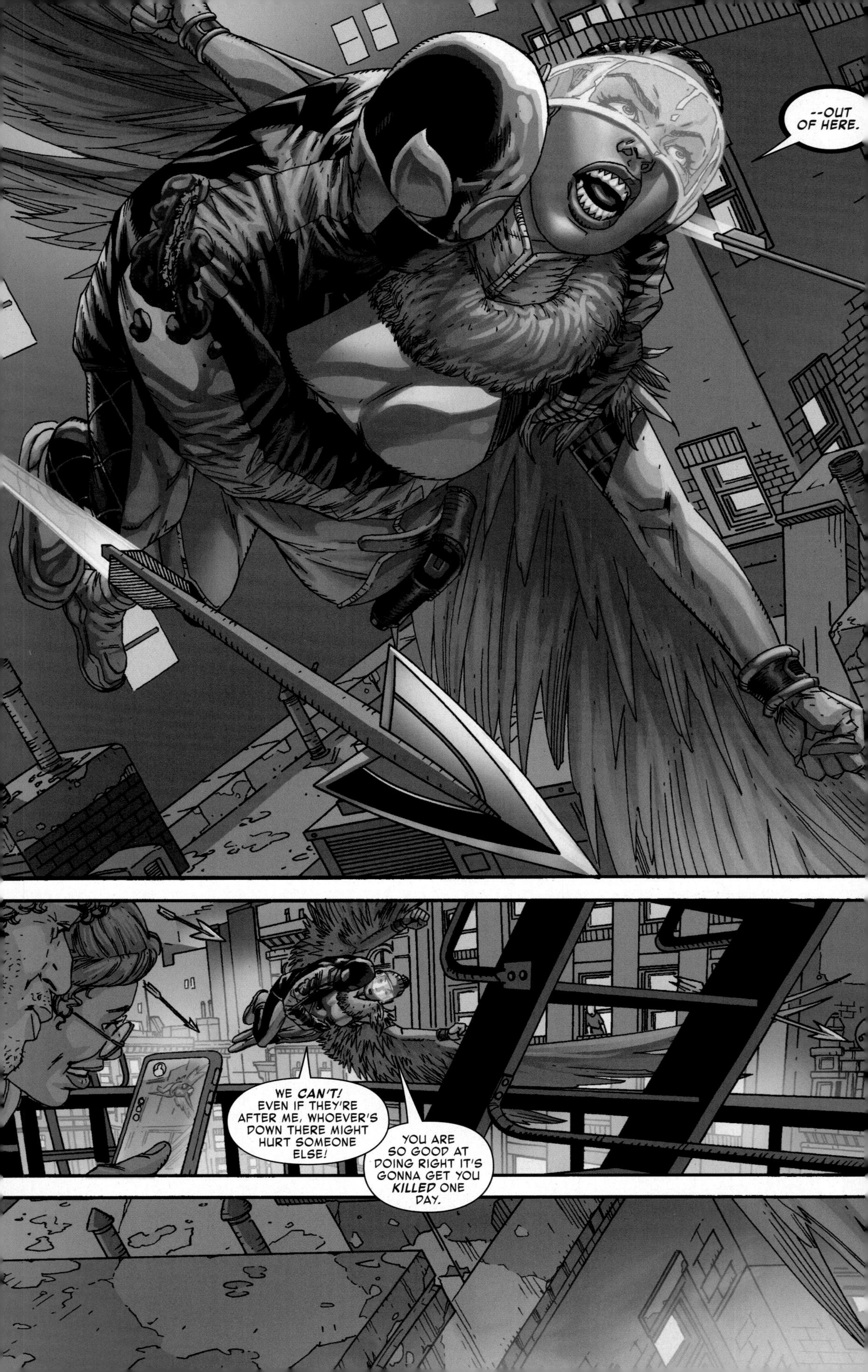

--OUT OF HERE.
WE CAN'T! EVEN IF THEY'RE AFTER ME, WHOEVER'S DOWN THERE MIGHT HURT SOMEONE ELSE!
YOU ARE SO GOOD AT DOING RIGHT IT'S GONNA GET YOU KILLED ONE DAY.

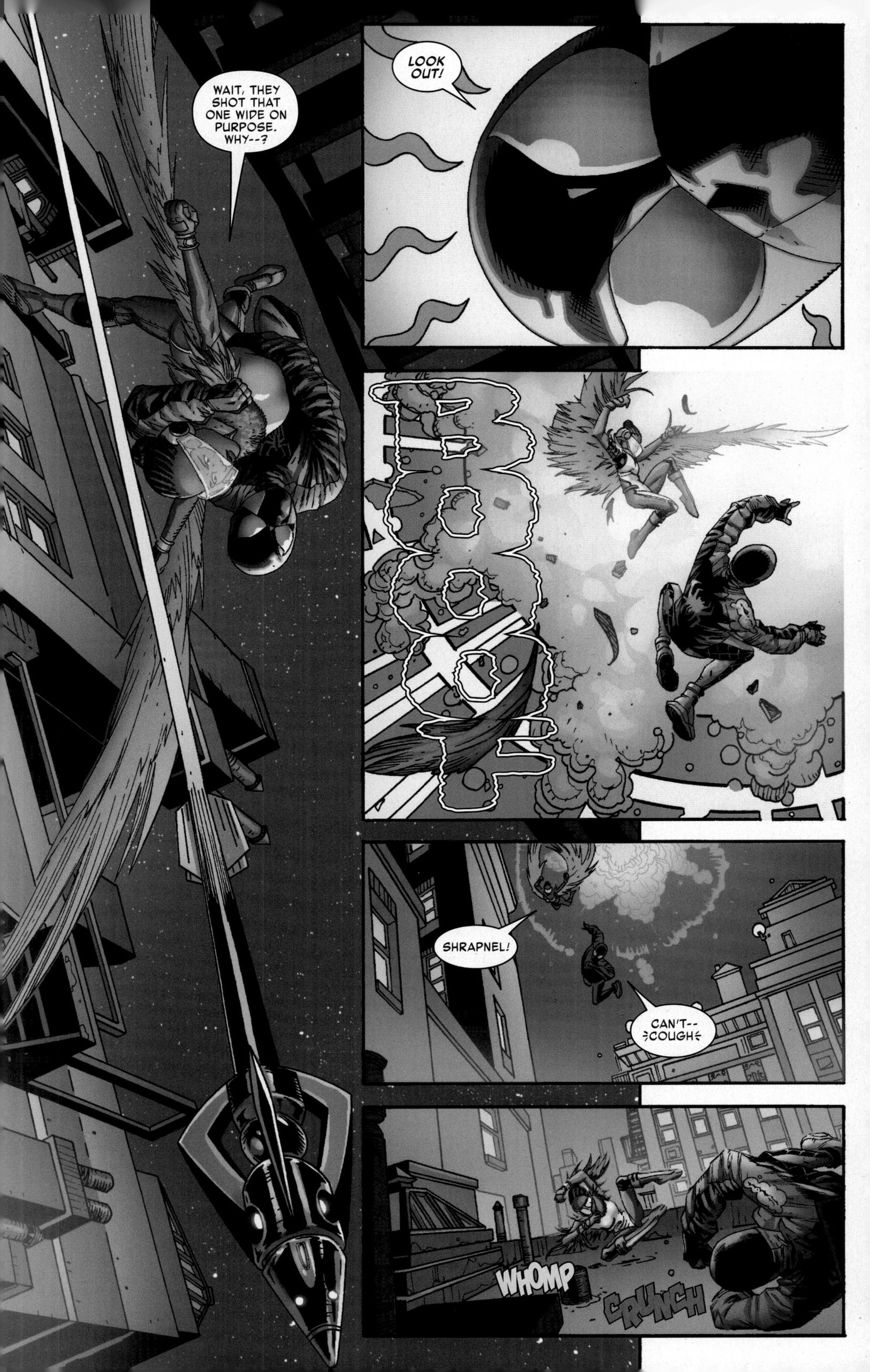
WAIT, THEY SHOT THAT ONE WIDE ON PURPOSE. WHY--?
LOOK OUT!
SHRAPNEL!
CAN'T-- ≈COUGH≈
WHOMP
CRUNCH

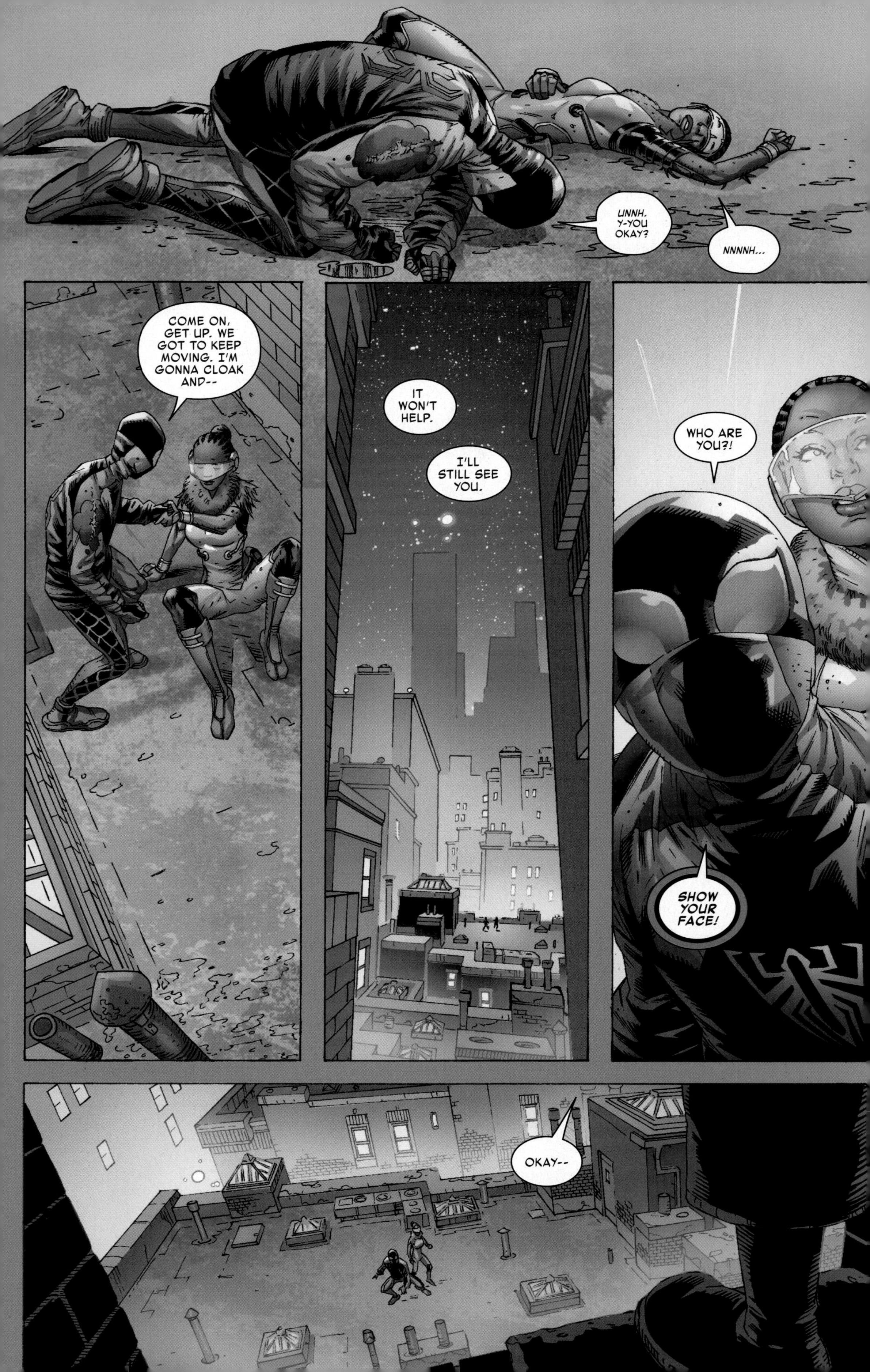
UNNH. Y-YOU OKAY?
NNNNH...
COME ON, GET UP. WE GOT TO KEEP MOVING. I'M GONNA CLOAK AND--
IT WON'T HELP.
I'LL STILL SEE YOU.
WHO ARE YOU?!
SHOW YOUR FACE!
OKAY--

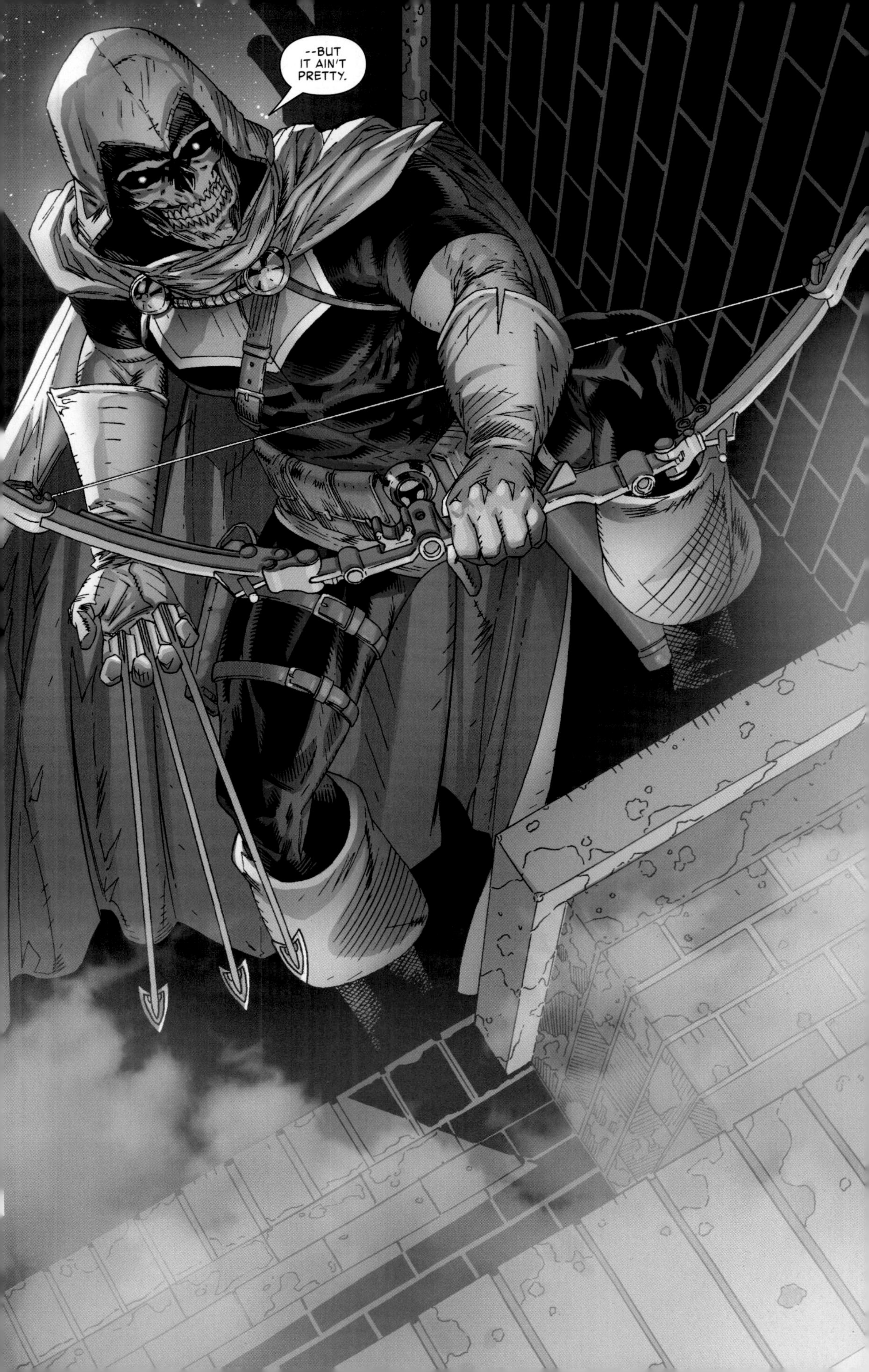
--BUT IT AIN'T PRETTY.

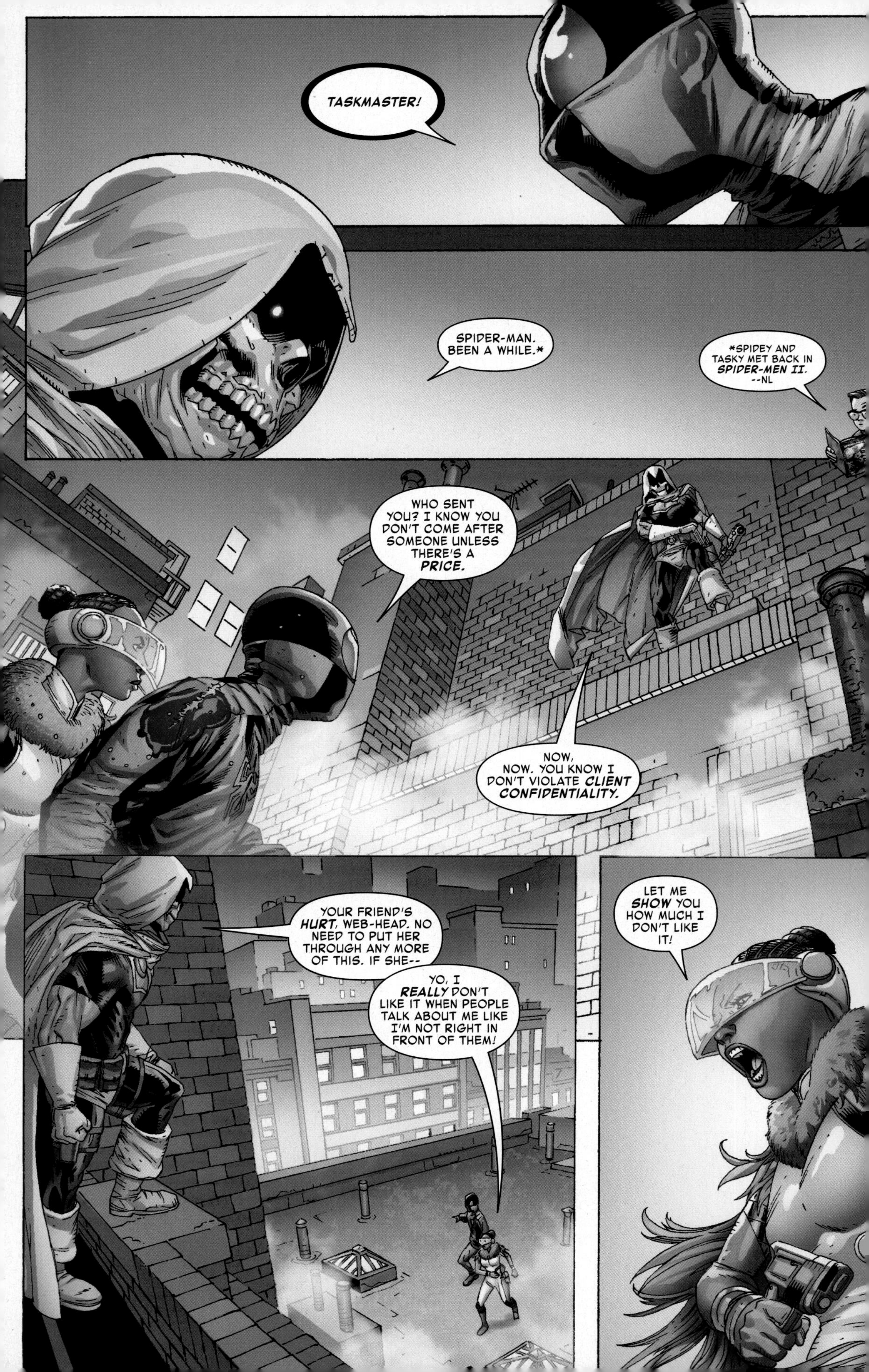
TASKMASTER!
SPIDER-MAN. BEEN A WHILE.*
*SPIDEY AND TASKY MET BACK IN SPIDER-MEN II. --NL
WHO SENT YOU? I KNOW YOU DON'T COME AFTER SOMEONE UNLESS THERE'S A PRICE.
NOW, NOW. YOU KNOW I DON'T VIOLATE CLIENT CONFIDENTIALITY.
YOUR FRIEND'S HURT, WEB-HEAD. NO NEED TO PUT HER THROUGH ANY MORE OF THIS. IF SHE--
YO, I REALLY DON'T LIKE IT WHEN PEOPLE TALK ABOUT ME LIKE I'M NOT RIGHT IN FRONT OF THEM!
LET ME SHOW YOU HOW MUCH I DON'T LIKE IT!

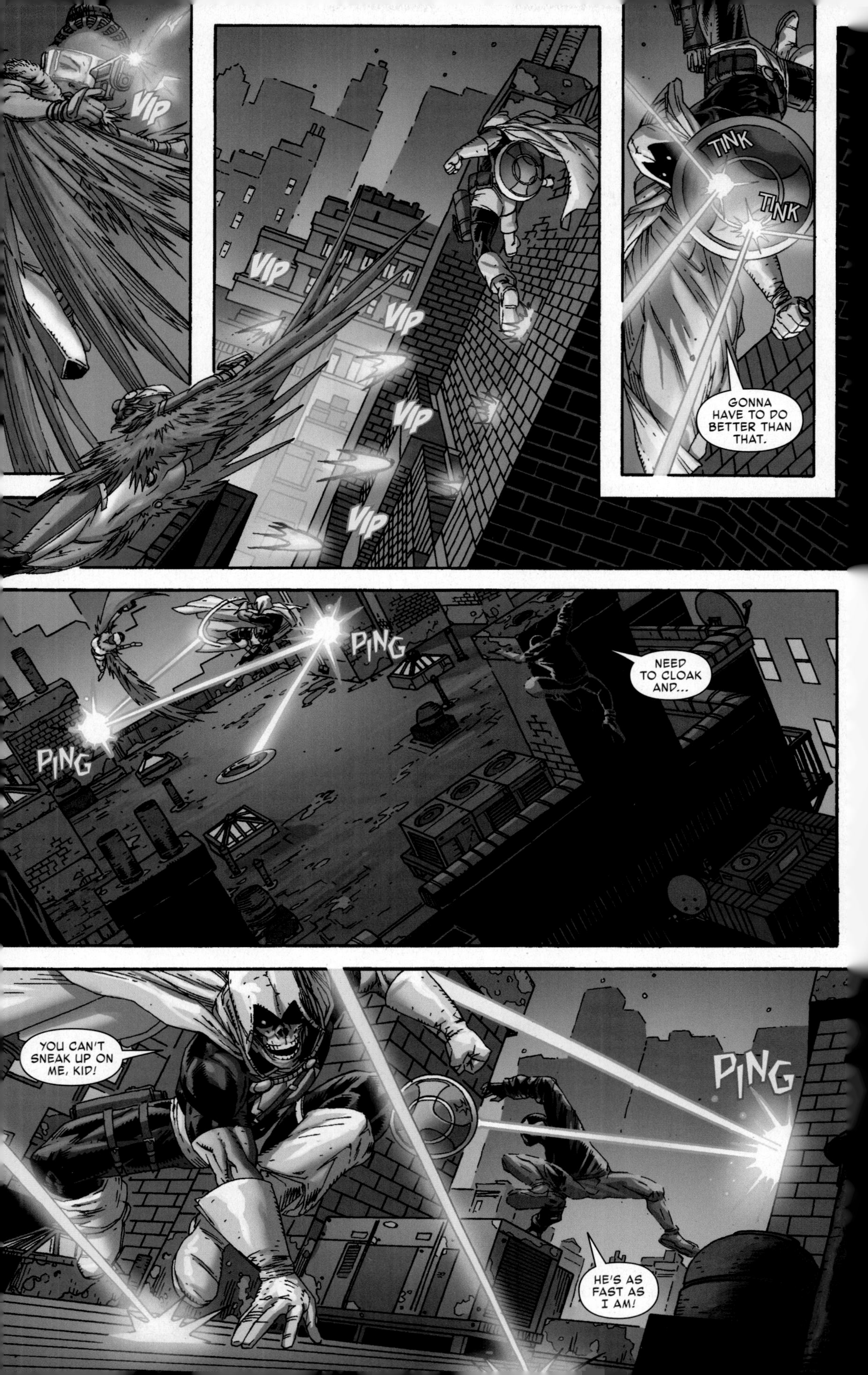
VIP
VIP
VIP
VIP
VIP
TINK
TINK
GONNA HAVE TO DO BETTER THAN THAT.
PING
PING
NEED TO CLOAK AND...
YOU CAN'T SNEAK UP ON ME, KID!
PING
HE'S AS FAST AS I AM!

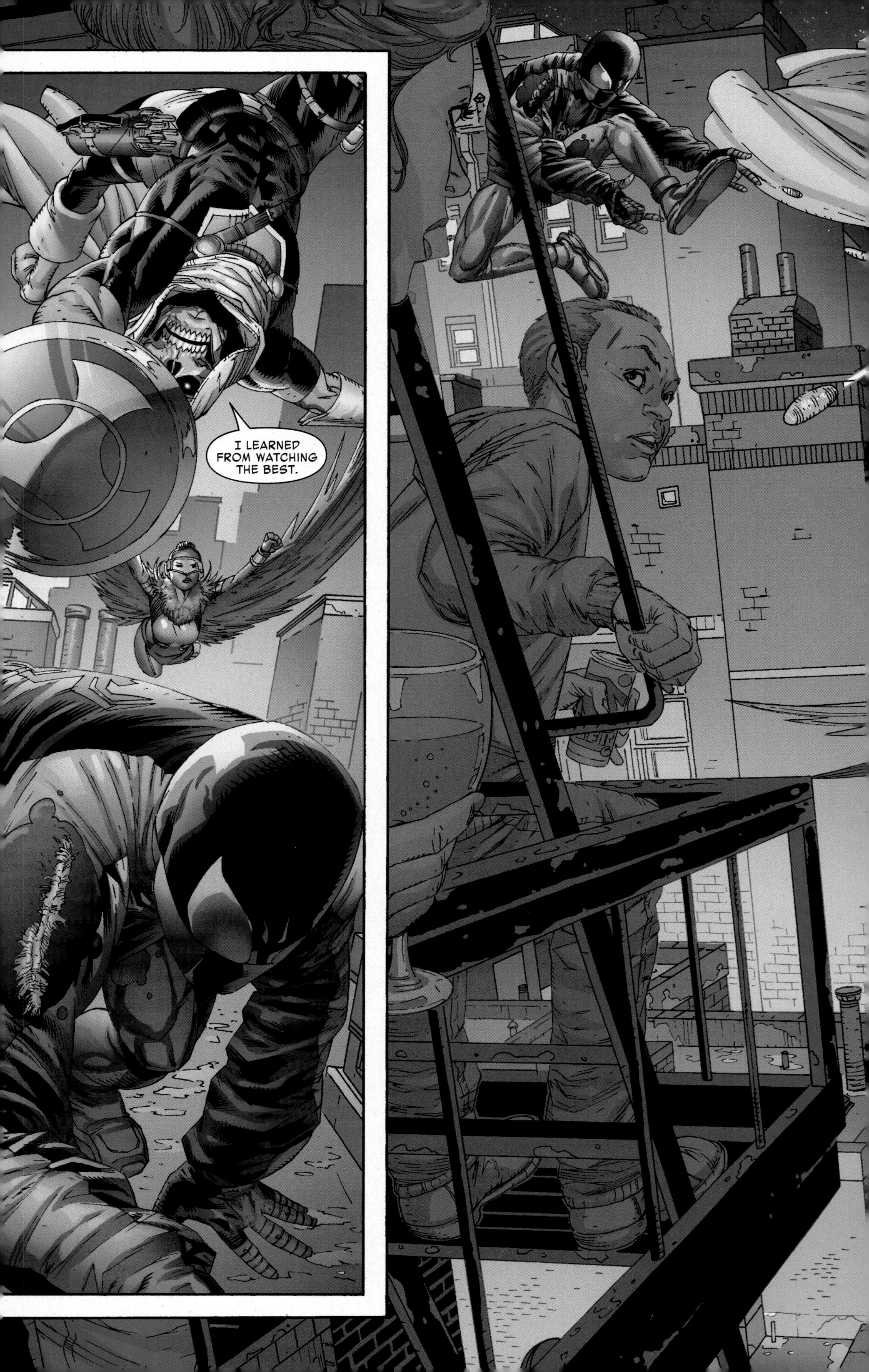
I LEARNED FROM WATCHING THE BEST.

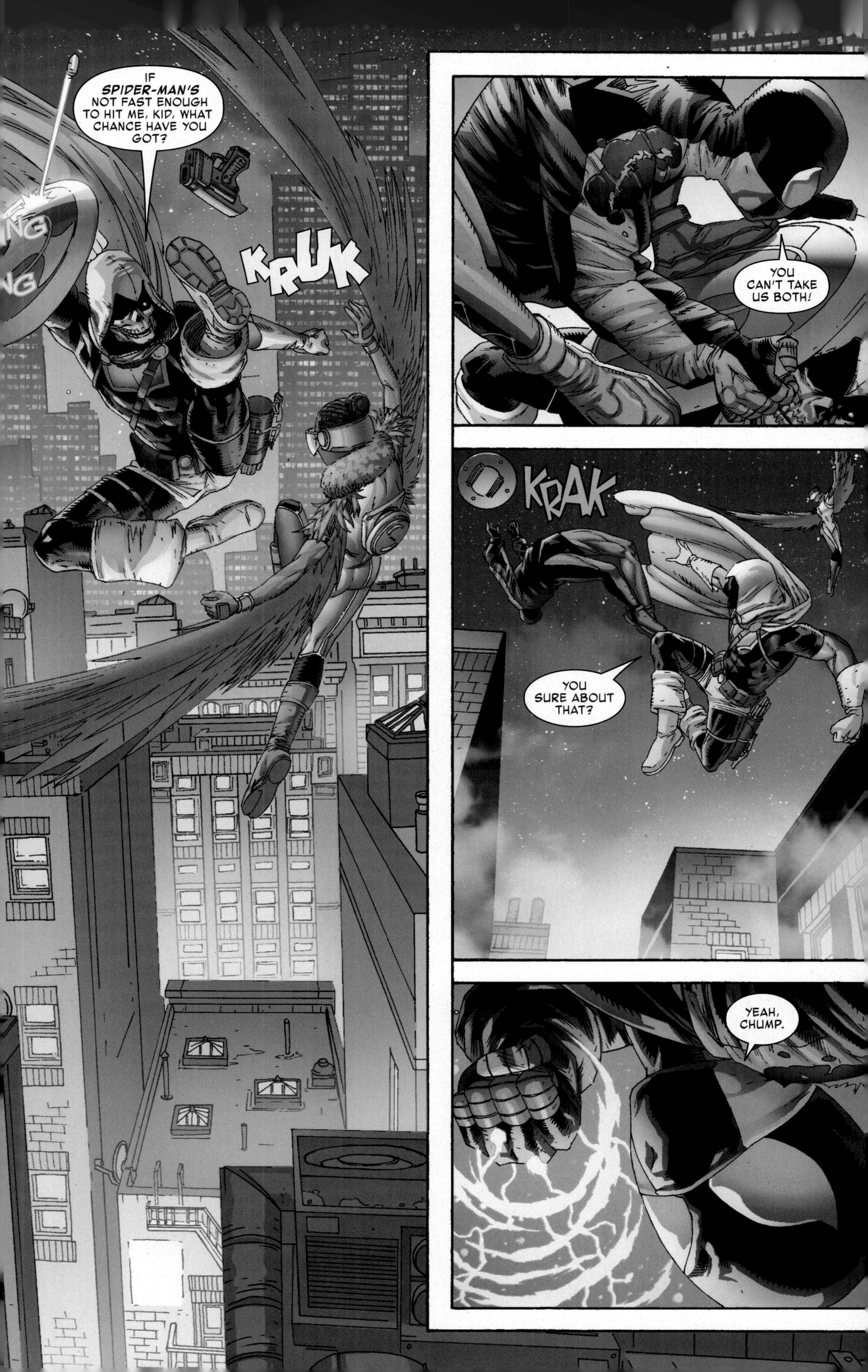
IF SPIDER-MAN'S NOT FAST ENOUGH TO HIT ME, KID, WHAT CHANCE HAVE YOU GOT?
KRUK
YOU CAN'T TAKE US BOTH!
KRAK
YOU SURE ABOUT THAT?
YEAH, CHUMP.

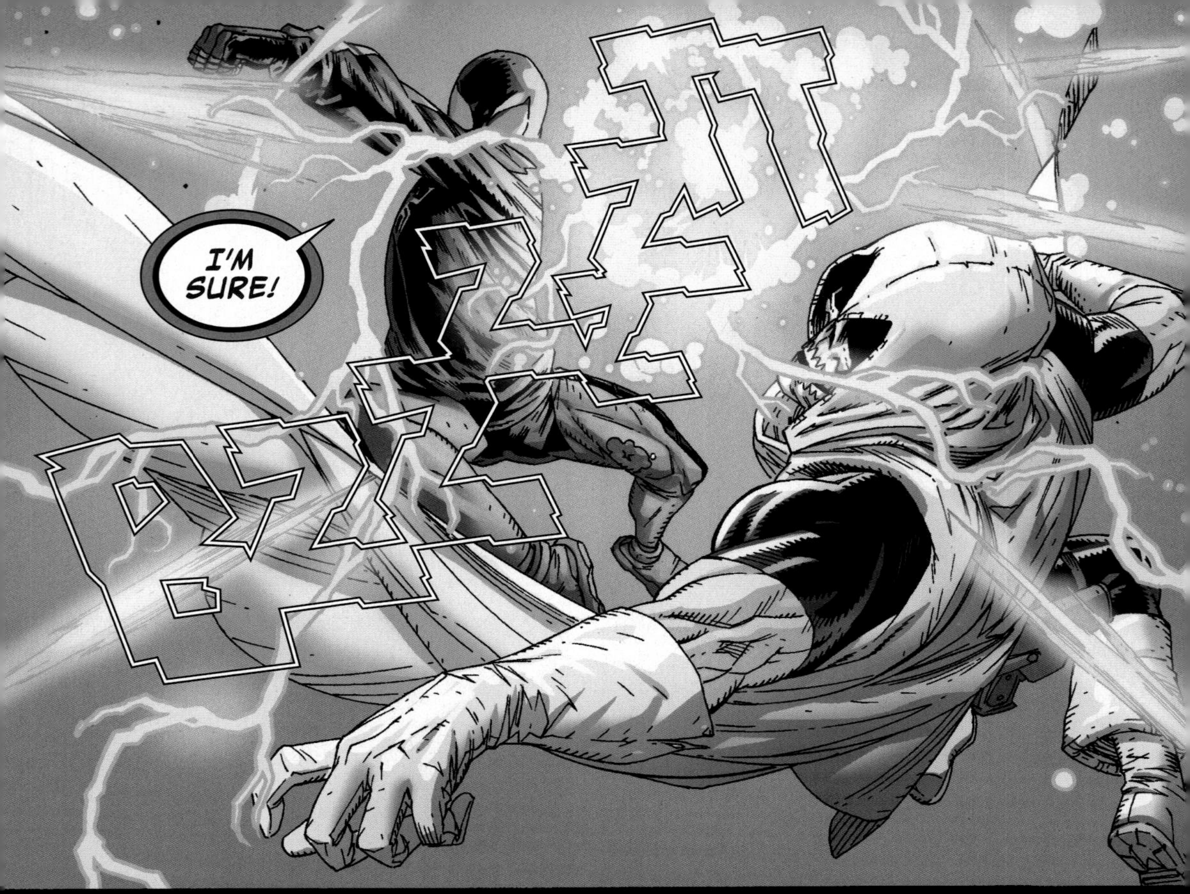
I'M SURE!

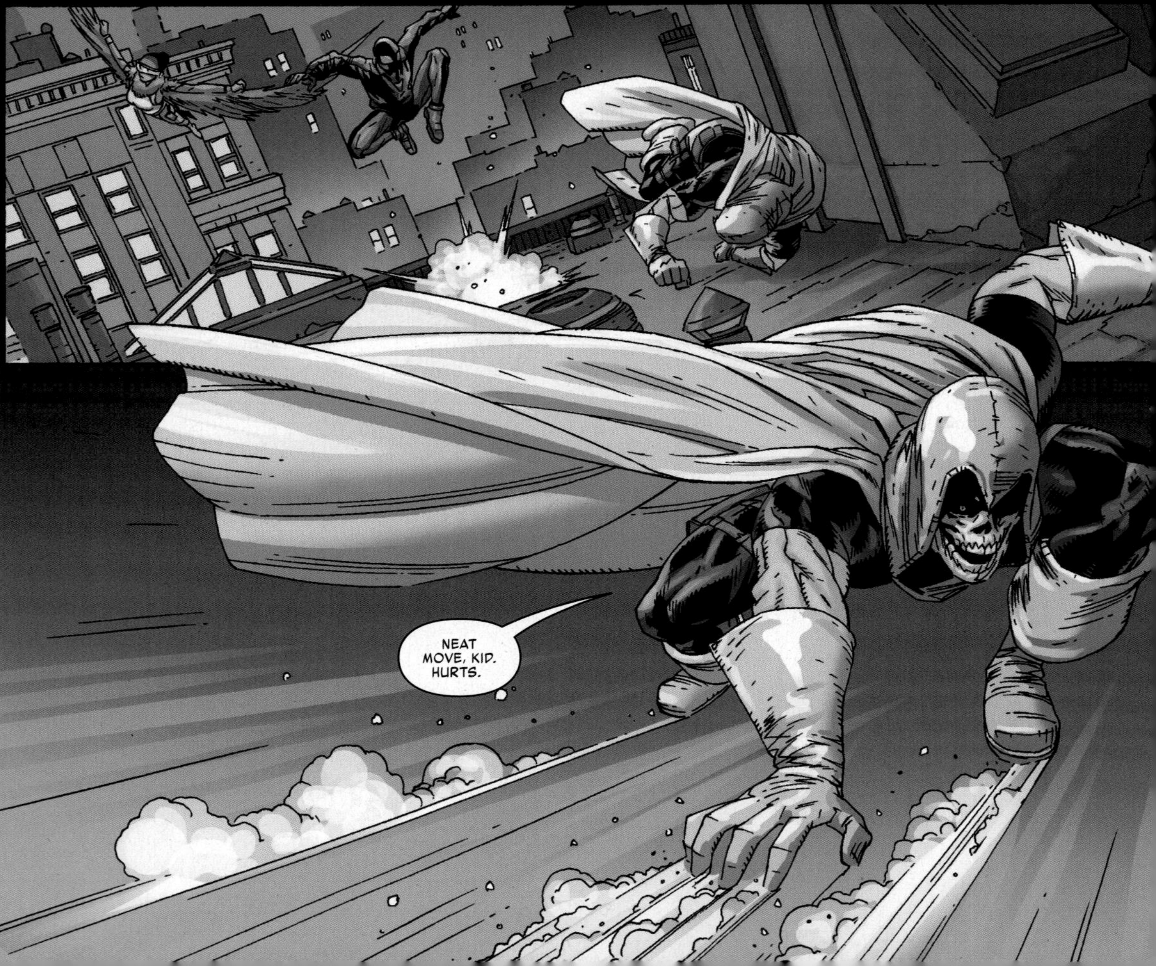
NEAT MOVE, KID. HURTS.

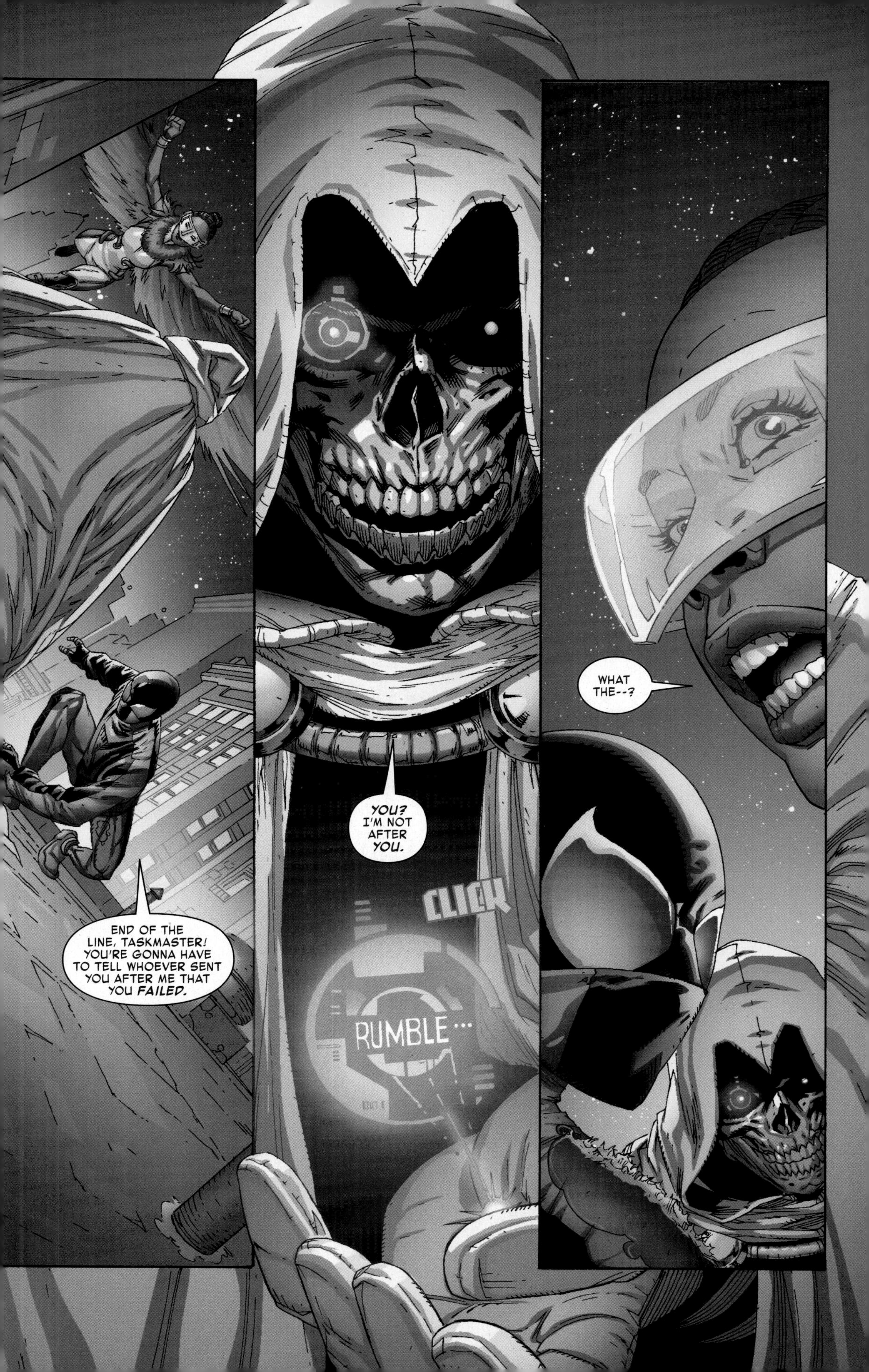

END OF THE LINE, TASKMASTER! YOU'RE GONNA HAVE TO TELL WHOEVER SENT YOU AFTER ME THAT YOU FAILED.
YOU? I'M NOT AFTER YOU.
CLICK
RUMBLE...
WHAT THE--?

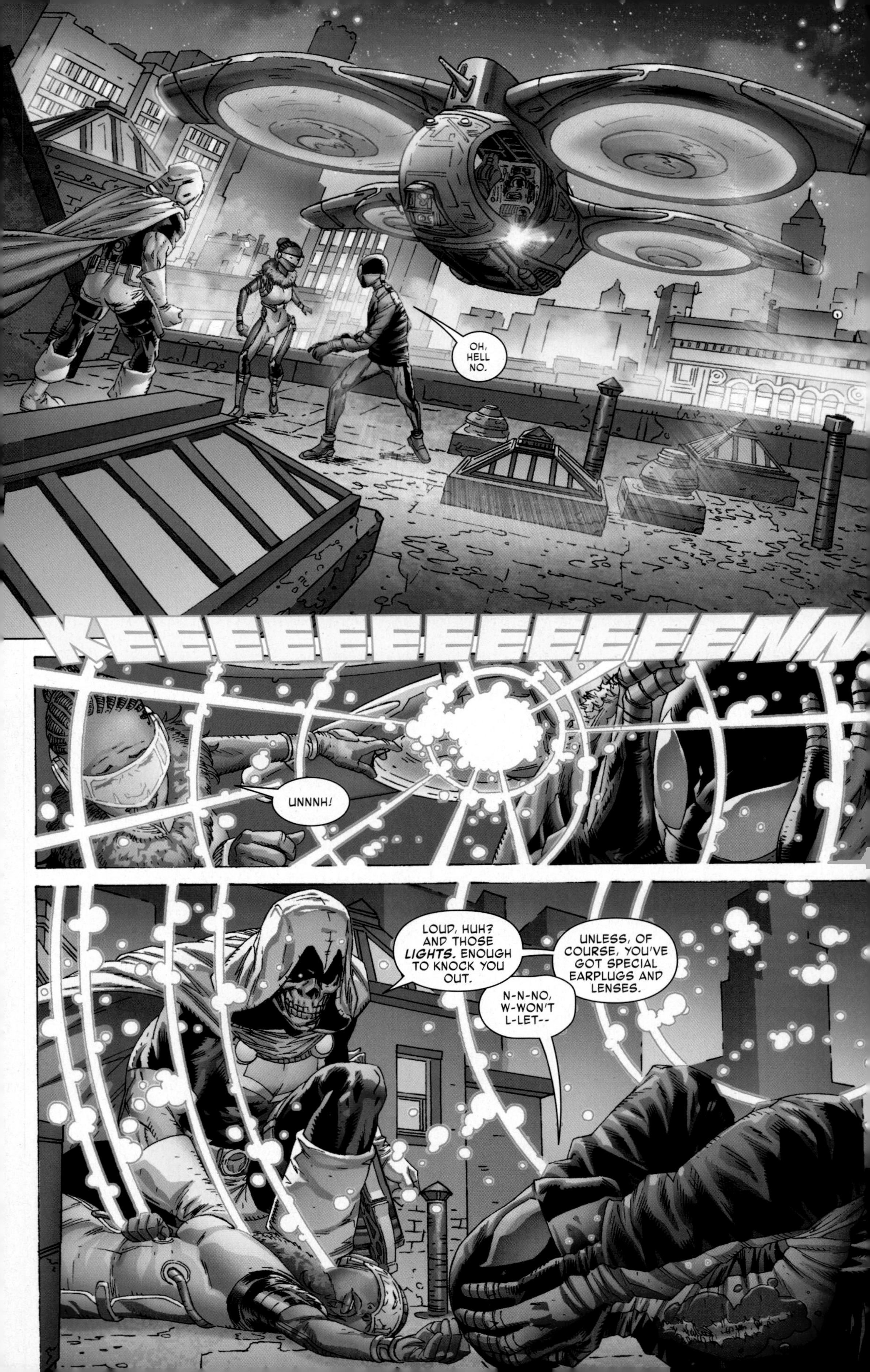
OH, HELL NO.
KEEEEEEEEEEEEENN
UNNNH!
LOUD, HUH? AND THOSE LIGHTS. ENOUGH TO KNOCK YOU OUT.
UNLESS, OF COURSE, YOU'VE GOT SPECIAL EARPLUGS AND LENSES.
N-N-NO, W-WON'T L-LET--

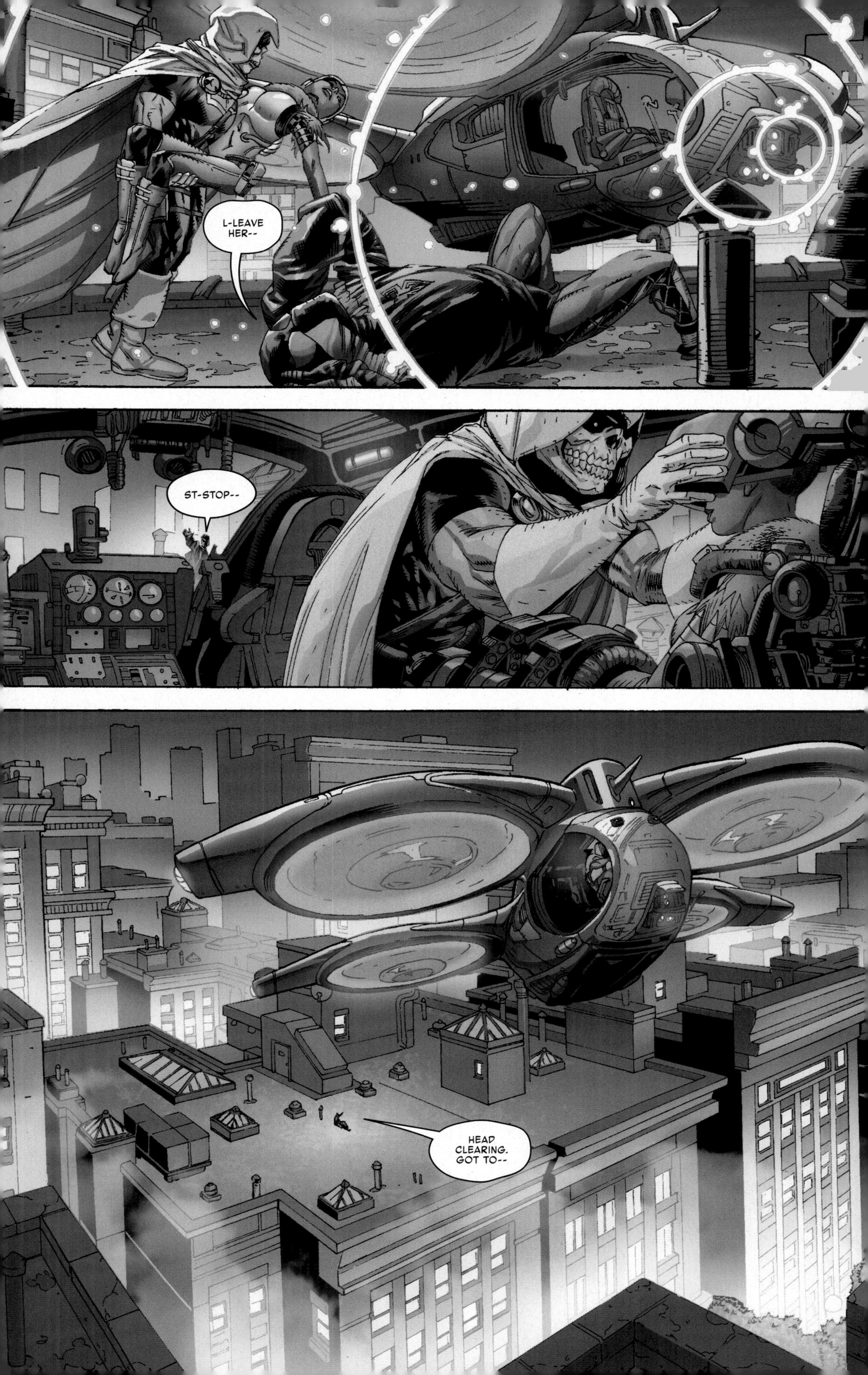
L-LEAVE HER--
ST-STOP--
HEAD CLEARING. GOT TO--

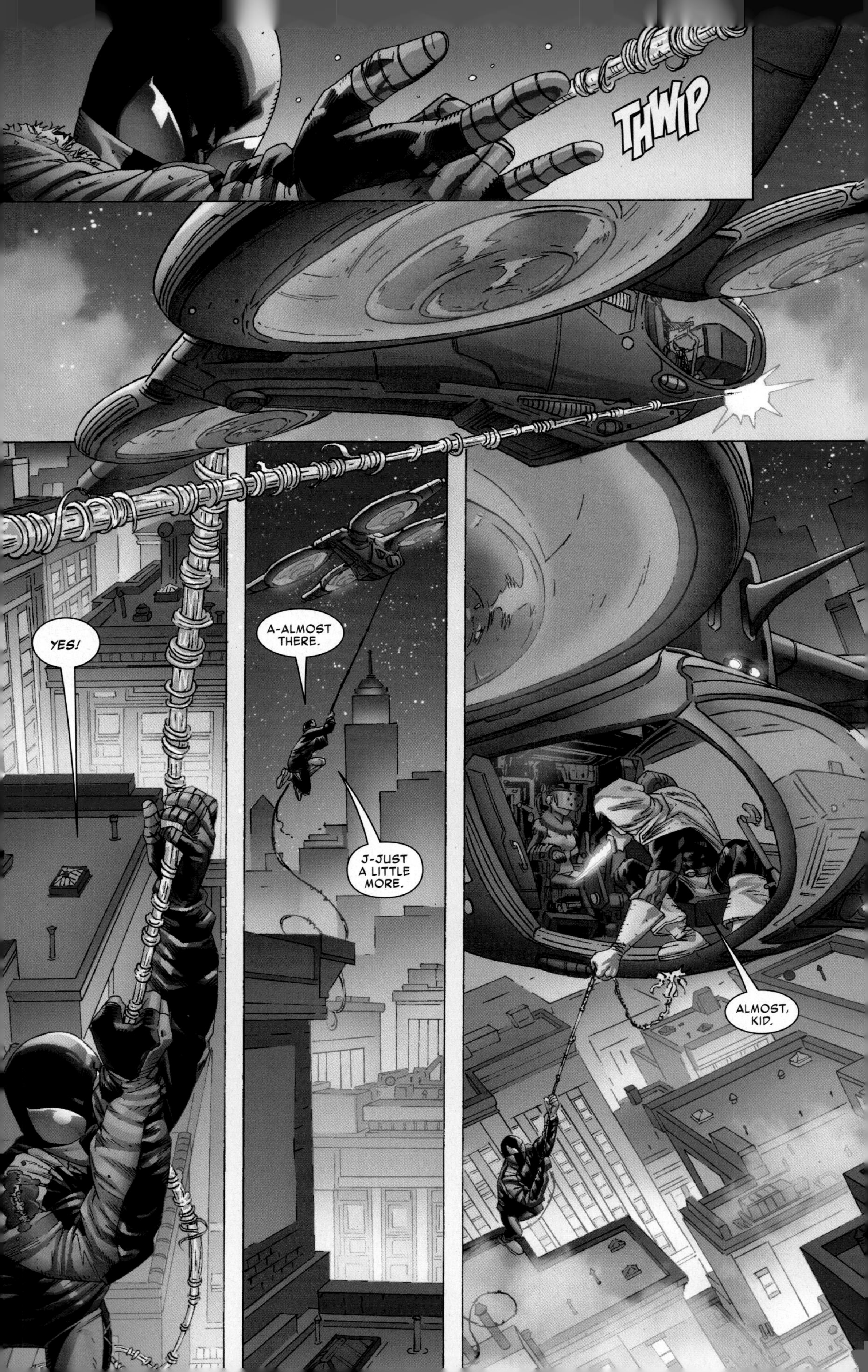
THWIP
YES!
A-ALMOST THERE.
J-JUST A LITTLE MORE.
ALMOST, KID.

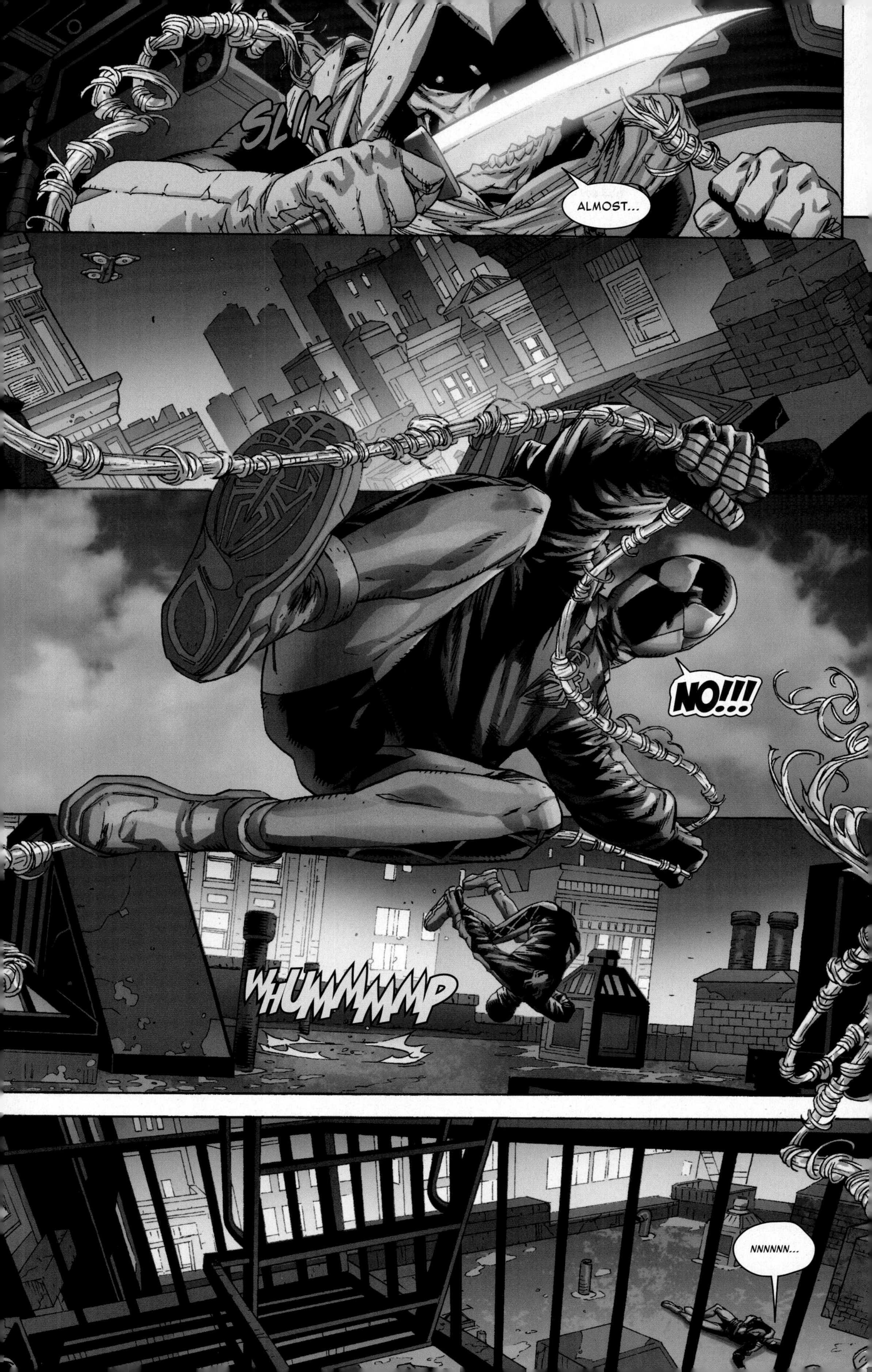
SLIK
ALMOST...
NO!!!
WHUMMMMP
NNNNNN...

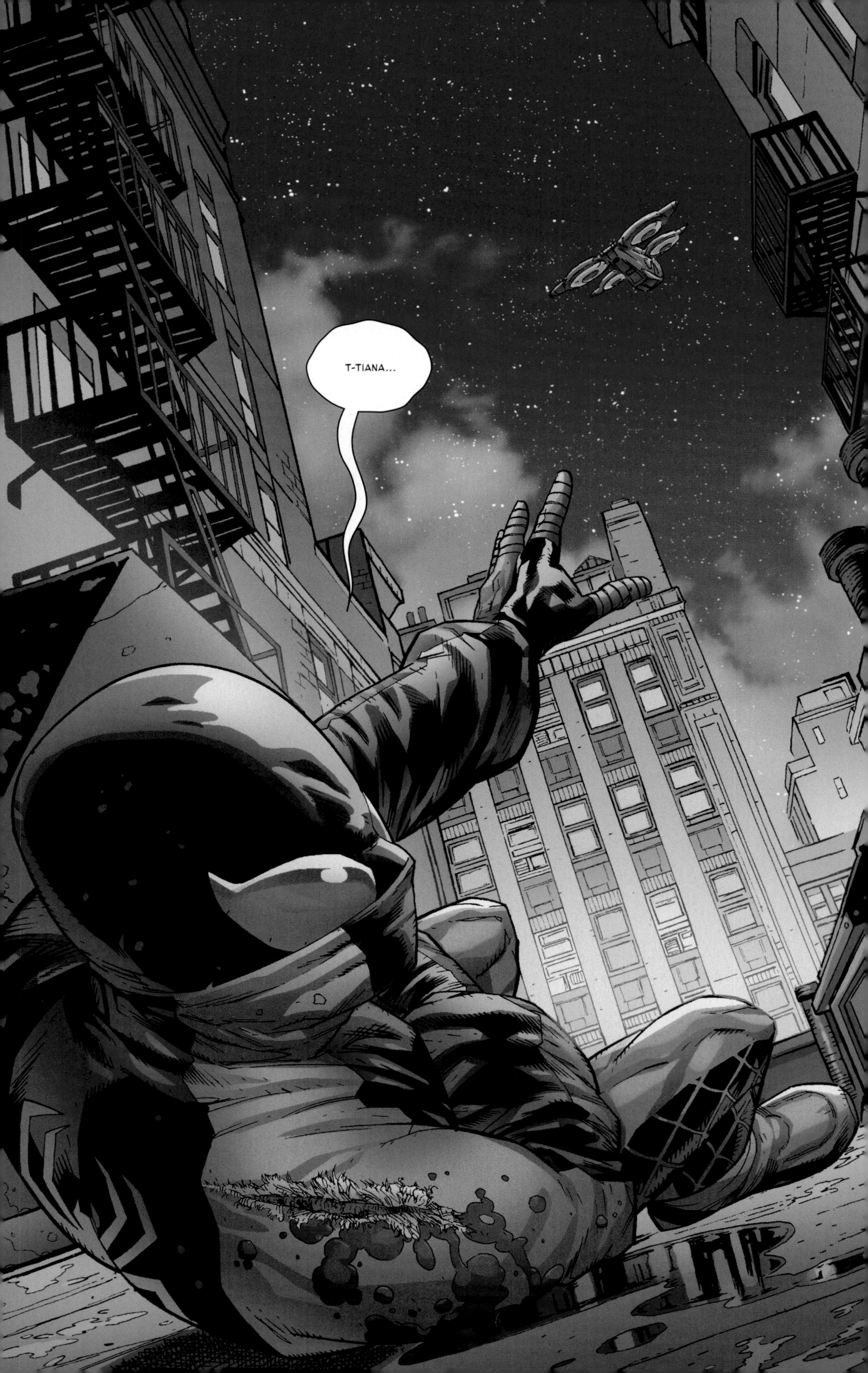
T-TIANA...

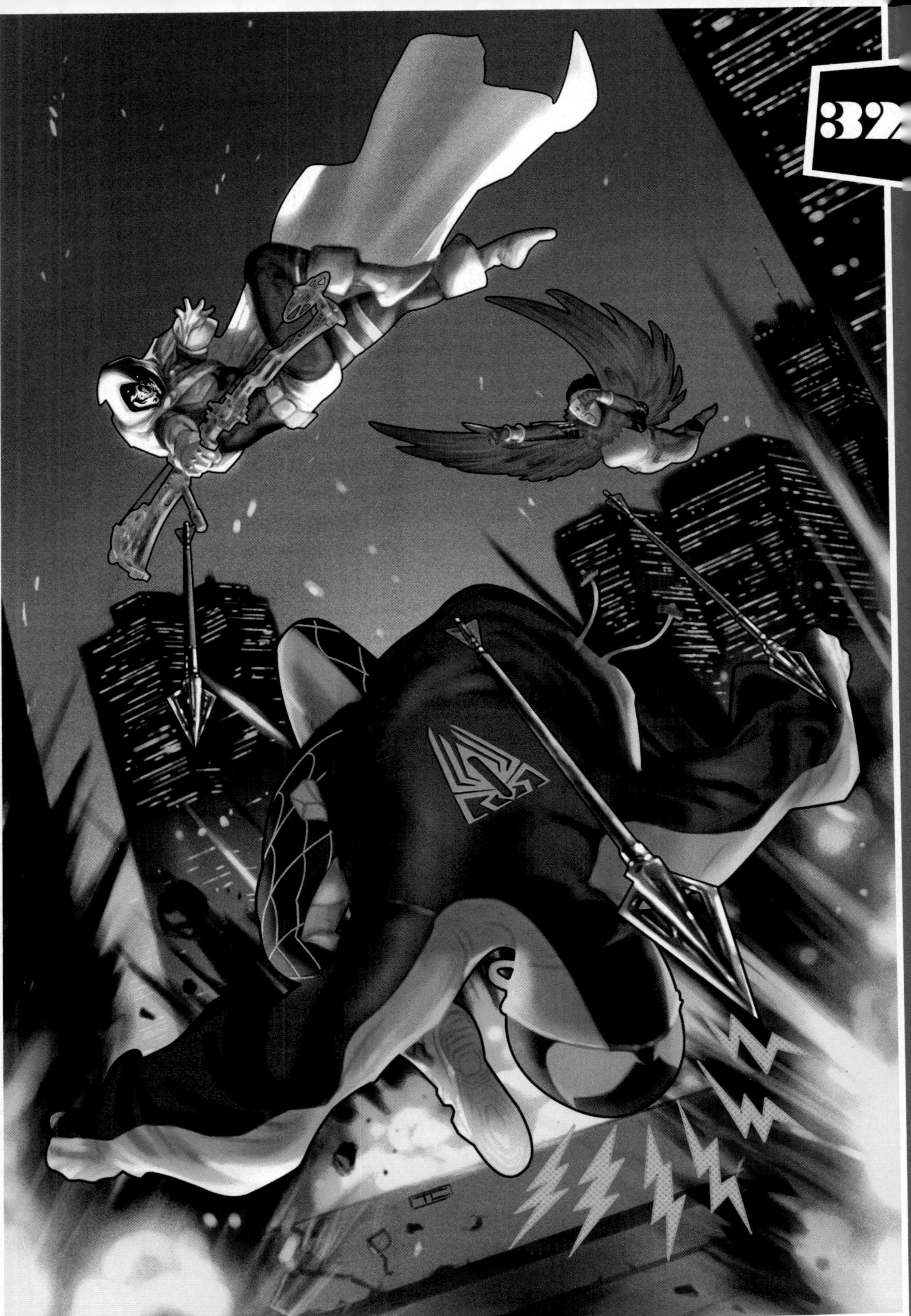
32

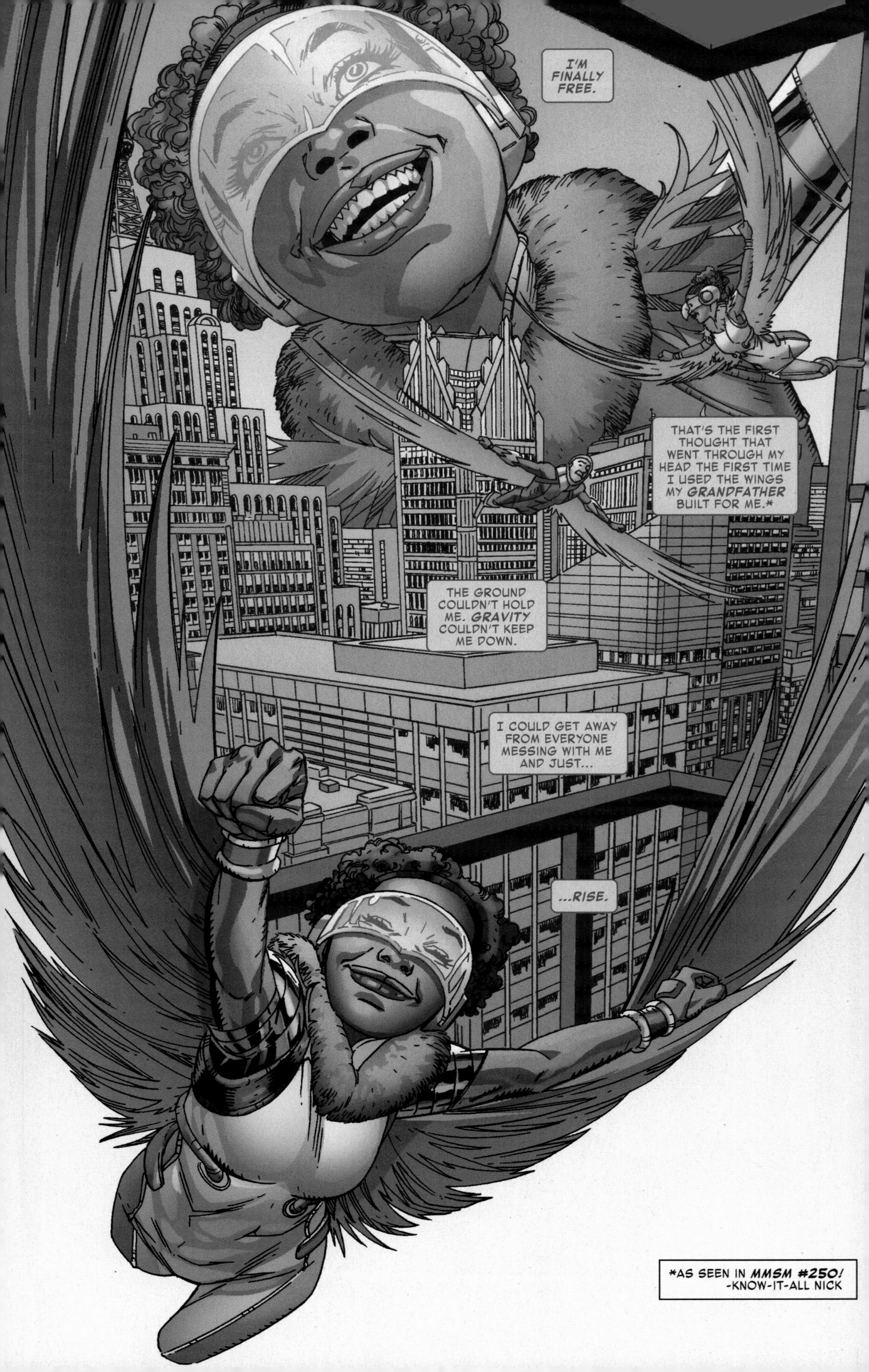
I'M FINALLY FREE.
THAT'S THE FIRST THOUGHT THAT WENT THROUGH MY HEAD THE FIRST TIME I USED THE WINGS MY GRANDFATHER BUILT FOR ME.*
THE GROUND COULDN'T HOLD ME. GRAVITY COULDN'T KEEP ME DOWN.
I COULD GET AWAY FROM EVERYONE MESSING WITH ME AND JUST...
...RISE.
*AS SEEN IN MMSM #250! -KNOW-IT-ALL NICK

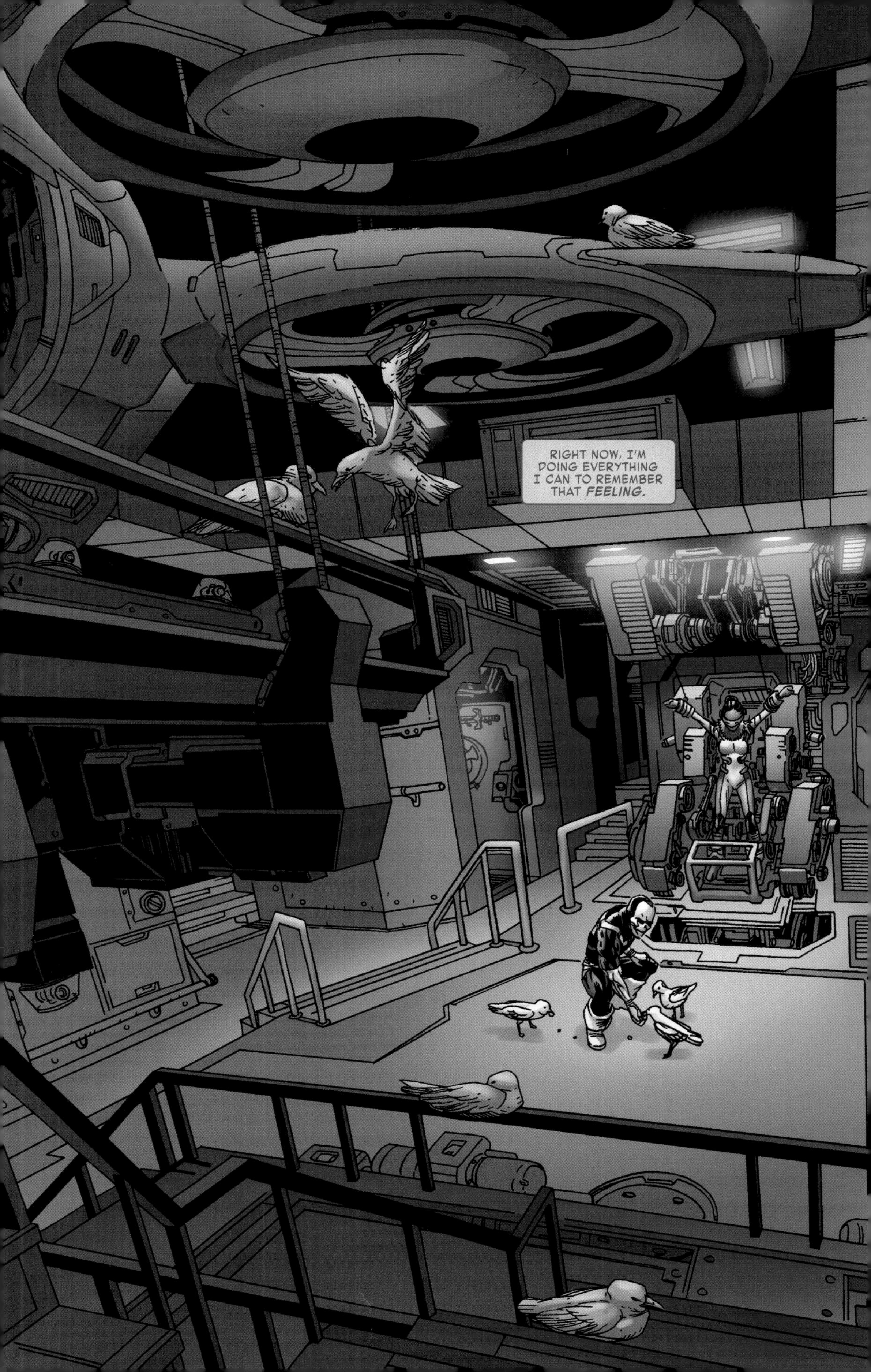
RIGHT NOW, I'M DOING EVERYTHING I CAN TO REMEMBER THAT FEELING.

FINALLY WAKING UP?

AWAKE ENOUGH TO KICK *YOUR* %&&$@ SOON AS I GET OUT OF THIS!

THAT'S NOT GONNA HAPPEN.

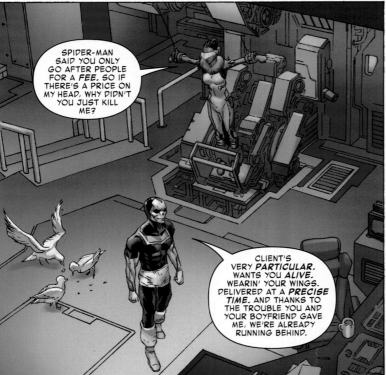

SPIDER-MAN SAID YOU ONLY GO AFTER PEOPLE FOR A *FEE*. SO IF THERE'S A PRICE ON MY HEAD, WHY DIDN'T YOU JUST KILL ME?

CLIENT'S VERY *PARTICULAR*. WANTS YOU *ALIVE*. WEARIN' YOUR WINGS. DELIVERED AT A *PRECISE TIME*. AND THANKS TO THE TROUBLE YOU AND YOUR BOYFRIEND GAVE ME, WE'RE ALREADY RUNNING BEHIND.

WH-WHAT CLIENT?

OH, YOU'LL FIND OUT *REAL* SOON.

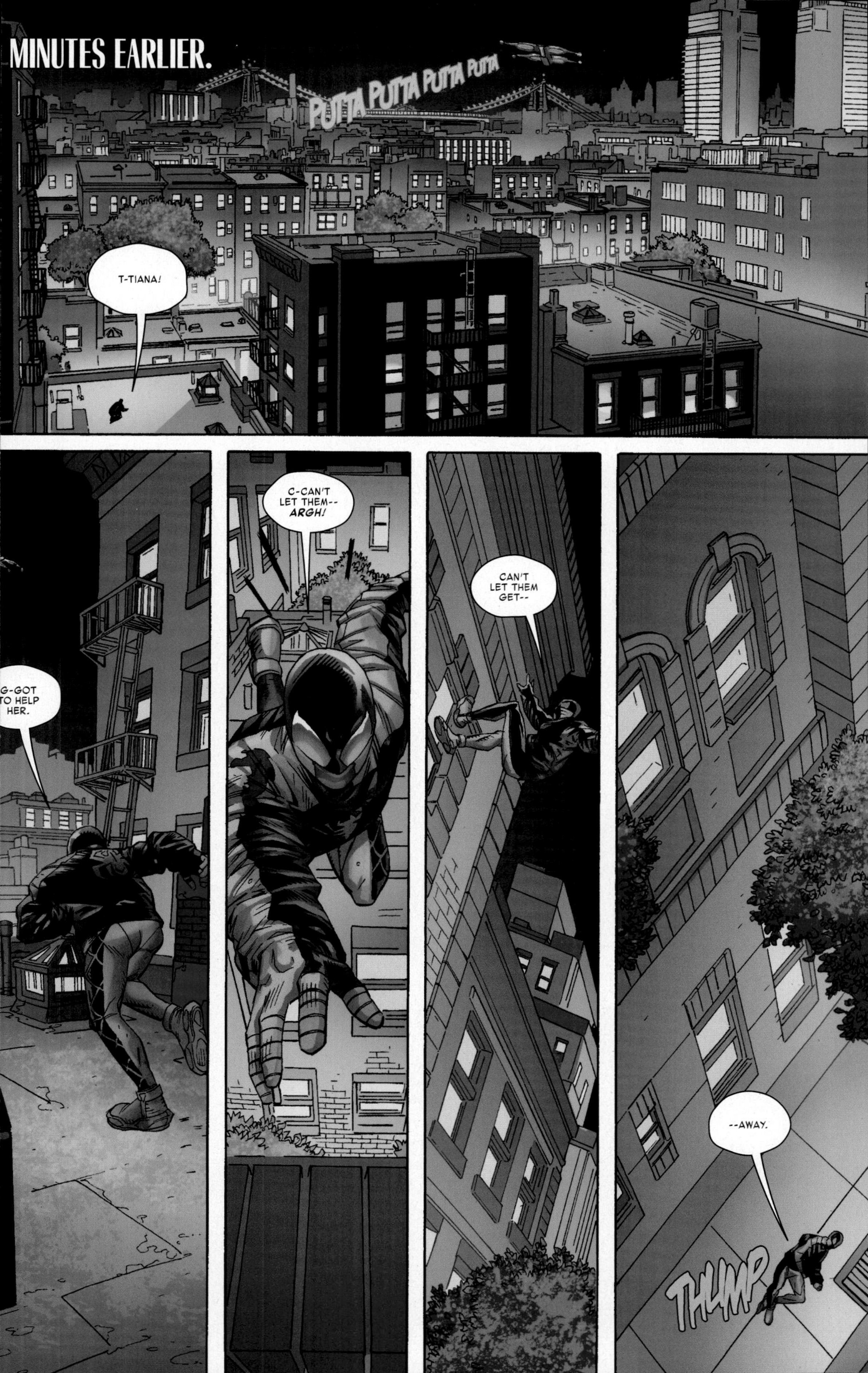
MINUTES EARLIER.
PUTTA PUTTA PUTTA PUTTA
T-TIANA!
G-GOT TO HELP HER.
C-CAN'T LET THEM-- ARGH!
CAN'T LET THEM GET--
--AWAY.
THUMP

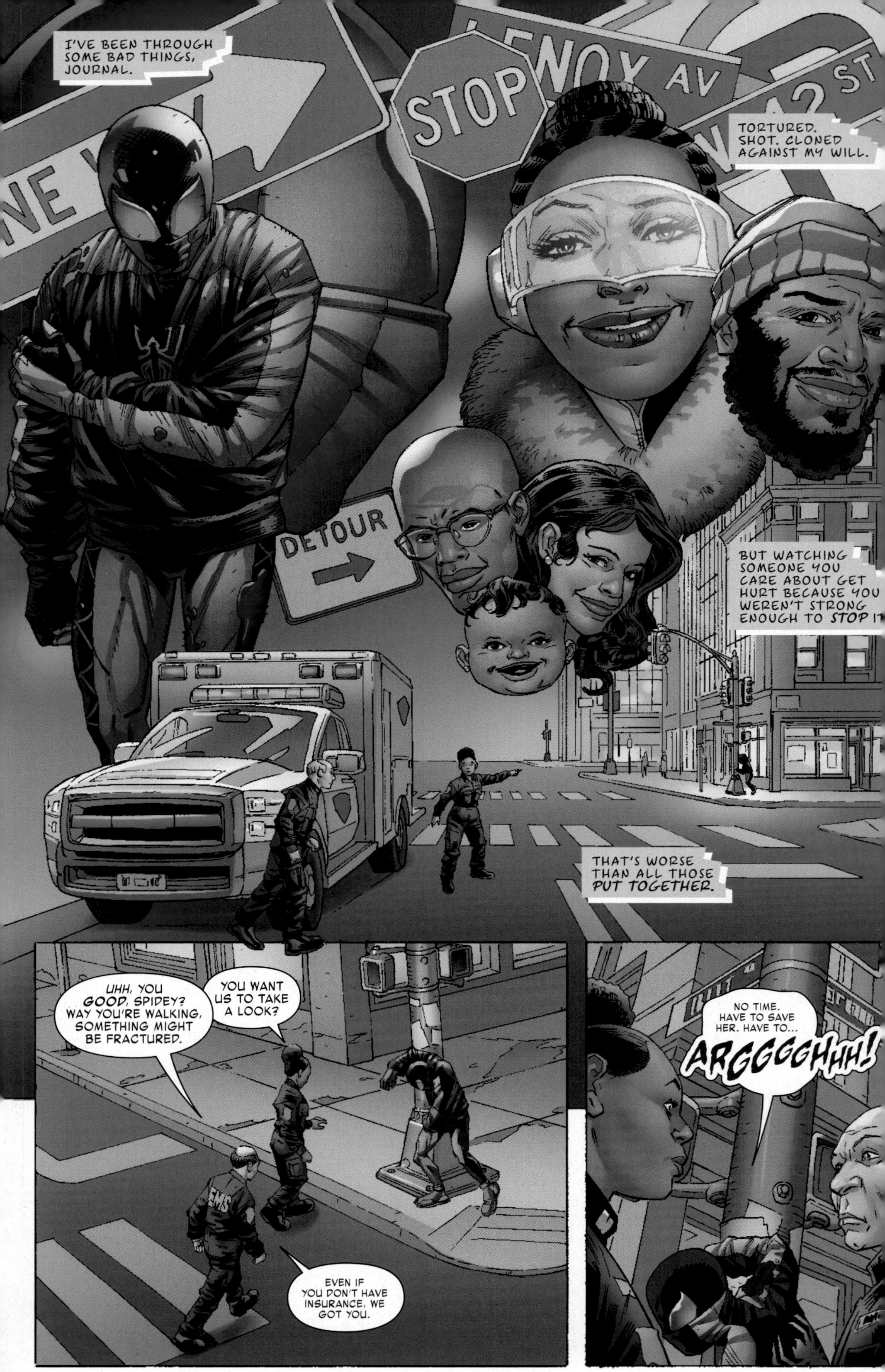
I'VE BEEN THROUGH SOME BAD THINGS, JOURNAL.
ONE WAY
STOP
LENOX AV
W 142 ST
TORTURED. SHOT. CLONED AGAINST MY WILL.
DETOUR
BUT WATCHING SOMEONE YOU CARE ABOUT GET HURT BECAUSE YOU WEREN'T STRONG ENOUGH TO STOP IT
THAT'S WORSE THAN ALL THOSE PUT TOGETHER.
UHH, YOU GOOD, SPIDEY? WAY YOU'RE WALKING, SOMETHING MIGHT BE FRACTURED.
YOU WANT US TO TAKE A LOOK?
EVEN IF YOU DON'T HAVE INSURANCE, WE GOT YOU.
EMS
NO TIME. HAVE TO SAVE HER. HAVE TO...
ARGGGGHHH!

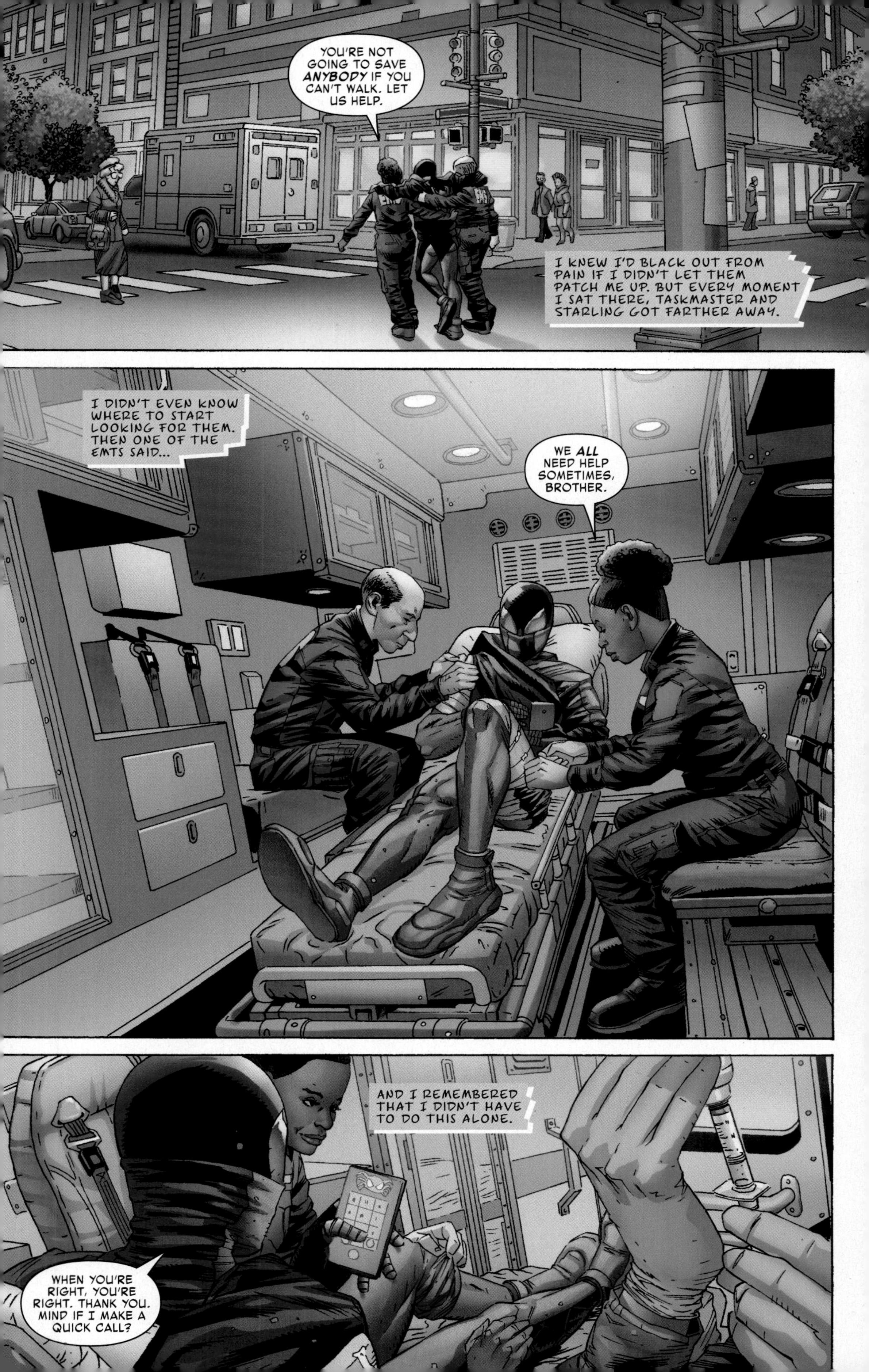
YOU'RE NOT GOING TO SAVE ANYBODY IF YOU CAN'T WALK. LET US HELP.
I KNEW I'D BLACK OUT FROM PAIN IF I DIDN'T LET THEM PATCH ME UP. BUT EVERY MOMENT I SAT THERE, TASKMASTER AND STARLING GOT FARTHER AWAY.
I DIDN'T EVEN KNOW WHERE TO START LOOKING FOR THEM. THEN ONE OF THE EMTS SAID...
WE ALL NEED HELP SOMETIMES, BROTHER.
AND I REMEMBERED THAT I DIDN'T HAVE TO DO THIS ALONE.
WHEN YOU'RE RIGHT, YOU'RE RIGHT. THANK YOU. MIND IF I MAKE A QUICK CALL?

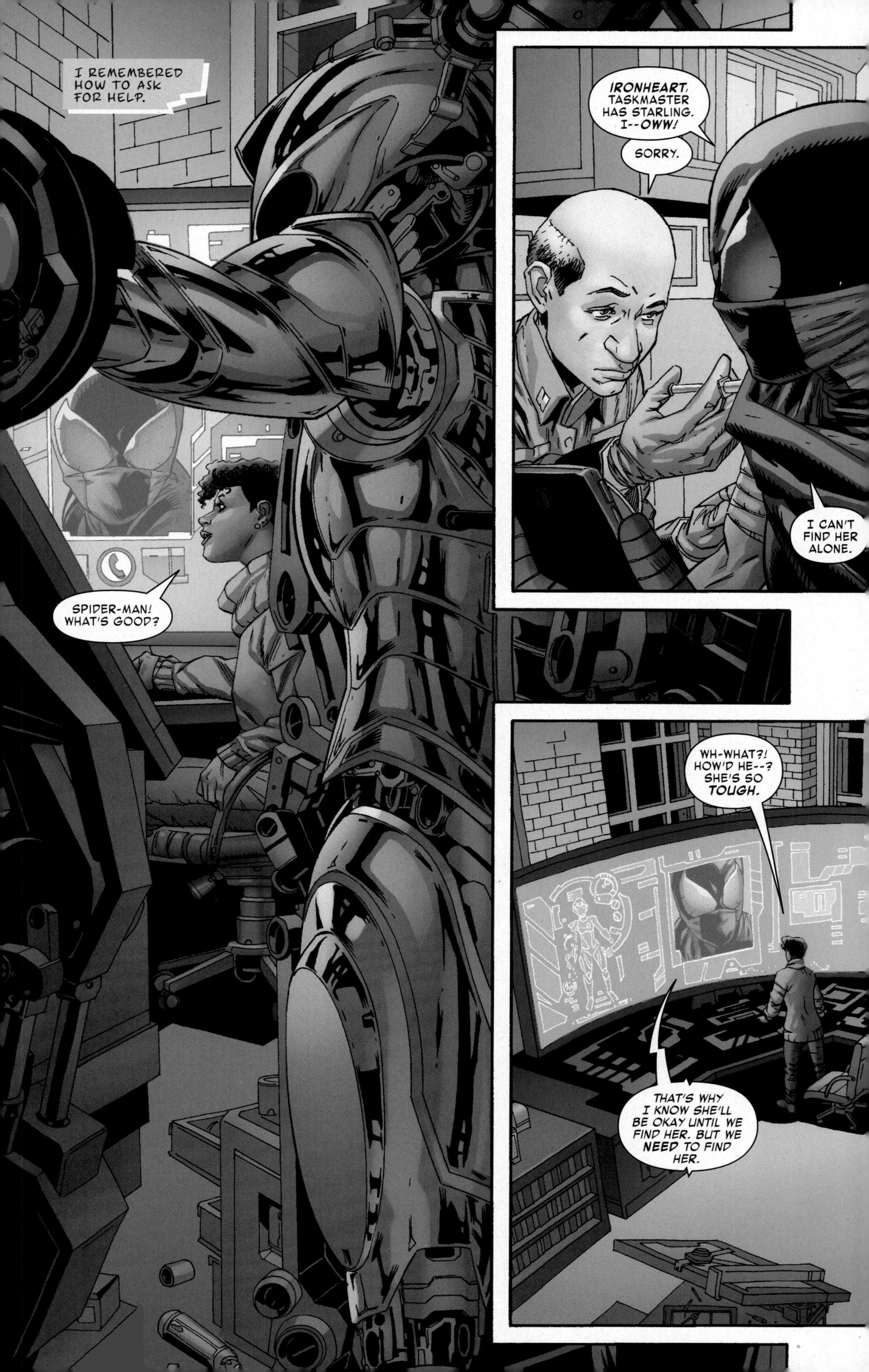

I REMEMBERED HOW TO ASK FOR HELP.
IRONHEART, TASKMASTER HAS STARLING. I--OWW!
SORRY.
I CAN'T FIND HER ALONE.
SPIDER-MAN! WHAT'S GOOD?
WH-WHAT?! HOW'D HE--? SHE'S SO TOUGH.
THAT'S WHY I KNOW SHE'LL BE OKAY UNTIL WE FIND HER. BUT WE NEED TO FIND HER.

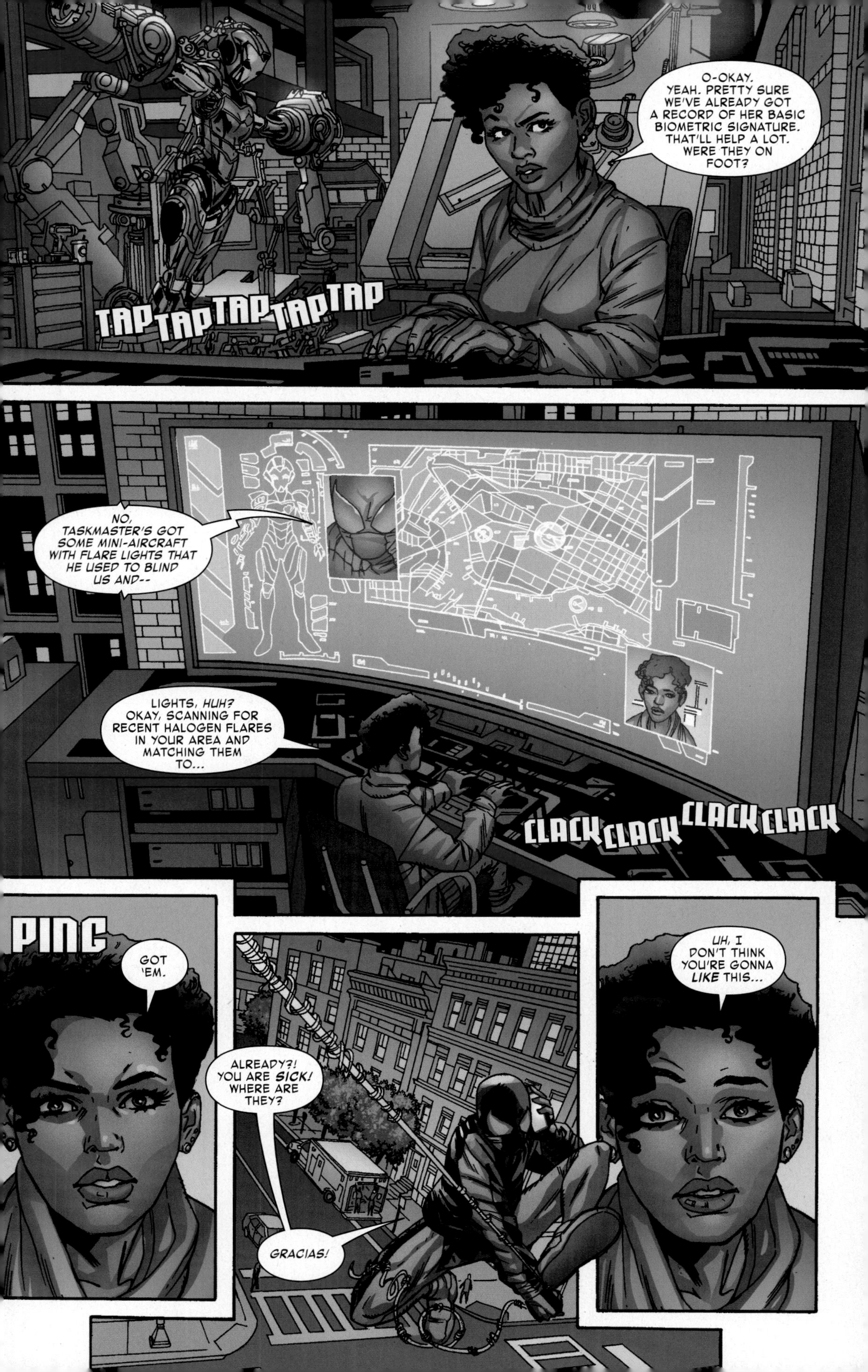
O-OKAY. YEAH. PRETTY SURE WE'VE ALREADY GOT A RECORD OF HER BASIC BIOMETRIC SIGNATURE. THAT'LL HELP A LOT. WERE THEY ON FOOT?
TAPTAPTAPTAPTAP
NO, TASKMASTER'S GOT SOME MINI-AIRCRAFT WITH FLARE LIGHTS THAT HE USED TO BLIND US AND--
LIGHTS, HUH? OKAY, SCANNING FOR RECENT HALOGEN FLARES IN YOUR AREA AND MATCHING THEM TO...
CLACKCLACKCLACKCLACK
PING
GOT 'EM.
ALREADY?! YOU ARE SICK! WHERE ARE THEY?
GRACIAS!
UH, I DON'T THINK YOU'RE GONNA LIKE THIS...

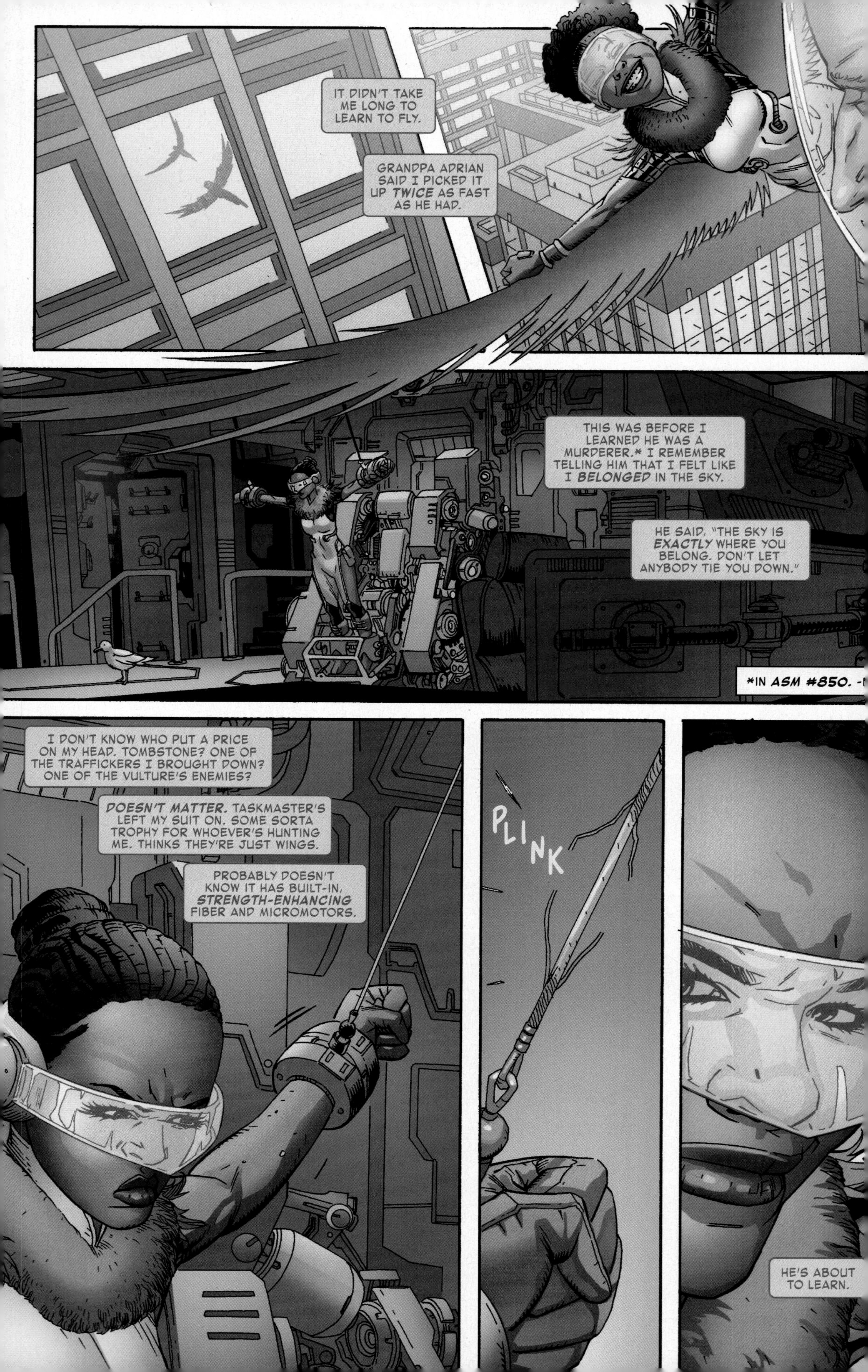
IT DIDN'T TAKE ME LONG TO LEARN TO FLY.
GRANDPA ADRIAN SAID I PICKED IT UP *TWICE* AS FAST AS HE HAD.
THIS WAS BEFORE I LEARNED HE WAS A MURDERER.* I REMEMBER TELLING HIM THAT I FELT LIKE I *BELONGED* IN THE SKY.
HE SAID, "THE SKY IS *EXACTLY* WHERE YOU BELONG. DON'T LET ANYBODY TIE YOU DOWN."
*IN *ASM #850.*
I DON'T KNOW WHO PUT A PRICE ON MY HEAD. TOMBSTONE? ONE OF THE TRAFFICKERS I BROUGHT DOWN? ONE OF THE VULTURE'S ENEMIES?
DOESN'T MATTER. TASKMASTER'S LEFT MY SUIT ON. SOME SORTA TROPHY FOR WHOEVER'S HUNTING ME. THINKS THEY'RE JUST WINGS.
PROBABLY DOESN'T KNOW IT HAS BUILT-IN, *STRENGTH-ENHANCING* FIBER AND MICROMOTORS.
PLINK
HE'S ABOUT TO LEARN.

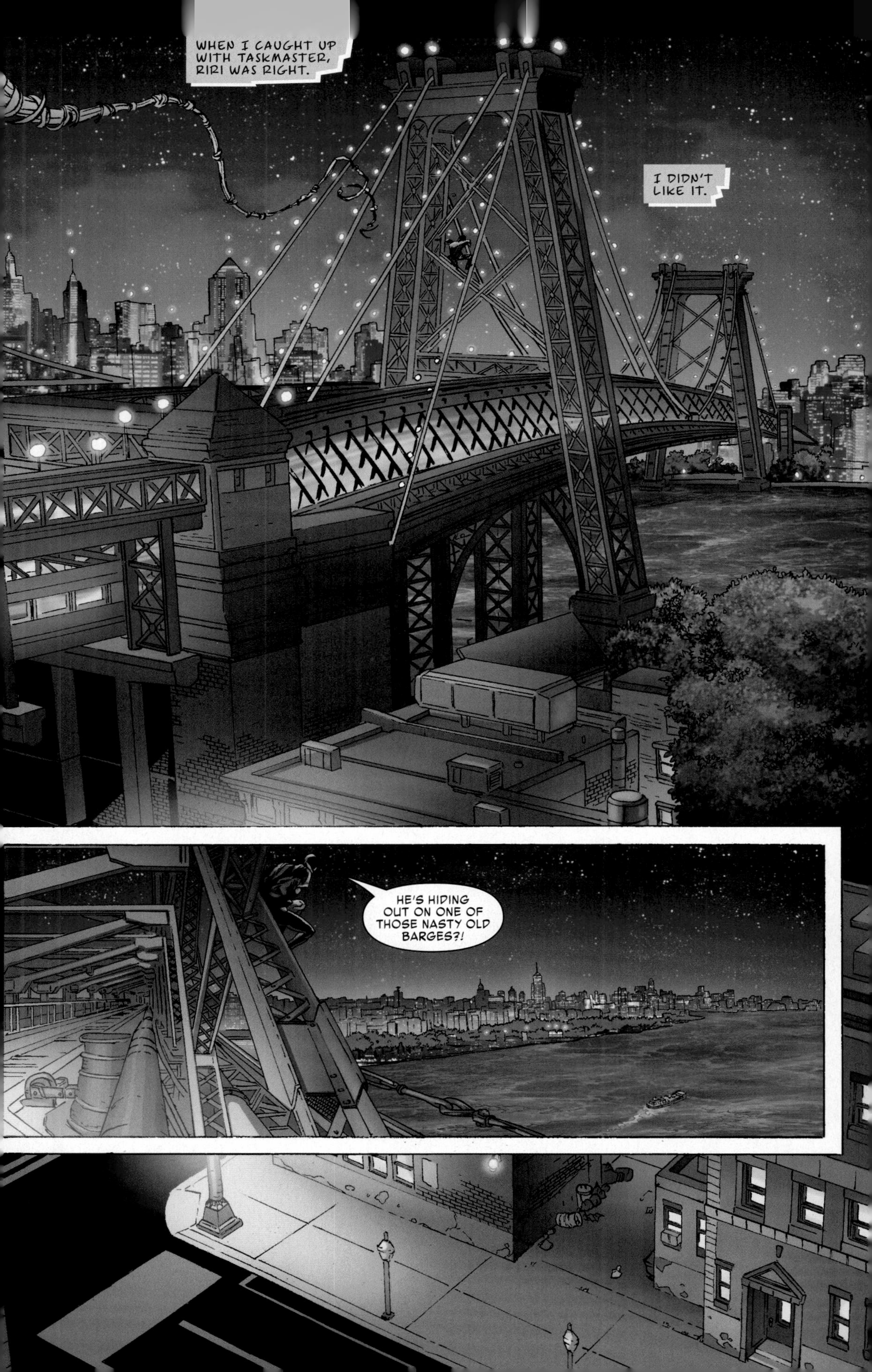
WHEN I CAUGHT UP WITH TASKMASTER, RIRI WAS RIGHT.
I DIDN'T LIKE IT.
HE'S HIDING OUT ON ONE OF THOSE NASTY OLD BARGES?!

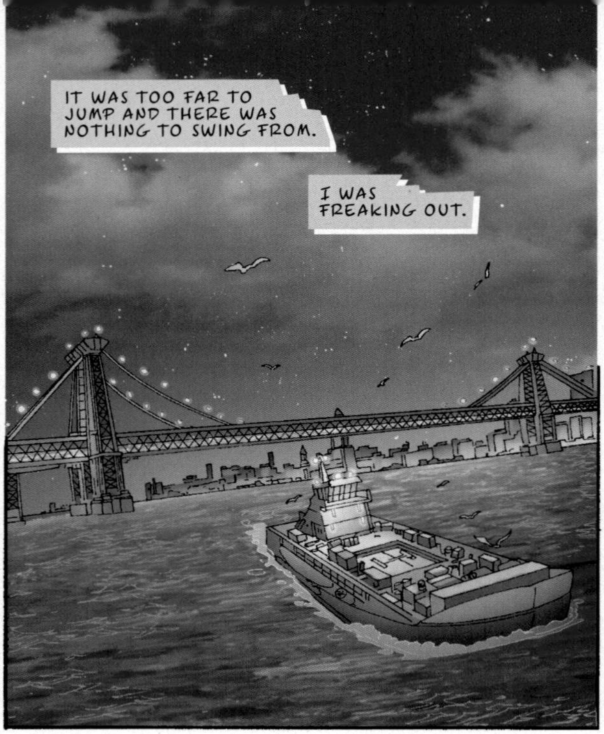
IT WAS TOO FAR TO JUMP AND THERE WAS NOTHING TO SWING FROM.
I WAS FREAKING OUT.

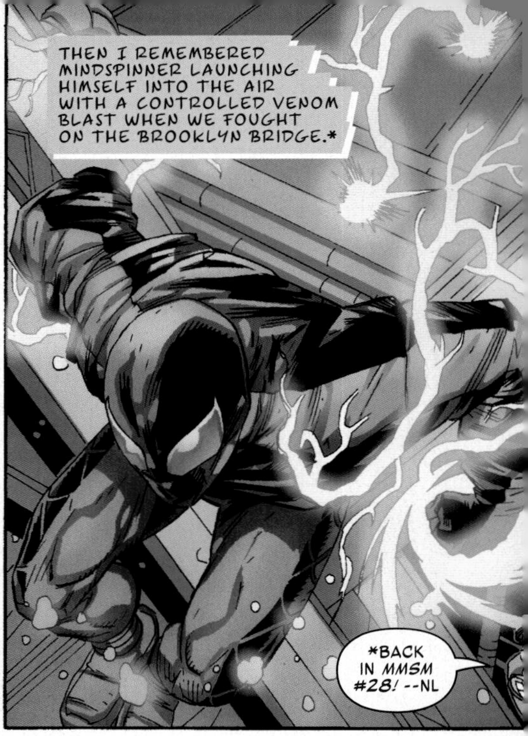
THEN I REMEMBERED MINDSPINNER LAUNCHING HIMSELF INTO THE AIR WITH A CONTROLLED VENOM BLAST WHEN WE FOUGHT ON THE BROOKLYN BRIDGE.*
*BACK IN MMSM #28! --NL

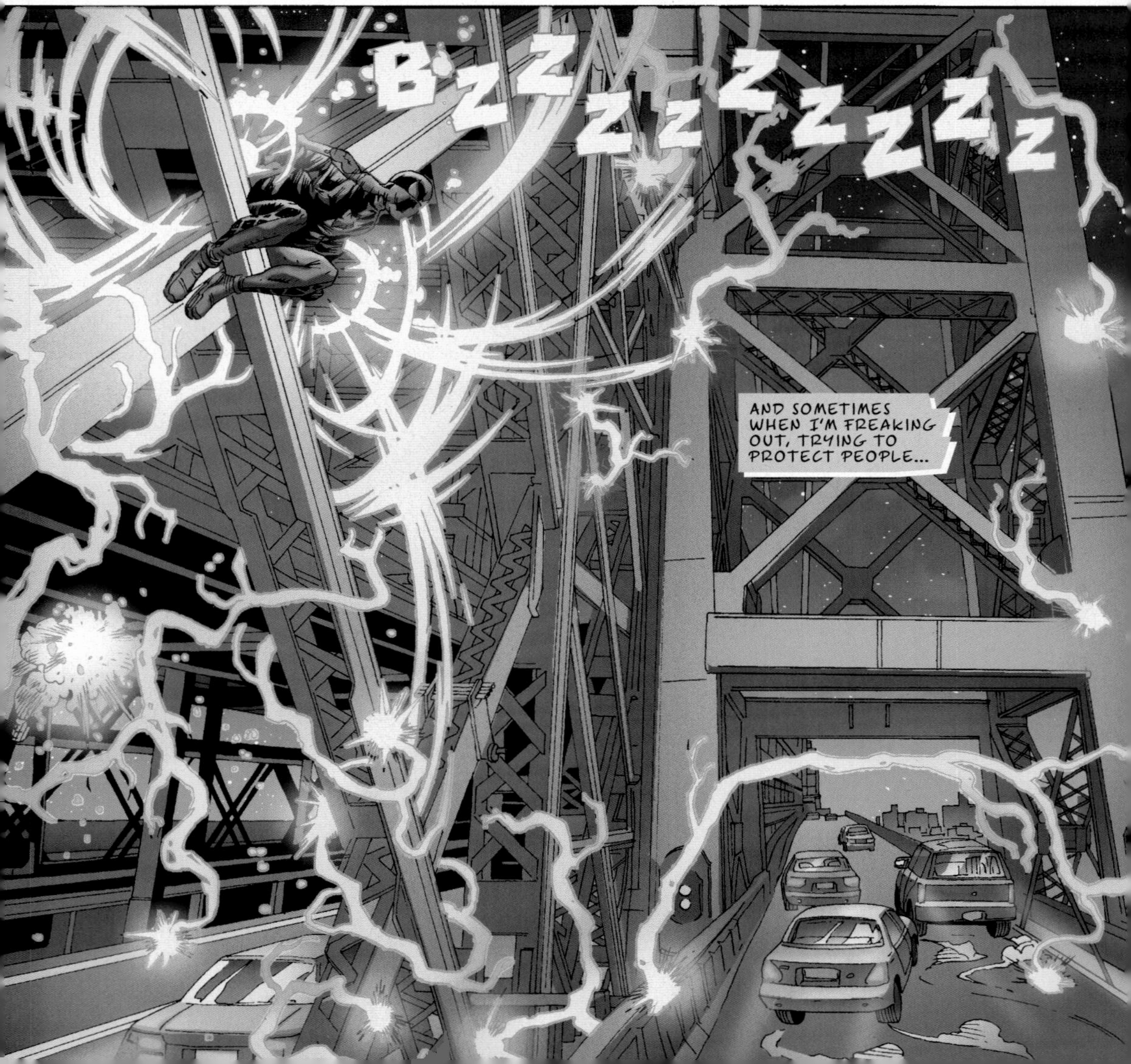
BZZZZZZZZZZz
AND SOMETIMES WHEN I'M FREAKING OUT, TRYING TO PROTECT PEOPLE...

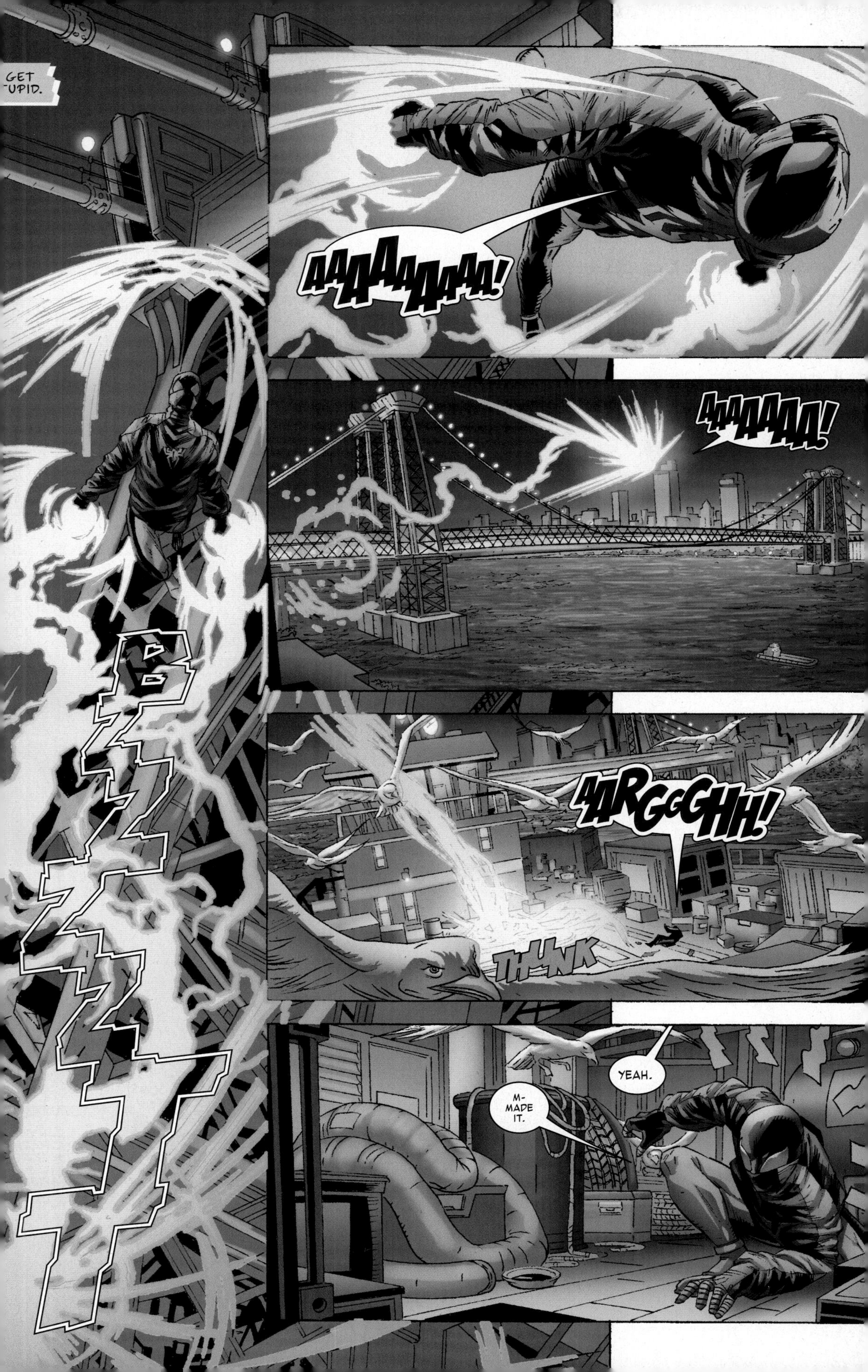

GET
TUPID.
AAAAAAAAAA!
AAAAAAA!
AARGGGHH!
THUNK
YEAH.
M-
MADE
IT.

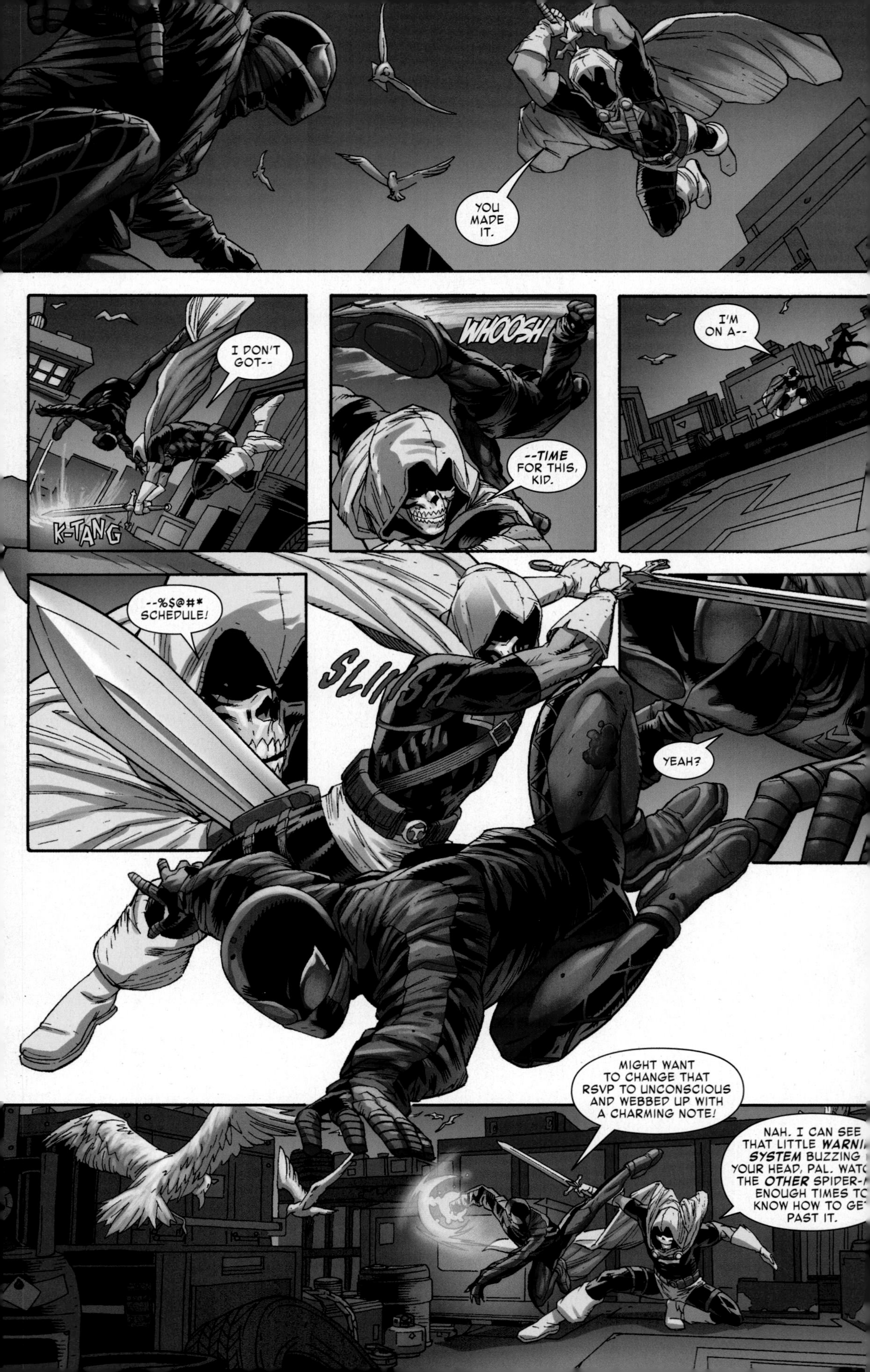
YOU MADE IT.
I DON'T GOT--
K-TANG
WHOOSH
--TIME FOR THIS, KID.
I'M ON A--
--%$@#* SCHEDULE!
SLINSH
YEAH?
MIGHT WANT TO CHANGE THAT RSVP TO UNCONSCIOUS AND WEBBED UP WITH A CHARMING NOTE!
NAH. I CAN SEE THAT LITTLE WARNI SYSTEM BUZZING YOUR HEAD, PAL. WATC THE OTHER SPIDER-M ENOUGH TIMES TO KNOW HOW TO GET PAST IT.

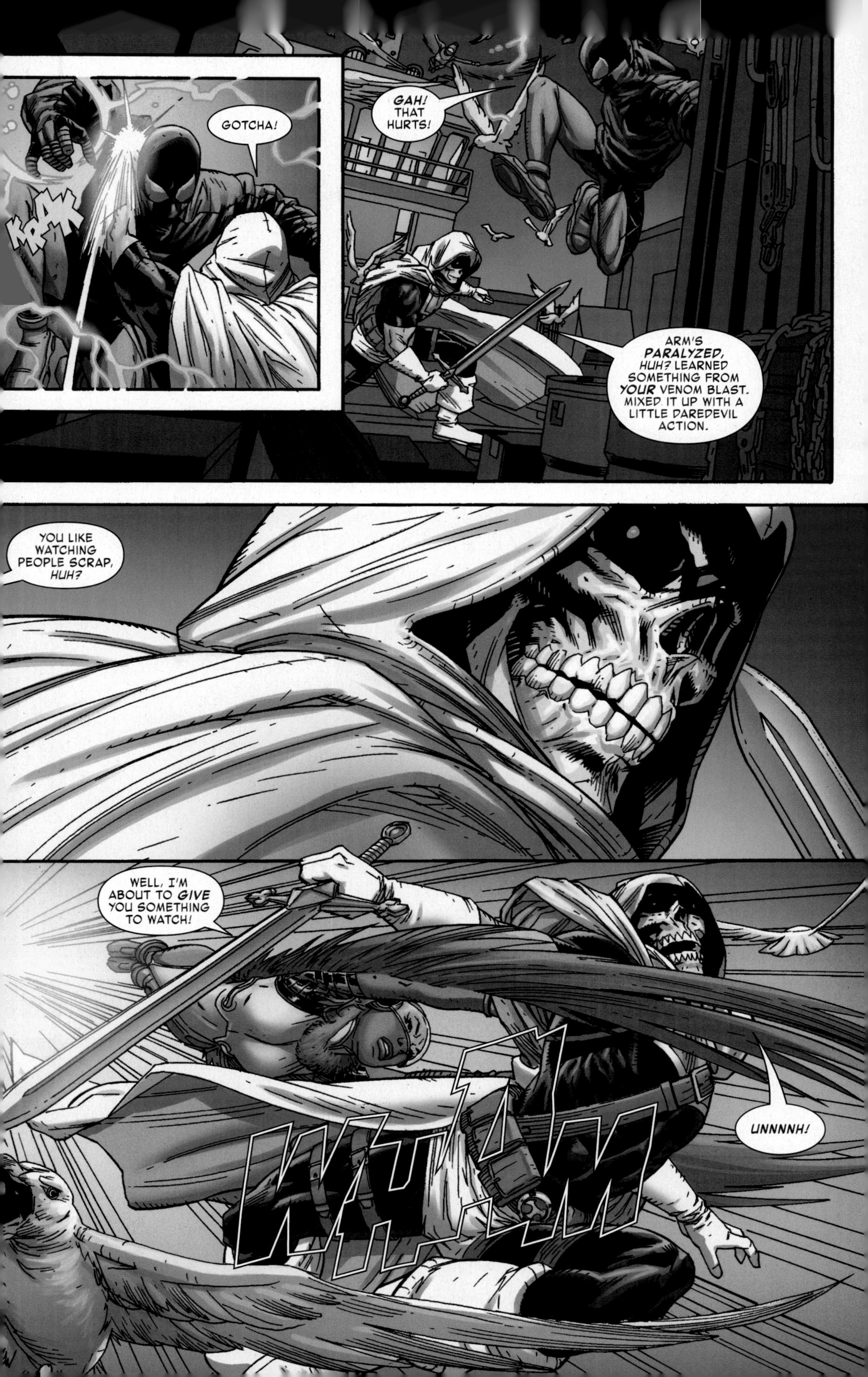
GOTCHA!
KRAK
GAH! THAT HURTS!
ARM'S PARALYZED, HUH? LEARNED SOMETHING FROM YOUR VENOM BLAST. MIXED IT UP WITH A LITTLE DAREDEVIL ACTION.
YOU LIKE WATCHING PEOPLE SCRAP, HUH?
WELL, I'M ABOUT TO GIVE YOU SOMETHING TO WATCH!
UNNNNH!
WHAM

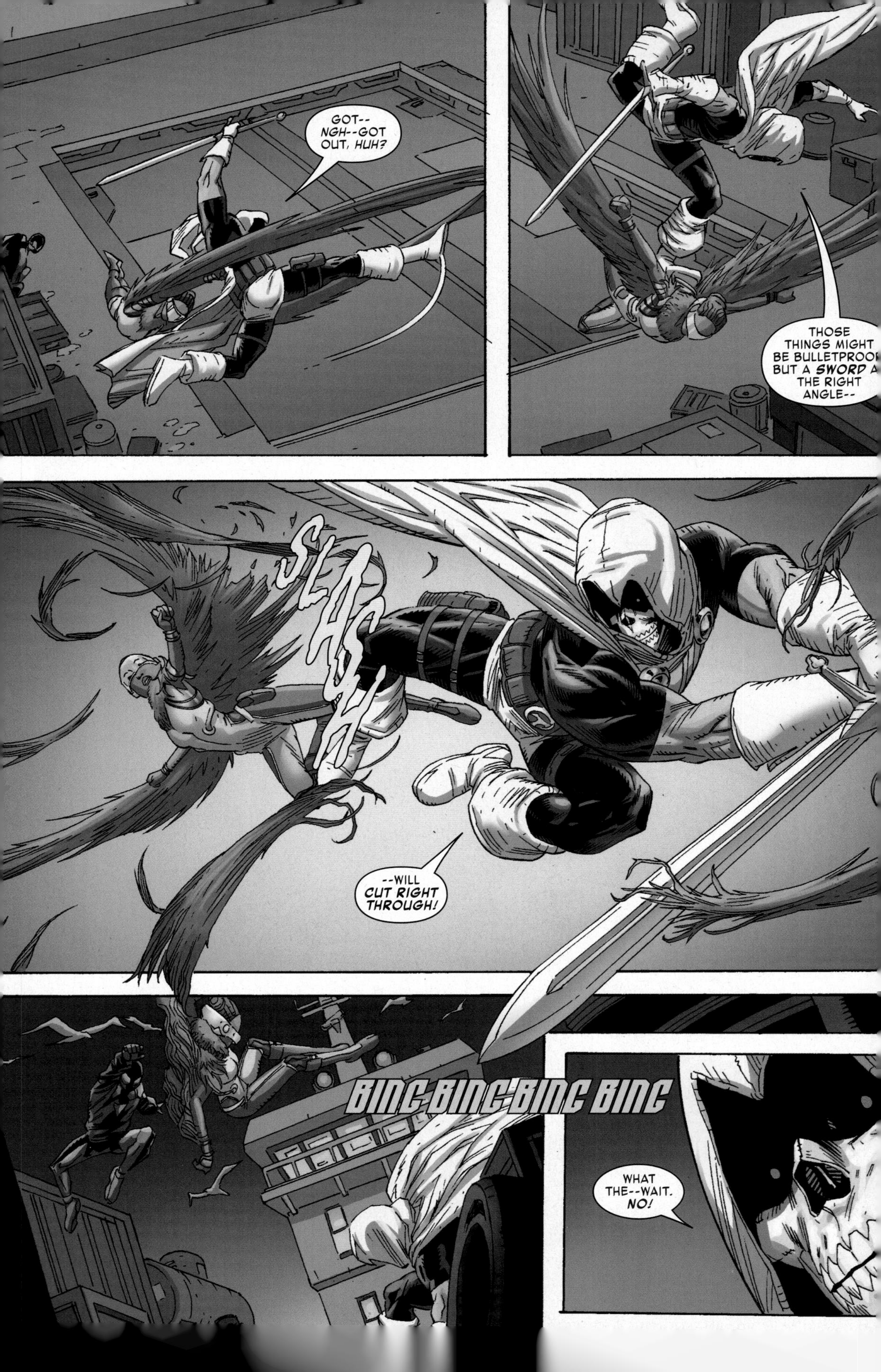
GOT--
NGH--GOT
OUT, HUH?
THOSE
THINGS MIGHT
BE BULLETPROOF
BUT A SWORD AT
THE RIGHT
ANGLE--
SLASH
--WILL
CUT RIGHT
THROUGH!
BING BING BING BING
WHAT
THE--WAIT.
NO!

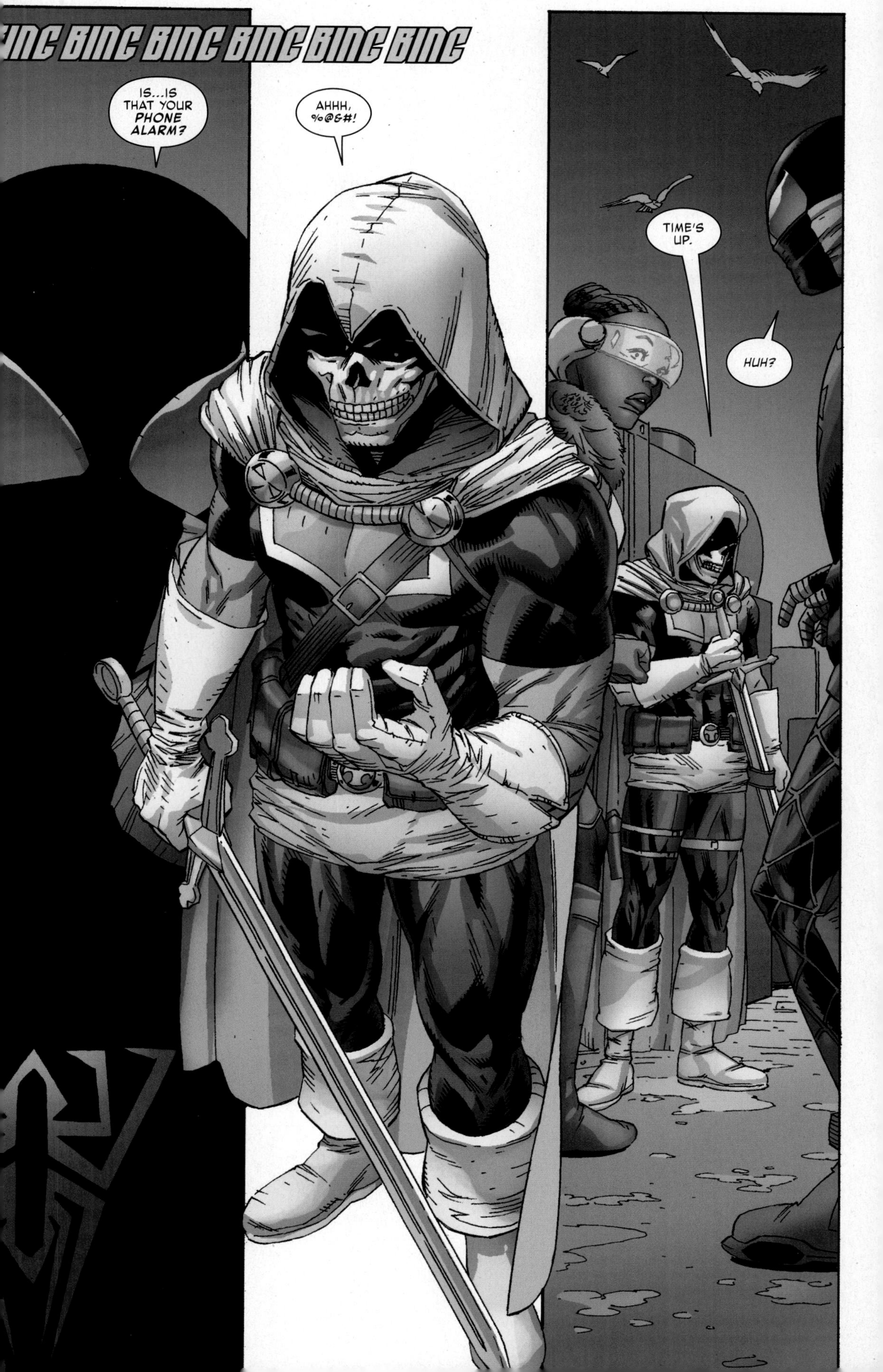
BING BING BING BING BING BING
IS...IS THAT YOUR PHONE ALARM?
AHHH, %@&#!
TIME'S UP.
HUH?

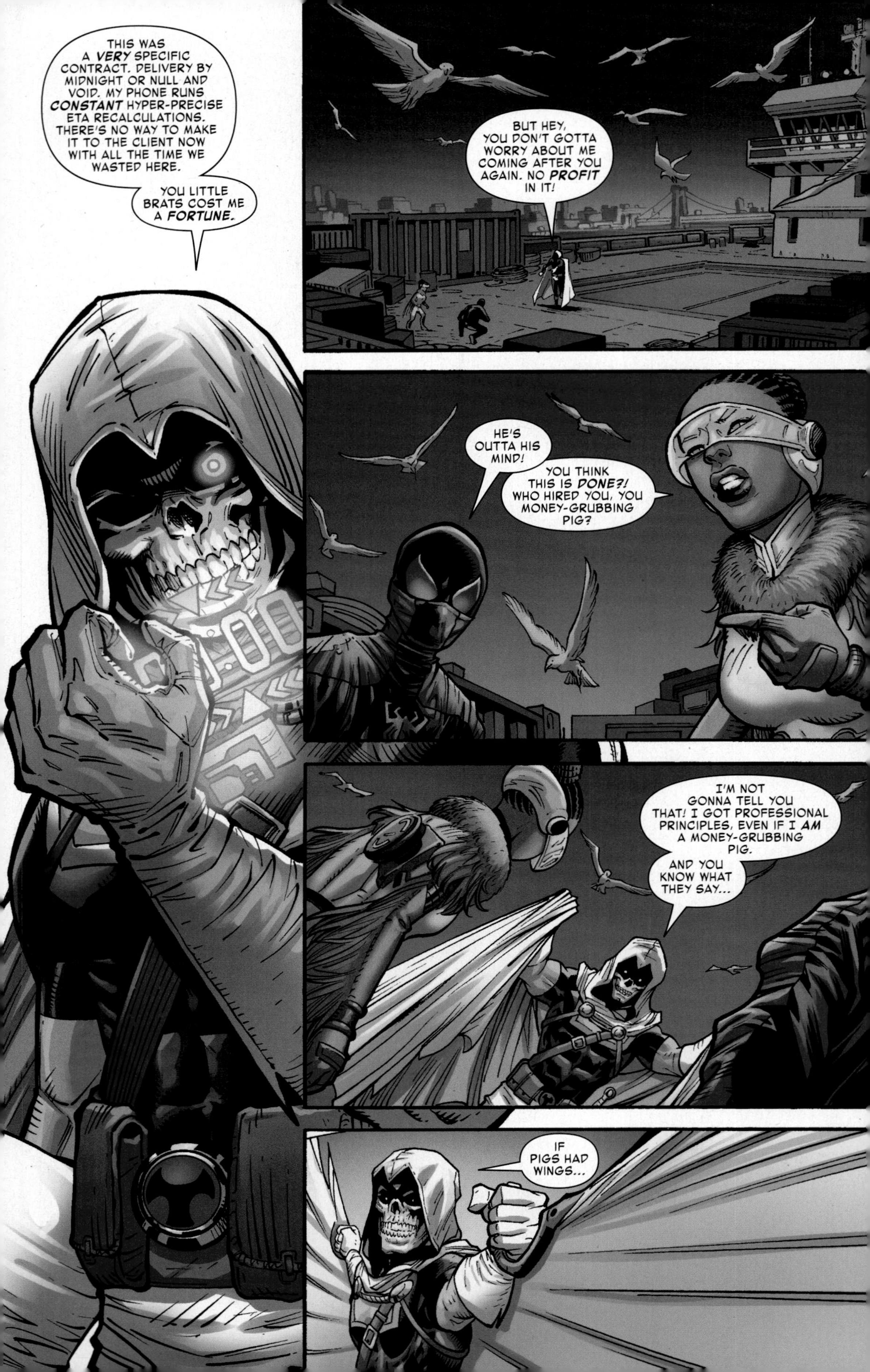

THIS WAS A *VERY* SPECIFIC CONTRACT. DELIVERY BY MIDNIGHT OR NULL AND VOID. MY PHONE RUNS *CONSTANT* HYPER-PRECISE ETA RECALCULATIONS. THERE'S NO WAY TO MAKE IT TO THE CLIENT NOW WITH ALL THE TIME WE WASTED HERE.
YOU LITTLE BRATS COST ME A *FORTUNE.*
BUT HEY, YOU DON'T GOTTA WORRY ABOUT ME COMING AFTER YOU AGAIN. NO *PROFIT* IN IT!
HE'S OUTTA HIS MIND!
YOU THINK THIS IS *DONE?!* WHO HIRED YOU, YOU MONEY-GRUBBING PIG?
I'M NOT GONNA TELL YOU THAT! I GOT PROFESSIONAL PRINCIPLES, EVEN IF I *AM* A MONEY-GRUBBING PIG.
AND YOU KNOW WHAT THEY SAY...
IF PIGS HAD WINGS...

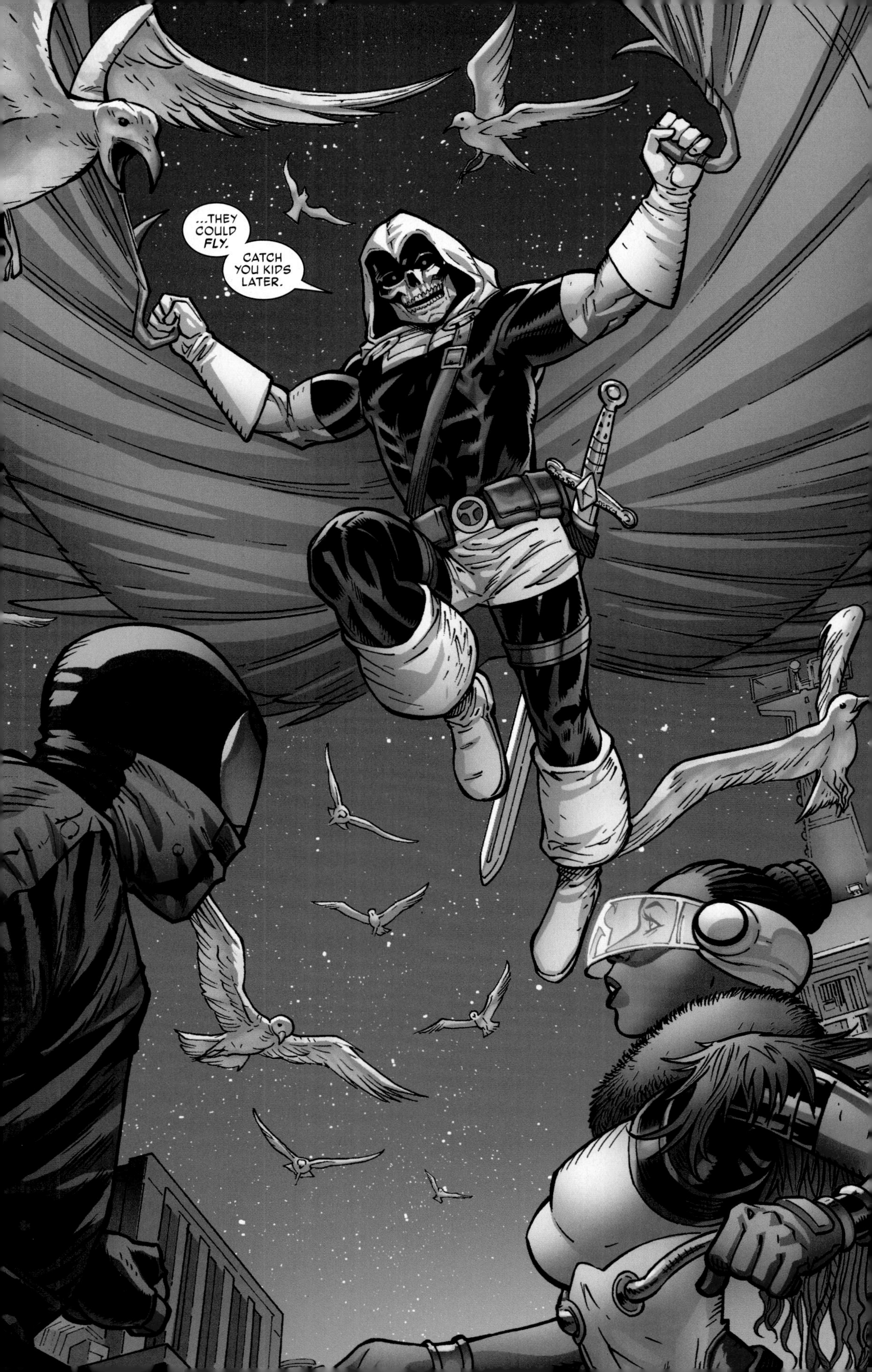
...THEY COULD FLY.
CATCH YOU KIDS LATER.

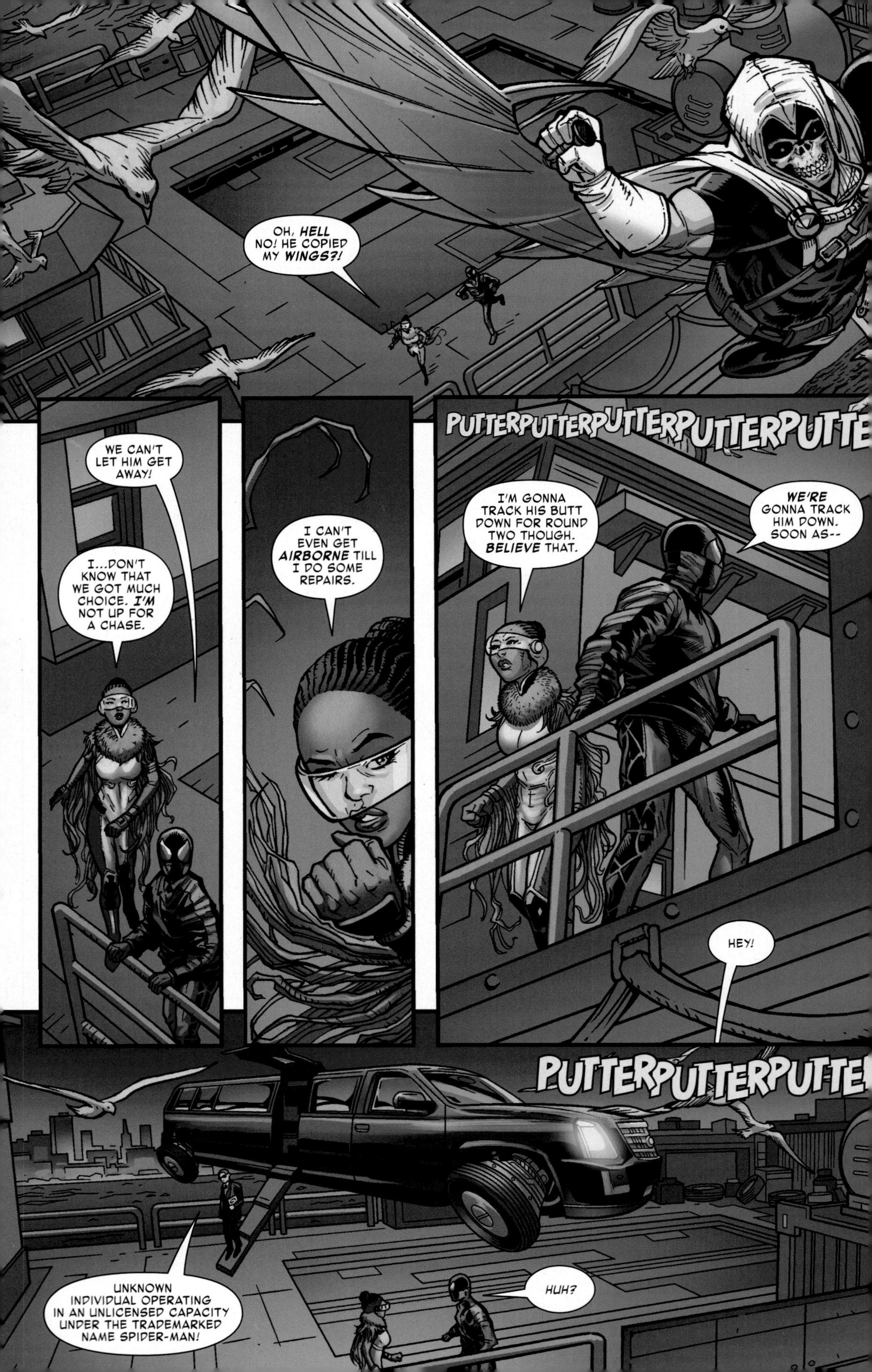
OH, HELL NO! HE COPIED MY WINGS?!
WE CAN'T LET HIM GET AWAY!
I...DON'T KNOW THAT WE GOT MUCH CHOICE. I'M NOT UP FOR A CHASE.
I CAN'T EVEN GET AIRBORNE TILL I DO SOME REPAIRS.
PUTTERPUTTERPUTTERPUTTERPUTTE
I'M GONNA TRACK HIS BUTT DOWN FOR ROUND TWO THOUGH. BELIEVE THAT.
WE'RE GONNA TRACK HIM DOWN. SOON AS--
HEY!
PUTTERPUTTERPUTTE
UNKNOWN INDIVIDUAL OPERATING IN AN UNLICENSED CAPACITY UNDER THE TRADEMARKED NAME SPIDER-MAN!
HUH?

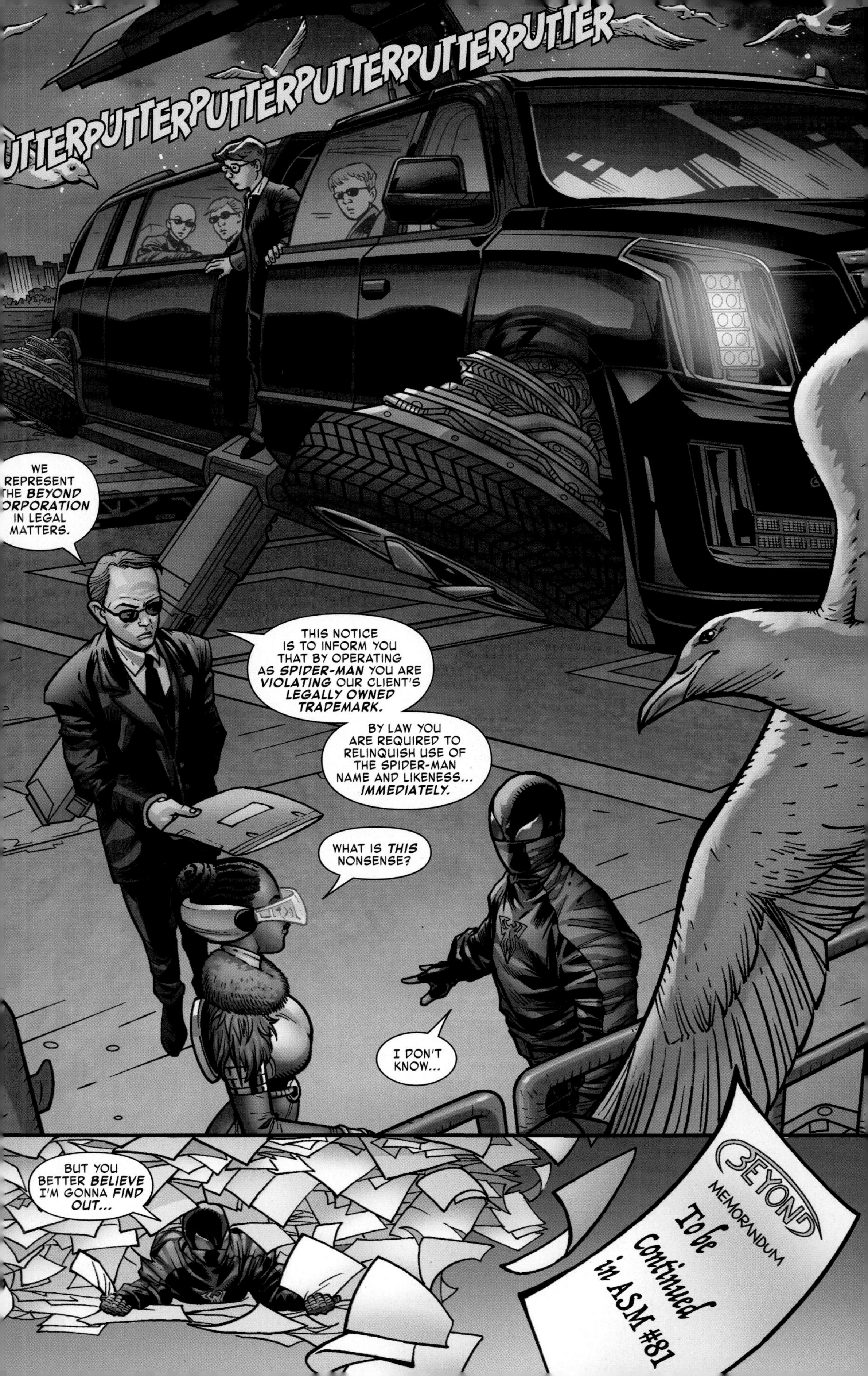

PUTTERPUTTERPUTTERPUTTERPUTTER
WE REPRESENT THE BEYOND CORPORATION IN LEGAL MATTERS.
THIS NOTICE IS TO INFORM YOU THAT BY OPERATING AS SPIDER-MAN YOU ARE VIOLATING OUR CLIENT'S LEGALLY OWNED TRADEMARK.
BY LAW YOU ARE REQUIRED TO RELINQUISH USE OF THE SPIDER-MAN NAME AND LIKENESS... IMMEDIATELY.
WHAT IS THIS NONSENSE?
I DON'T KNOW...
BUT YOU BETTER BELIEVE I'M GONNA FIND OUT...
BEYOND
MEMORANDUM
To be Continued in ASM #81

HEY WEB-HEADS!

We have a few more special stories in store for you! First, some of the minds behind the *Into the Spider-Verse* movie and the upcoming sequel have a story about a slightly alternate Miles Morales.

That's right, Phil Lord, Christopher Miller, (Academy Award Nominee) Kemp Powers and Jeff Loveness are dabbling in comics with none other than the co-creator of Miles herself, Sara Pichelli. Add Rachelle Rosenberg and Cory Petit, and you know you're in for a treat.

After that, we have a peek at a different time in Miles' life from two rising stars: Cody Ziglar (writer on the TV shows *She-Hulk* and *Rick and Morty*) and Anthony Piper (who's dabbled with Marvel work while creating his own comic *Trill League* and also working in animation).

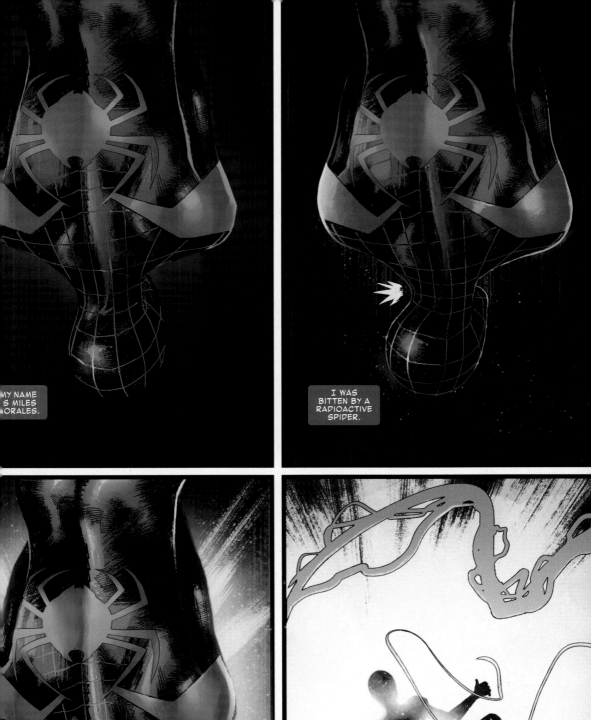

MY NAME IS MILES MORALES.

I WAS BITTEN BY A RADIOACTIVE SPIDER.

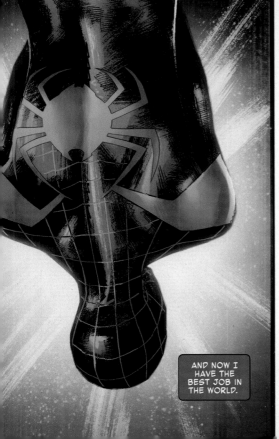

AND NOW I HAVE THE BEST JOB IN THE WORLD.

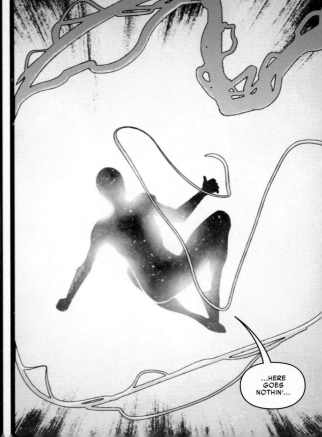

...HERE GOES NOTHIN'...

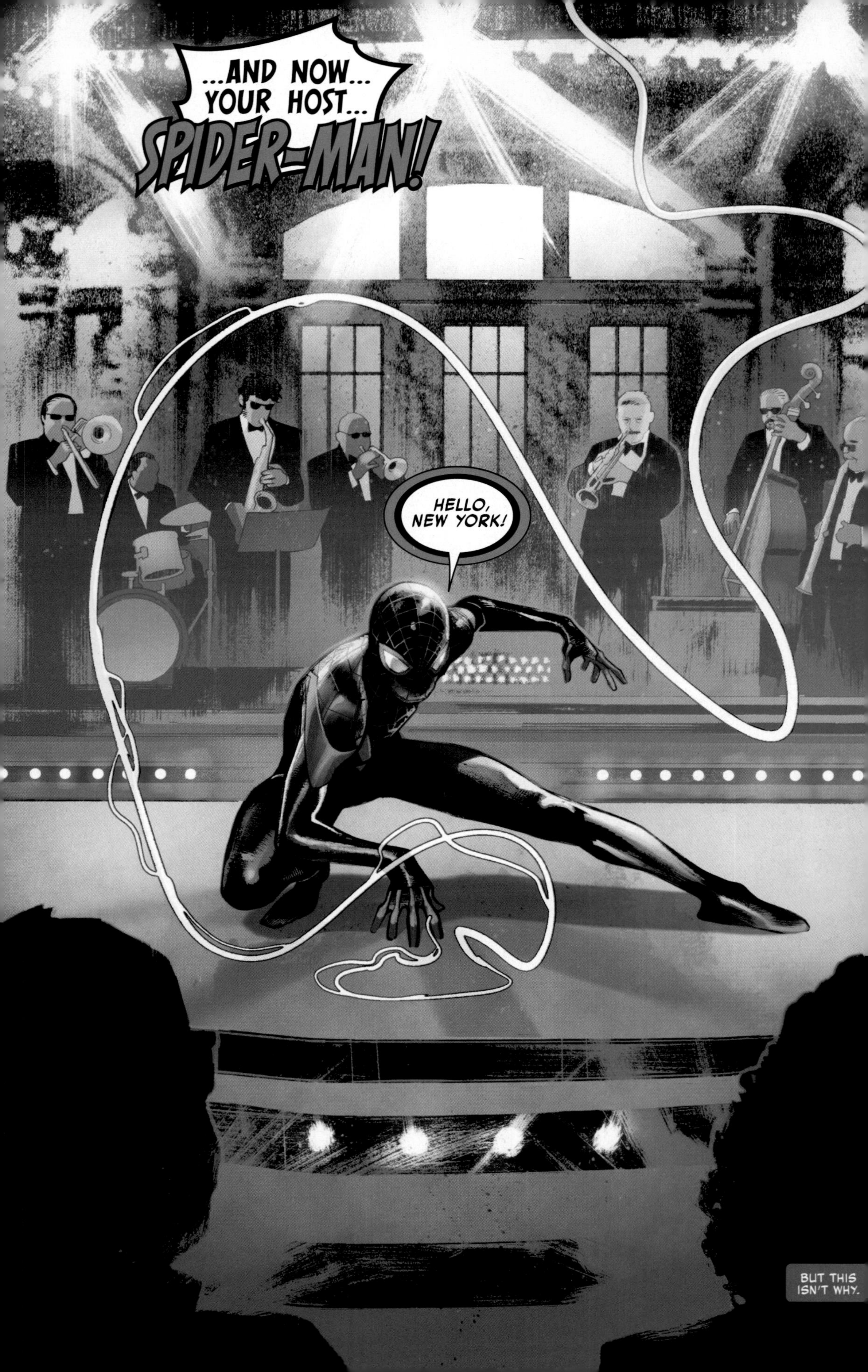
...AND NOW... YOUR HOST... SPIDER-MAN!
HELLO, NEW YORK!
BUT THIS ISN'T WHY.

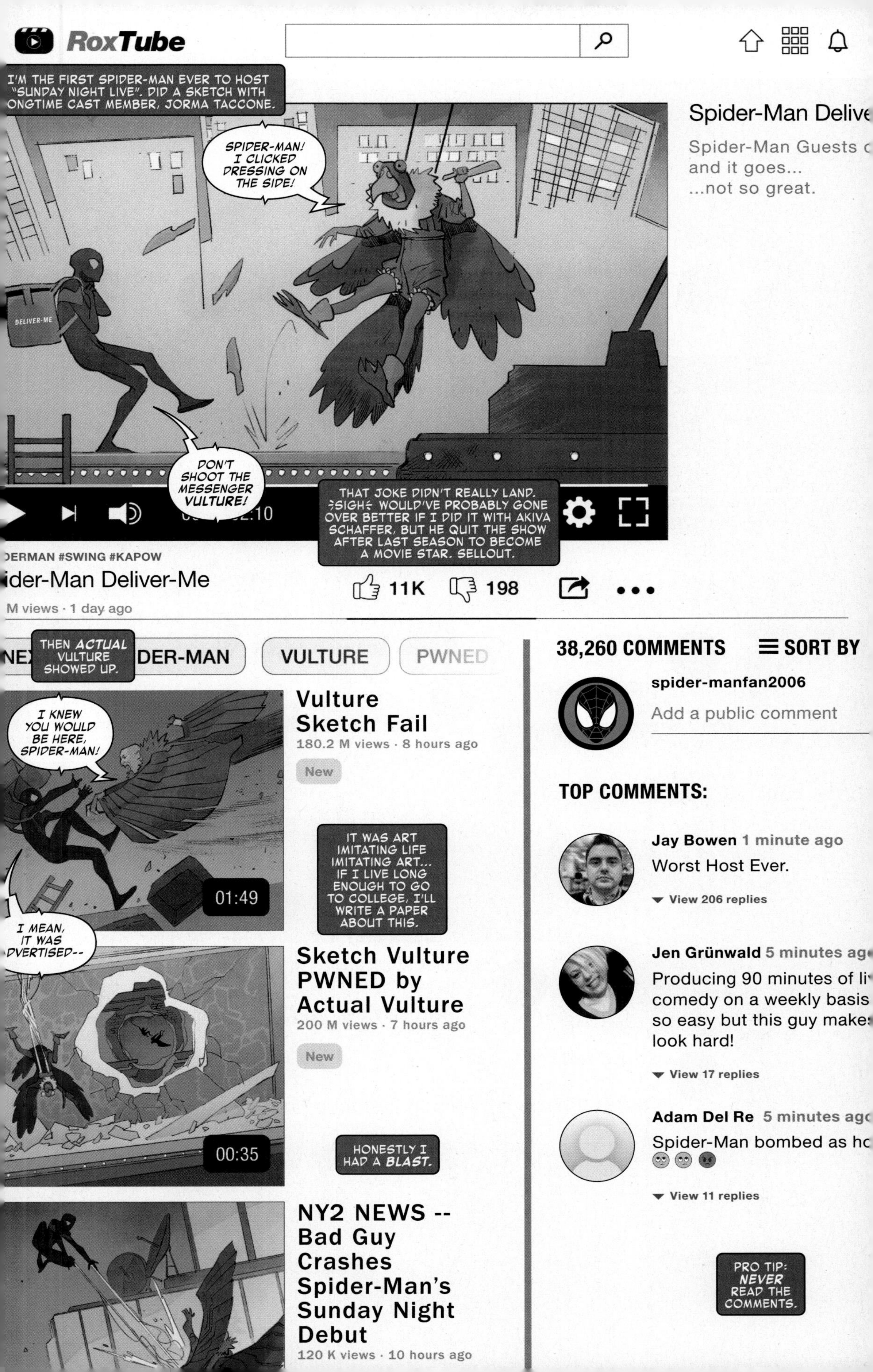
RoxTube
I'M THE FIRST SPIDER-MAN EVER TO HOST "SUNDAY NIGHT LIVE". DID A SKETCH WITH LONGTIME CAST MEMBER, JORMA TACCONE.
SPIDER-MAN! I CLICKED DRESSING ON THE SIDE!
DELIVER-ME
DON'T SHOOT THE MESSENGER VULTURE!
THAT JOKE DIDN'T REALLY LAND. ⸗SIGH⸗ WOULD'VE PROBABLY GONE OVER BETTER IF I DID IT WITH AKIVA SCHAFFER, BUT HE QUIT THE SHOW AFTER LAST SEASON TO BECOME A MOVIE STAR. SELLOUT.
Spider-Man Delive
Spider-Man Guests o
and it goes...
...not so great.
DERMAN #SWING #KAPOW
ider-Man Deliver-Me
M views · 1 day ago
11K
198
THEN ACTUAL VULTURE SHOWED UP.
DER-MAN
VULTURE
PWNED
38,260 COMMENTS
SORT BY
spider-manfan2006
Add a public comment
I KNEW YOU WOULD BE HERE, SPIDER-MAN!
Vulture Sketch Fail
180.2 M views · 8 hours ago
New
TOP COMMENTS:
Jay Bowen 1 minute ago
Worst Host Ever.
View 206 replies
01:49
IT WAS ART IMITATING LIFE IMITATING ART... IF I LIVE LONG ENOUGH TO GO TO COLLEGE, I'LL WRITE A PAPER ABOUT THIS.
I MEAN, IT WAS DVERTISED--
Sketch Vulture PWNED by Actual Vulture
200 M views · 7 hours ago
New
Jen Grünwald 5 minutes ag
Producing 90 minutes of li
comedy on a weekly basis
so easy but this guy make
look hard!
View 17 replies
Adam Del Re 5 minutes ago
Spider-Man bombed as ho
View 11 replies
00:35
HONESTLY I HAD A BLAST.
NY2 NEWS -- Bad Guy Crashes Spider-Man's Sunday Night Debut
120 K views · 10 hours ago
PRO TIP: NEVER READ THE COMMENTS.

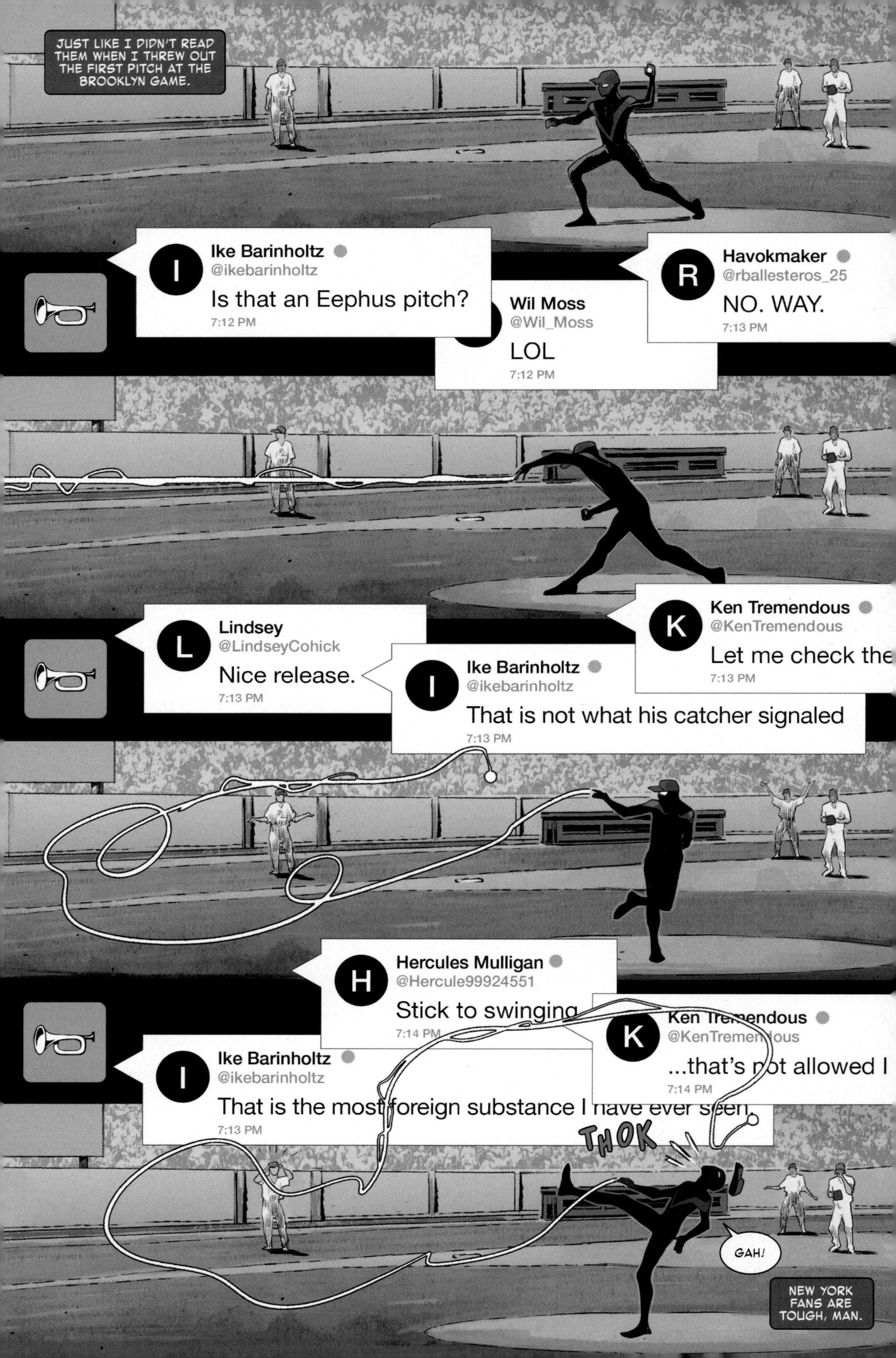

JUST LIKE I DIDN'T READ THEM WHEN I THREW OUT THE FIRST PITCH AT THE BROOKLYN GAME.
Ike Barinholtz @ikebarinholtz Is that an Eephus pitch? 7:12 PM
Wil Moss @Wil_Moss LOL 7:12 PM
Havokmaker @rballesteros_25 NO. WAY. 7:13 PM
Lindsey @LindseyCohick Nice release. 7:13 PM
Ken Tremendous @KenTremendous Let me check the 7:13 PM
Ike Barinholtz @ikebarinholtz That is not what his catcher signaled 7:13 PM
Hercules Mulligan @Hercule99924551 Stick to swinging 7:14 PM
Ike Barinholtz @ikebarinholtz That is the most foreign substance I have ever seen. 7:13 PM
Ken Tremendous @KenTremendous ...that's not allowed I 7:14 PM
THOK
GAH!
NEW YORK FANS ARE TOUGH, MAN.

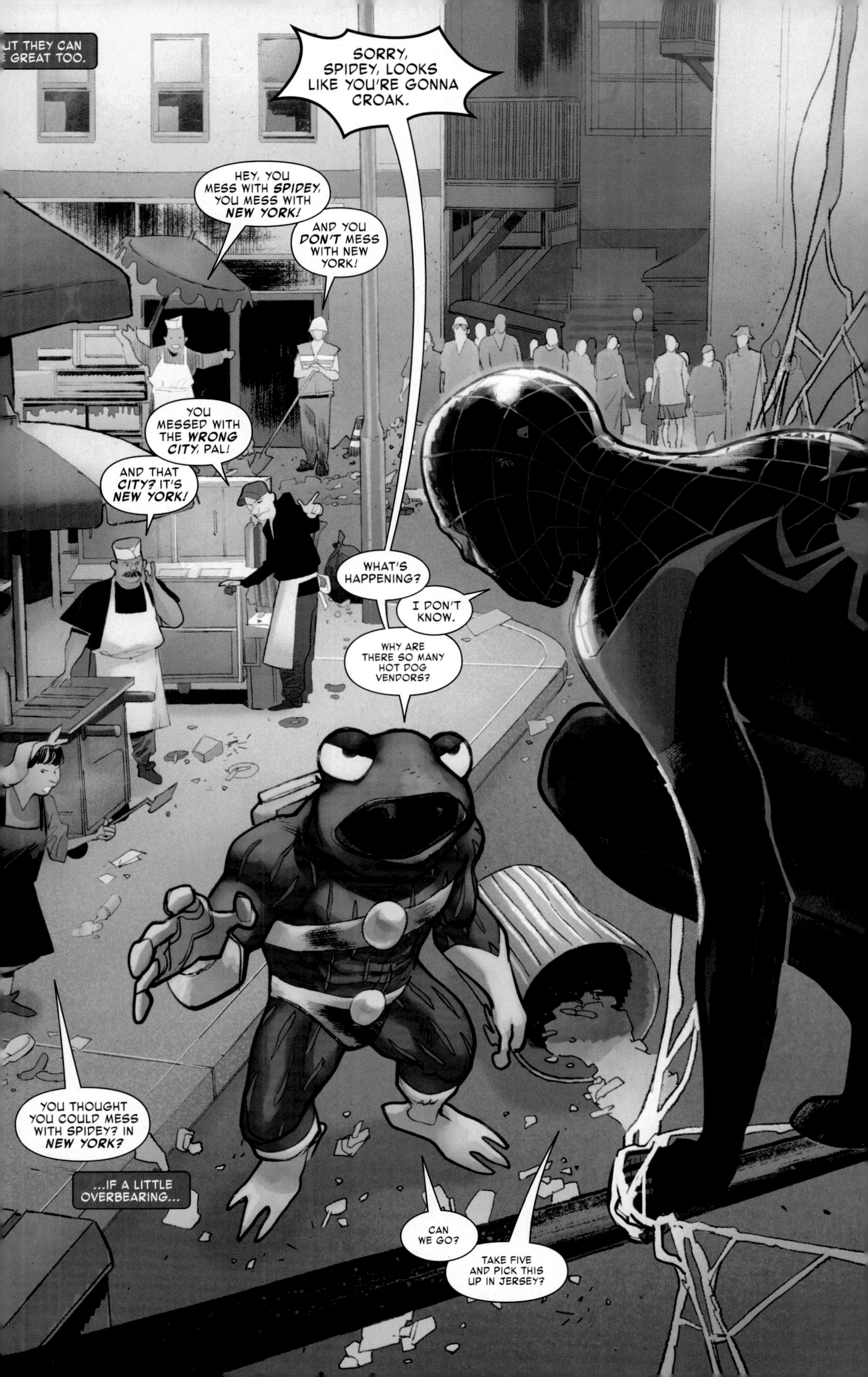

...BUT THEY CAN BE GREAT TOO.
SORRY, SPIDEY, LOOKS LIKE YOU'RE GONNA CROAK.
HEY, YOU MESS WITH SPIDEY, YOU MESS WITH NEW YORK!
AND YOU DON'T MESS WITH NEW YORK!
YOU MESSED WITH THE WRONG CITY, PAL!
AND THAT CITY? IT'S NEW YORK!
WHAT'S HAPPENING?
I DON'T KNOW.
WHY ARE THERE SO MANY HOT DOG VENDORS?
YOU THOUGHT YOU COULD MESS WITH SPIDEY? IN NEW YORK?
...IF A LITTLE OVERBEARING...
CAN WE GO?
TAKE FIVE AND PICK THIS UP IN JERSEY?

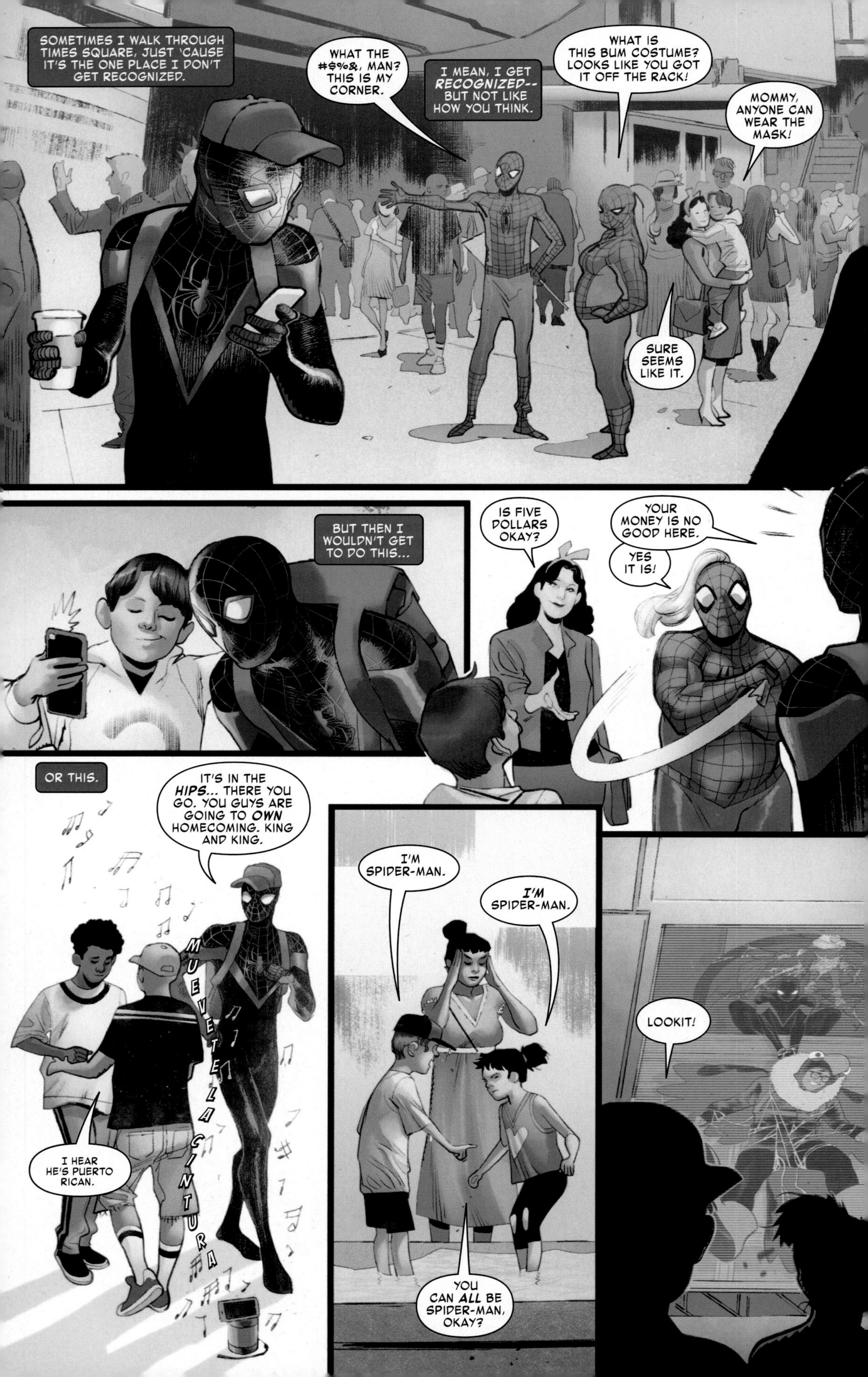
SOMETIMES I WALK THROUGH TIMES SQUARE, JUST 'CAUSE IT'S THE ONE PLACE I DON'T GET RECOGNIZED.
WHAT THE #$%&, MAN? THIS IS MY CORNER.
I MEAN, I GET RECOGNIZED-- BUT NOT LIKE HOW YOU THINK.
WHAT IS THIS BUM COSTUME? LOOKS LIKE YOU GOT IT OFF THE RACK!
MOMMY, ANYONE CAN WEAR THE MASK!
SURE SEEMS LIKE IT.
BUT THEN I WOULDN'T GET TO DO THIS...
IS FIVE DOLLARS OKAY?
YOUR MONEY IS NO GOOD HERE.
YES IT IS!
OR THIS.
IT'S IN THE HIPS... THERE YOU GO. YOU GUYS ARE GOING TO OWN HOMECOMING. KING AND KING.
MUEVETE LA CINTURA
I HEAR HE'S PUERTO RICAN.
I'M SPIDER-MAN.
I'M SPIDER-MAN.
YOU CAN ALL BE SPIDER-MAN, OKAY?
LOOKIT!

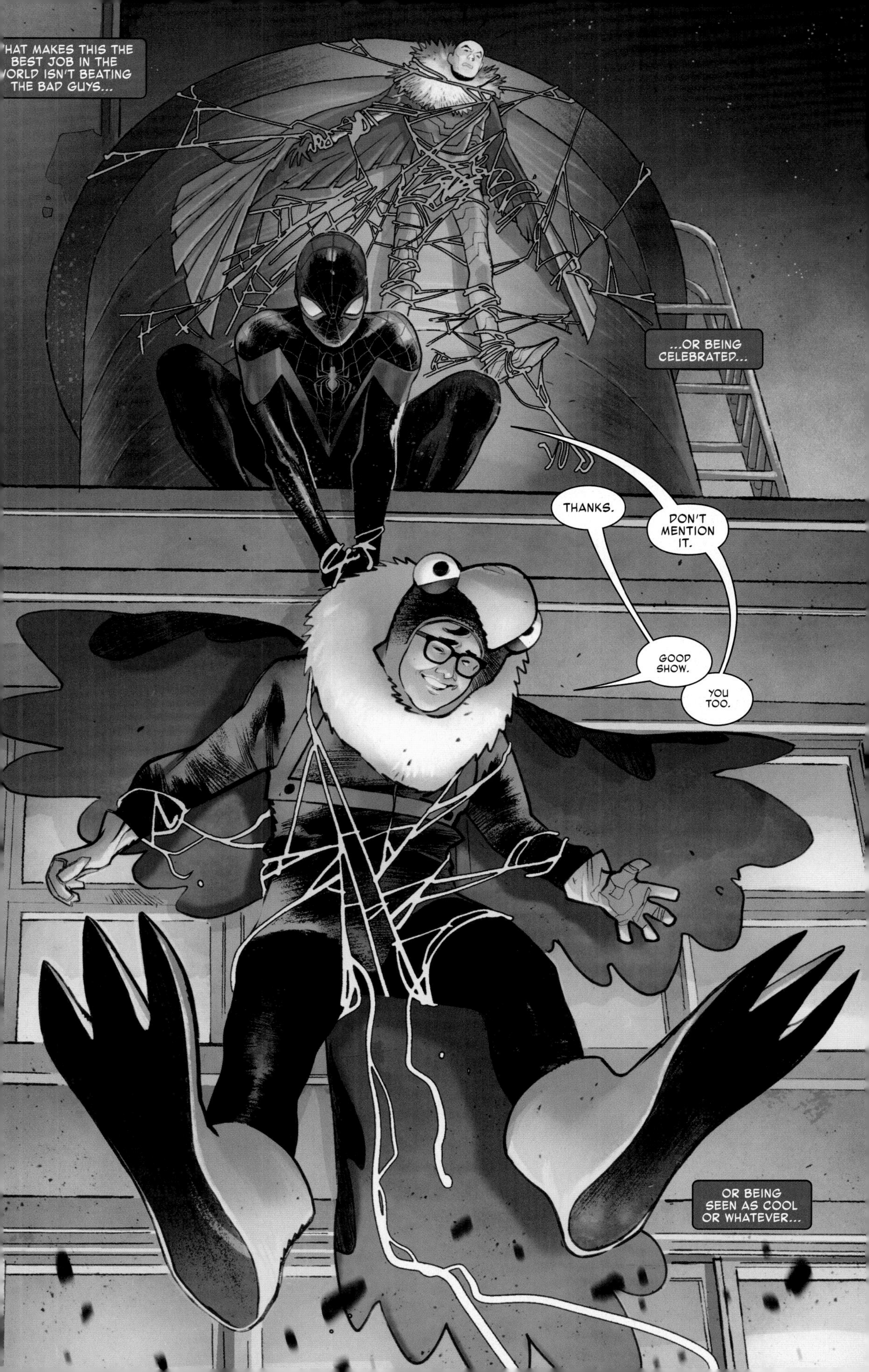
HAT MAKES THIS THE BEST JOB IN THE ORLD ISN'T BEATING THE BAD GUYS...
...OR BEING CELEBRATED...
THANKS.
DON'T MENTION IT.
GOOD SHOW.
YOU TOO.
OR BEING SEEN AS COOL OR WHATEVER...

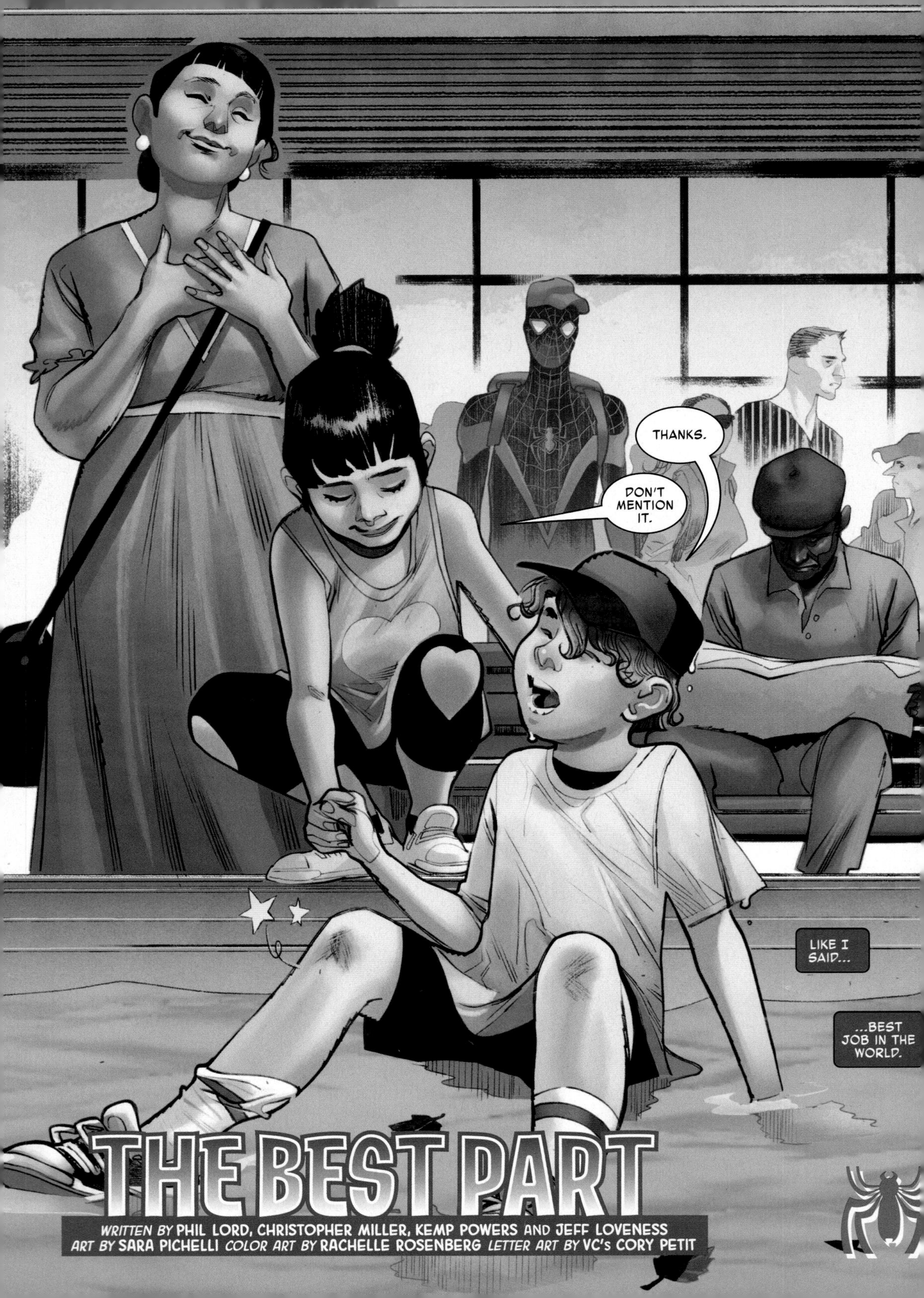
THANKS.
DON'T MENTION IT.
LIKE I SAID...
...BEST JOB IN THE WORLD.
THE BEST PART
WRITTEN BY PHIL LORD, CHRISTOPHER MILLER, KEMP POWERS AND JEFF LOVENESS
ART BY SARA PICHELLI COLOR ART BY RACHELLE ROSENBERG LETTER ART BY VC's CORY PETIT

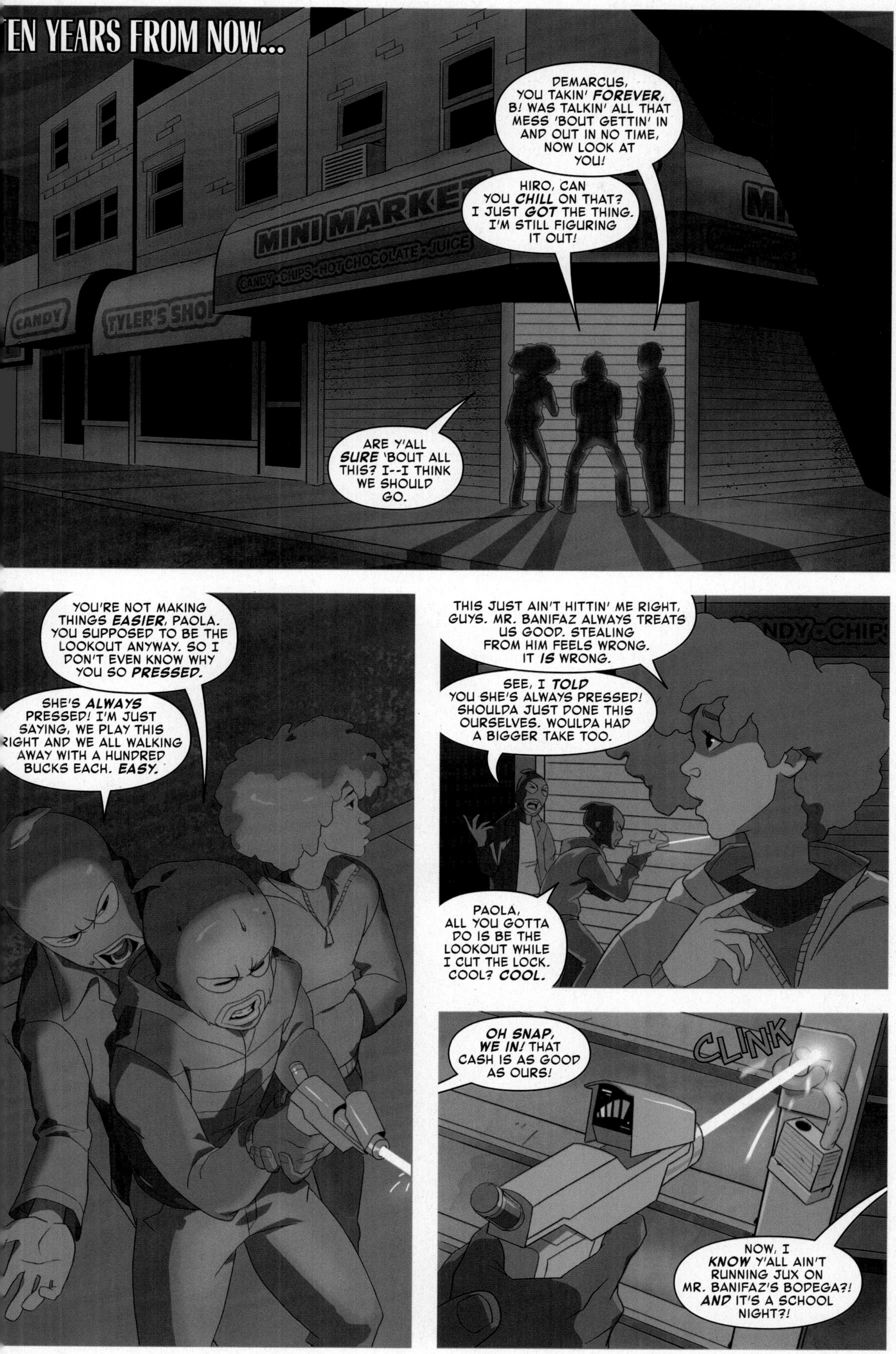
TEN YEARS FROM NOW...
DEMARCUS, YOU TAKIN' FOREVER, B! WAS TALKIN' ALL THAT MESS 'BOUT GETTIN' IN AND OUT IN NO TIME, NOW LOOK AT YOU!
HIRO, CAN YOU CHILL ON THAT? I JUST GOT THE THING. I'M STILL FIGURING IT OUT!
ARE Y'ALL SURE 'BOUT ALL THIS? I--I THINK WE SHOULD GO.
MINI MARKET
CANDY · CHIPS · HOT CHOCOLATE · JUICE
CANDY
TYLER'S SHO
YOU'RE NOT MAKING THINGS EASIER, PAOLA. YOU SUPPOSED TO BE THE LOOKOUT ANYWAY. SO I DON'T EVEN KNOW WHY YOU SO PRESSED.
SHE'S ALWAYS PRESSED! I'M JUST SAYING, WE PLAY THIS RIGHT AND WE ALL WALKING AWAY WITH A HUNDRED BUCKS EACH. EASY.
THIS JUST AIN'T HITTIN' ME RIGHT, GUYS. MR. BANIFAZ ALWAYS TREATS US GOOD. STEALING FROM HIM FEELS WRONG. IT IS WRONG.
SEE, I TOLD YOU SHE'S ALWAYS PRESSED! SHOULDA JUST DONE THIS OURSELVES. WOULDA HAD A BIGGER TAKE TOO.
PAOLA, ALL YOU GOTTA DO IS BE THE LOOKOUT WHILE I CUT THE LOCK. COOL? COOL.
CLINK
OH SNAP, WE IN! THAT CASH IS AS GOOD AS OURS!
NOW, I KNOW Y'ALL AIN'T RUNNING JUX ON MR. BANIFAZ'S BODEGA?! AND IT'S A SCHOOL NIGHT?!

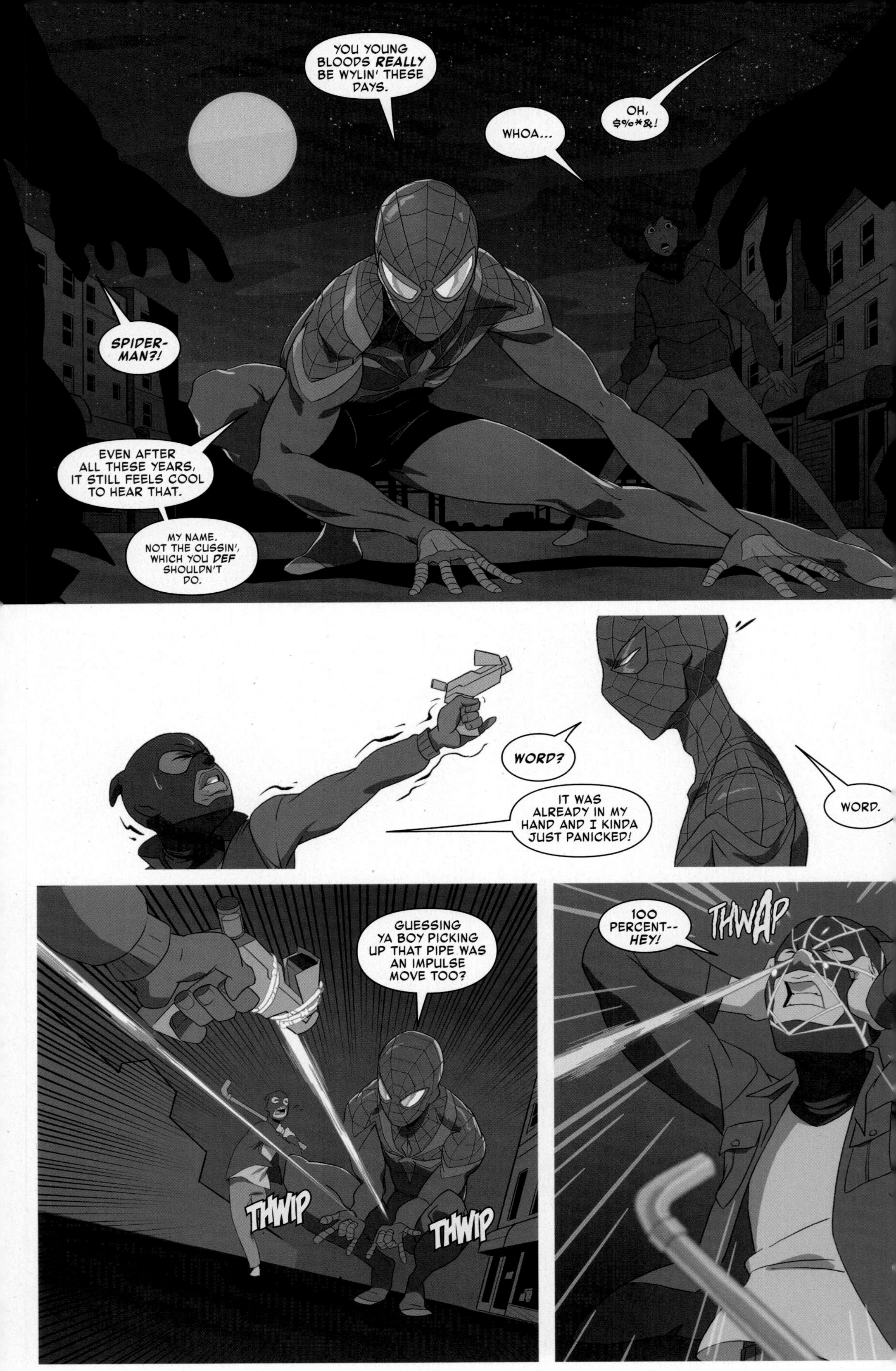
YOU YOUNG BLOODS *REALLY* BE WYLIN' THESE DAYS.
WHOA...
OH, $%*&!
SPIDER-MAN?!
EVEN AFTER ALL THESE YEARS, IT STILL FEELS COOL TO HEAR THAT.
MY NAME. NOT THE CUSSIN', WHICH YOU *DEF* SHOULDN'T DO.
WORD?
IT WAS ALREADY IN MY HAND AND I KINDA JUST PANICKED!
WORD.
GUESSING YA BOY PICKING UP THAT PIPE WAS AN IMPULSE MOVE TOO?
THWIP
THWIP
100 PERCENT-- *HEY!*
THWAP

BEEN AT THIS FOR A LONG TIME NOW. SQUARED UP WITH TASKMASTER, QUEEN GOBLIN, ZIP ZEPHYR, BLACK OBSIDIAN, AND WHOLE LOTTA OTHER CATS. Y'ALL REALLY TRYNA DO THIS?

UH, NO!

WE WANT ABSOLUTELY *NONE* OF THAT SMOKE!

SEEM LIKE GOOD KIDS. ALL THINGS CONSIDERED.

YOU HIDING A LASER CUTTER OR PIPE I SHOULD BE WORRIED ABOUT?

NAH, I CAN TELL YOU NOT 'BOUT THAT LIFE. WHICH BEGS THE QUESTION: WHY YOU HERE, KID?

I HEARD WHAT THEY WERE PLANNING AND THOUGHT MAYBE I COULD TALK 'EM OUT OF IT. STUPID, I KNOW.

BUT I JUST WOULD HAVE FELT SO *POWERLESS* IF I DIDN'T AT LEAST TRY.

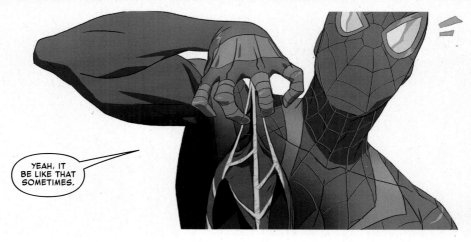

YEAH, IT BE LIKE THAT SOMETIMES.

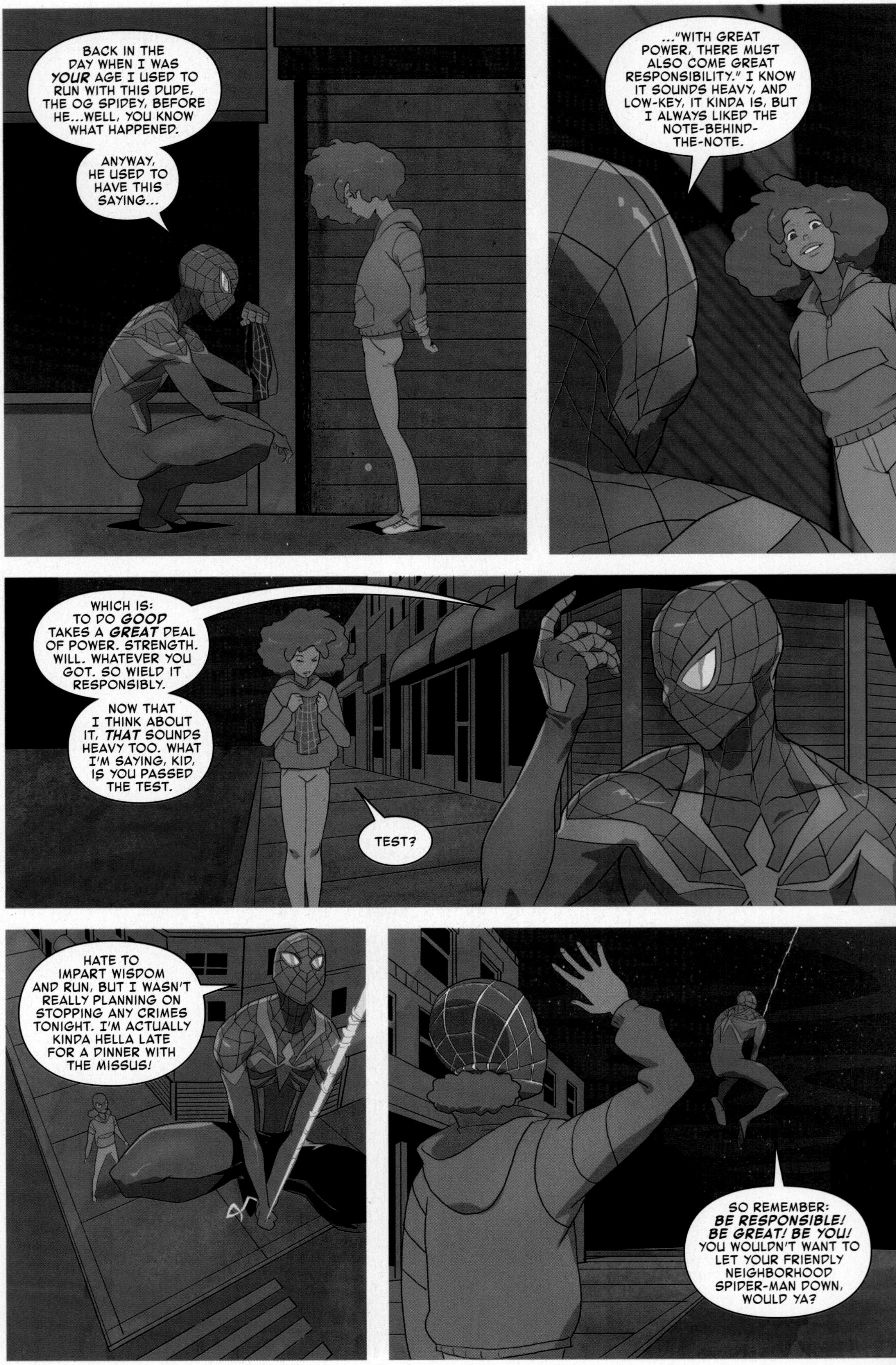
BACK IN THE DAY WHEN I WAS YOUR AGE I USED TO RUN WITH THIS DUDE, THE OG SPIDEY, BEFORE HE...WELL, YOU KNOW WHAT HAPPENED.
ANYWAY, HE USED TO HAVE THIS SAYING...
..."WITH GREAT POWER, THERE MUST ALSO COME GREAT RESPONSIBILITY." I KNOW IT SOUNDS HEAVY, AND LOW-KEY, IT KINDA IS, BUT I ALWAYS LIKED THE NOTE-BEHIND-THE-NOTE.
WHICH IS: TO DO GOOD TAKES A GREAT DEAL OF POWER. STRENGTH. WILL. WHATEVER YOU GOT. SO WIELD IT RESPONSIBLY.
NOW THAT I THINK ABOUT IT, THAT SOUNDS HEAVY TOO. WHAT I'M SAYING, KID, IS YOU PASSED THE TEST.
TEST?
HATE TO IMPART WISDOM AND RUN, BUT I WASN'T REALLY PLANNING ON STOPPING ANY CRIMES TONIGHT. I'M ACTUALLY KINDA HELLA LATE FOR A DINNER WITH THE MISSUS!
SO REMEMBER: BE RESPONSIBLE! BE GREAT! BE YOU! YOU WOULDN'T WANT TO LET YOUR FRIENDLY NEIGHBORHOOD SPIDER-MAN DOWN, WOULD YA?

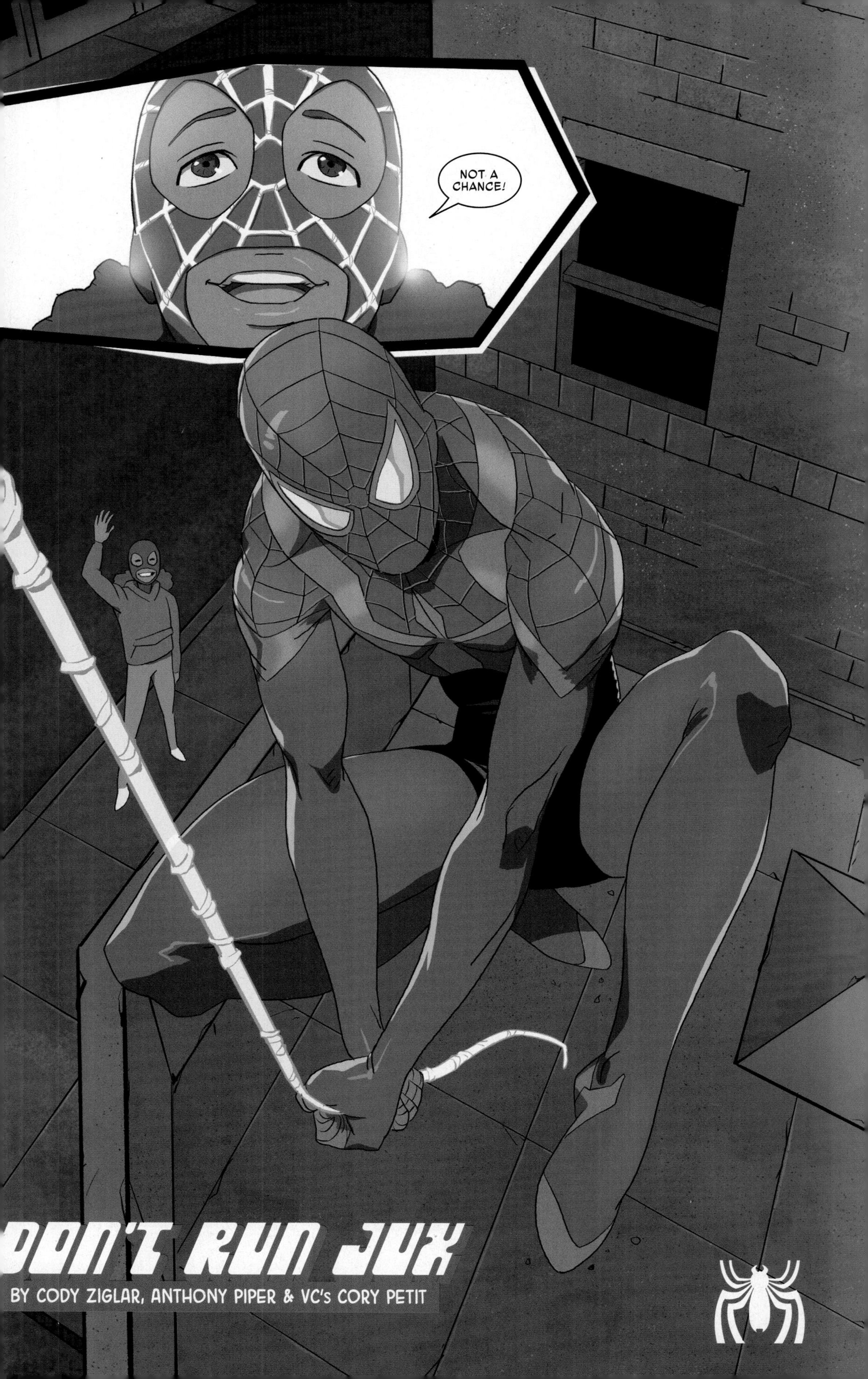
NOT A CHANCE!
DON'T RUN JUX
BY CODY ZIGLAR, ANTHONY PIPER & VC's CORY PETIT

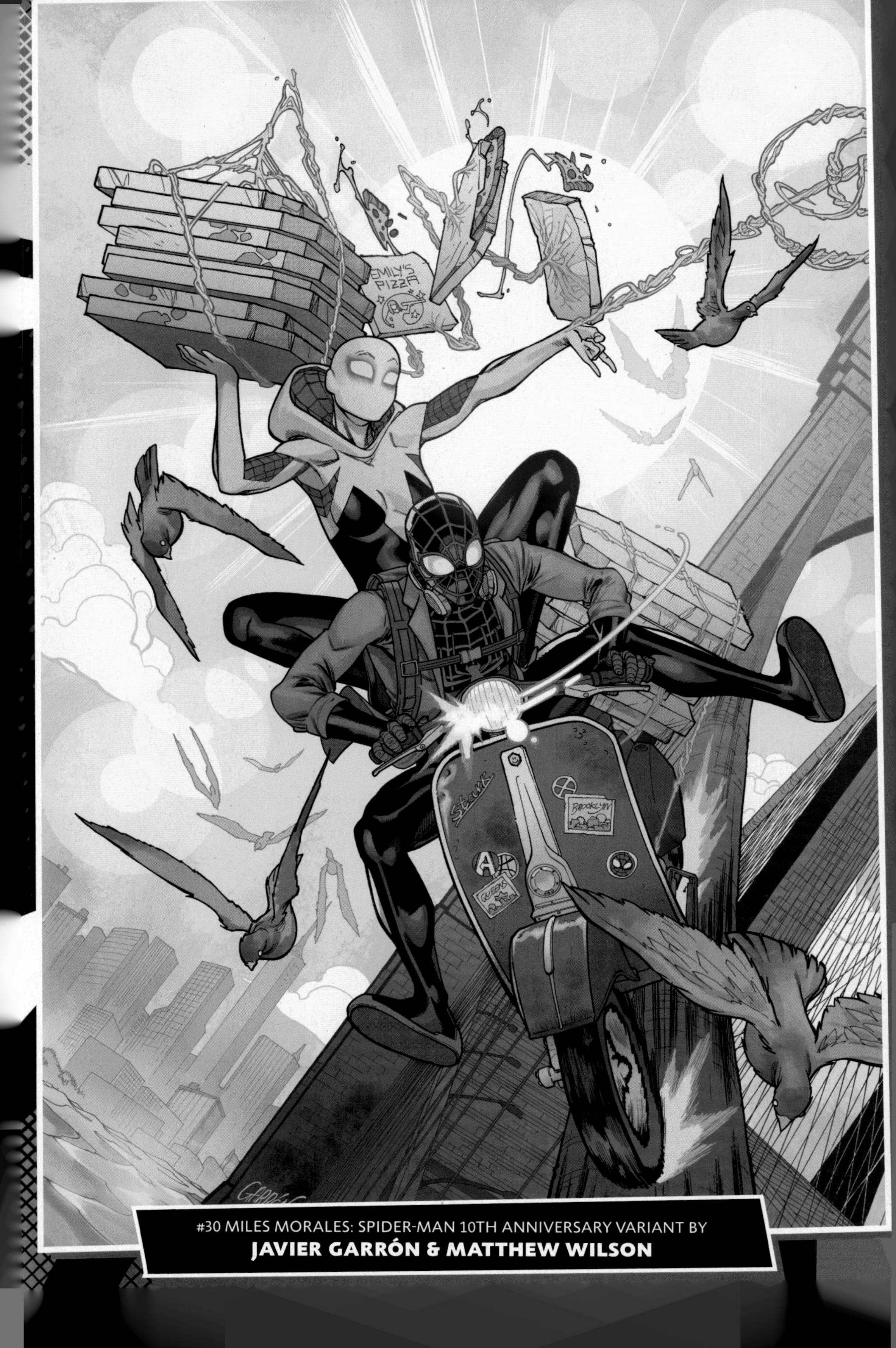
EMILY'S PIZZA
BROOKLYN
QUEENS

#30 MILES MORALES: SPIDER-MAN 10TH ANNIVERSARY VARIANT BY
JAVIER GARRÓN & MATTHEW WILSON

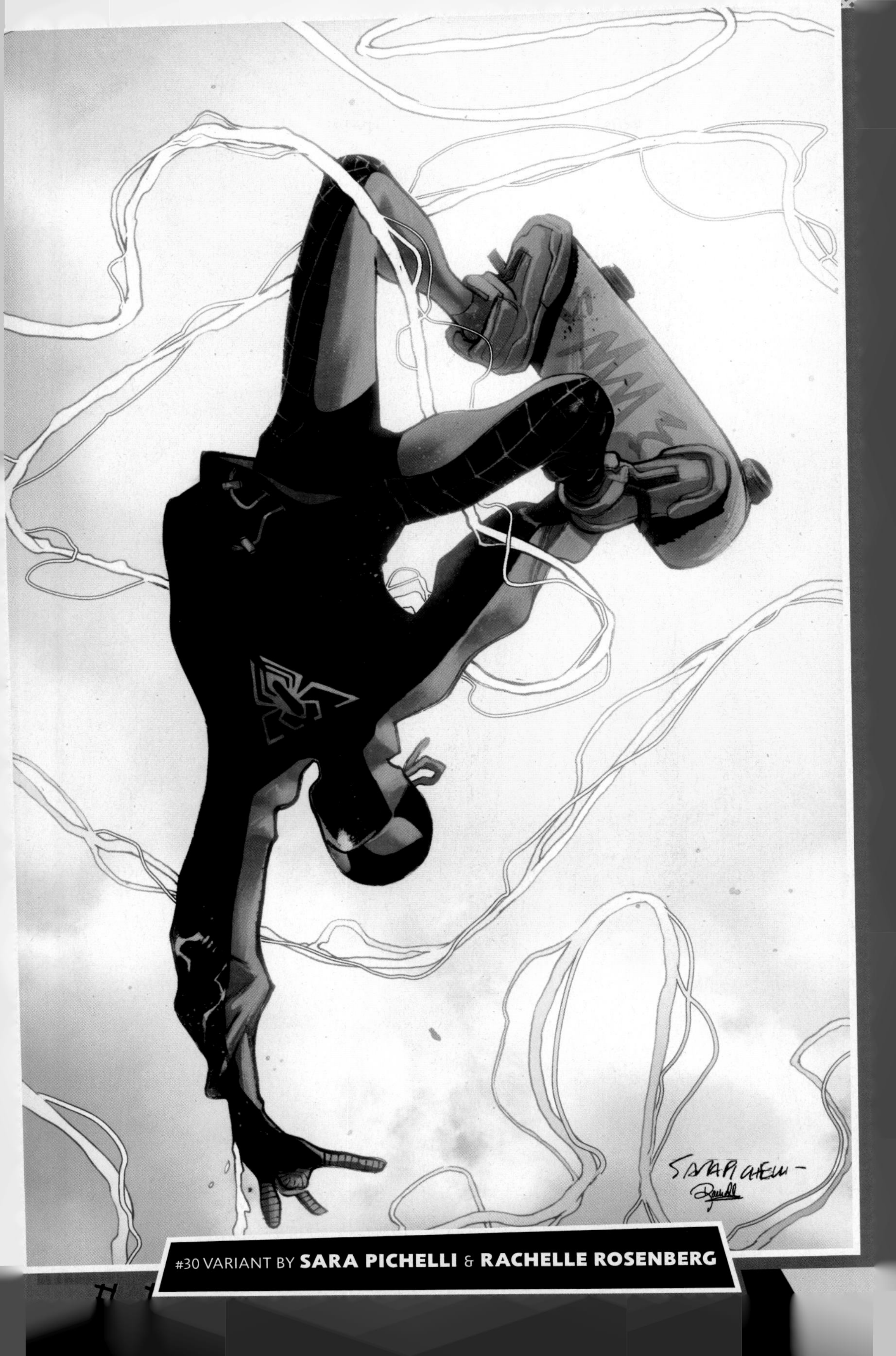

#30 VARIANT BY **SARA PICHELLI** & **RACHELLE ROSENBERG**

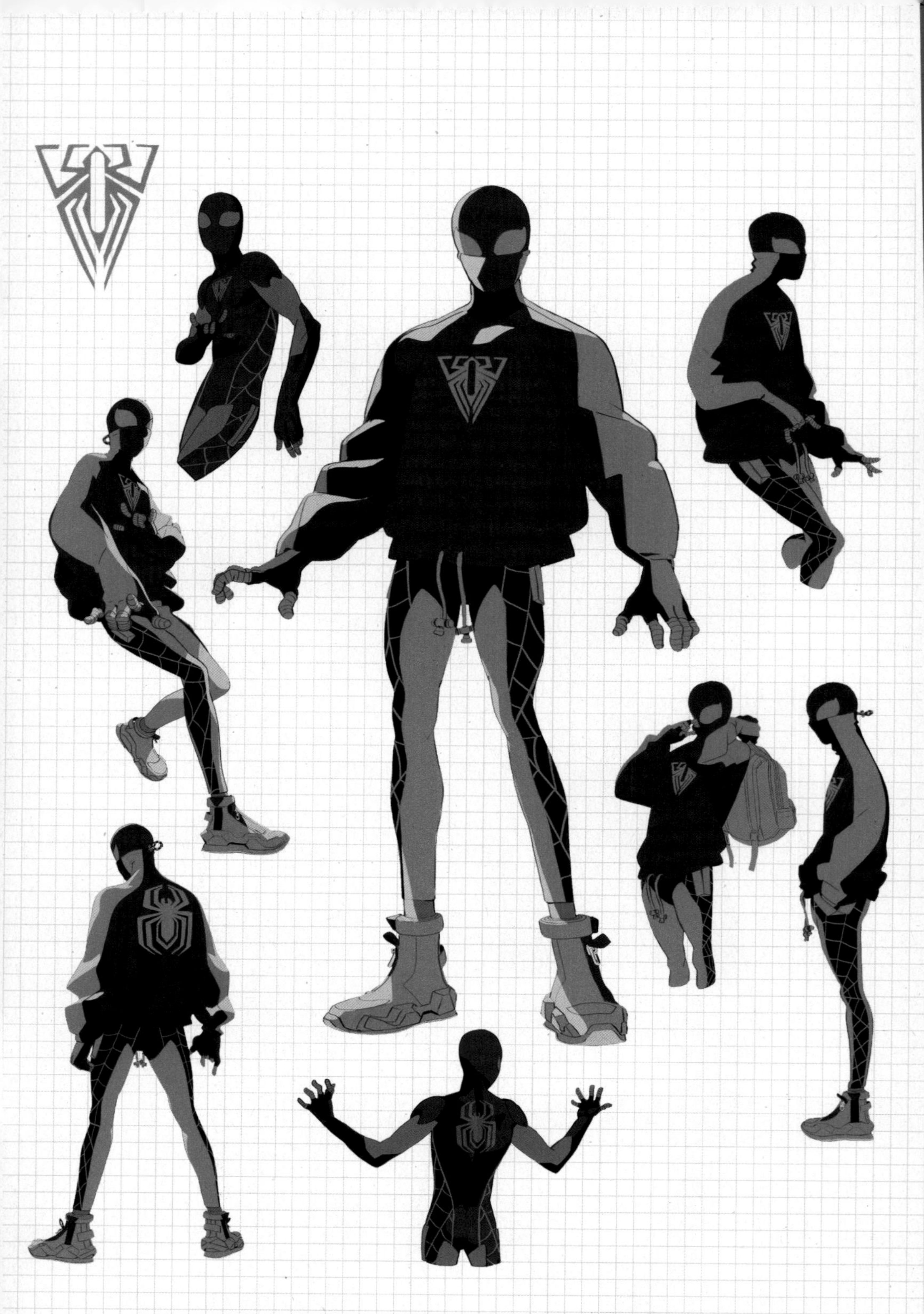

#30 DESIGN VARIANT BY **CHASE CONLEY**

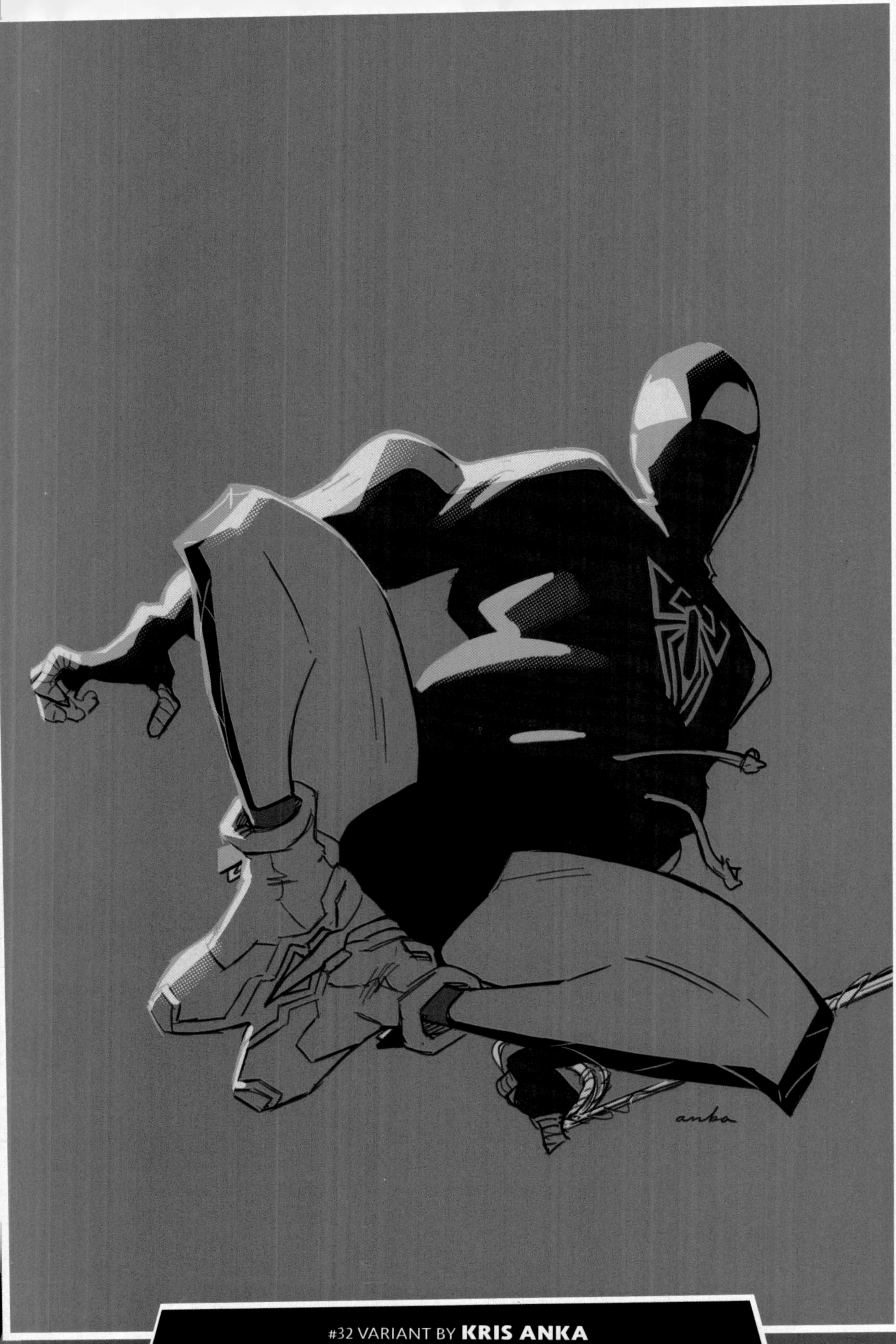
anka

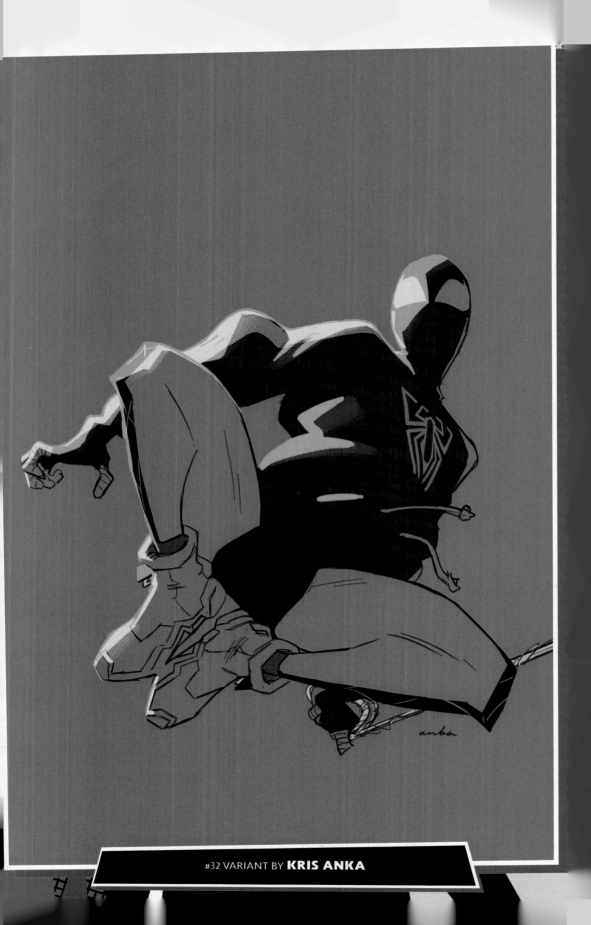

#32 VARIANT BY **KRIS ANKA**

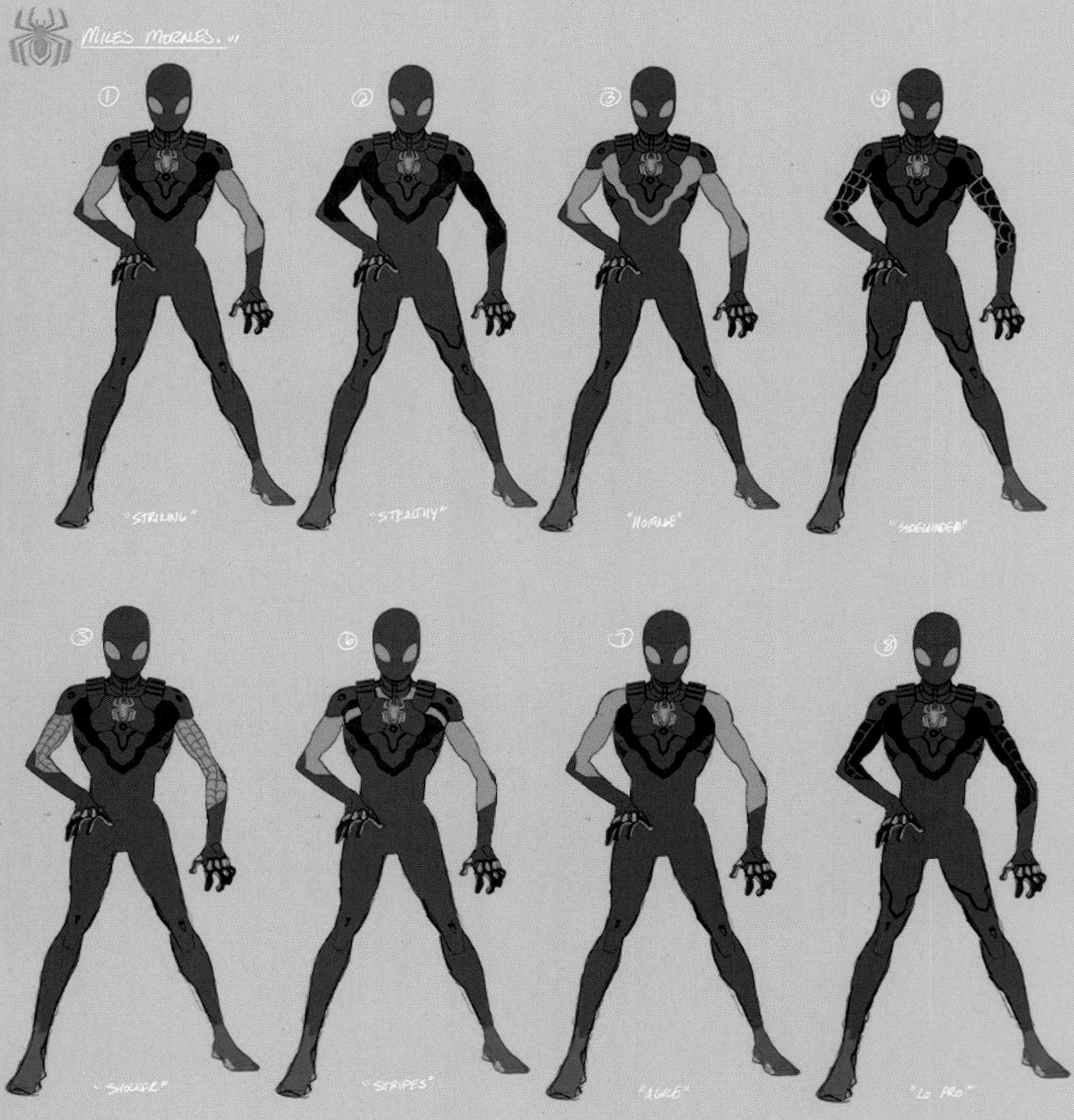
MILES MORALES. v1
①
②
③
④
"STRIKING"
"STEALTHY"
"HOMAGE"
"SIDEWINDER"
⑤
⑥
⑦
⑧
"SHOCKER"
"STRIPES"
"AGILE"
"LO PRO"

COSTUME DESIGNS BY **CHASE CONLEY**

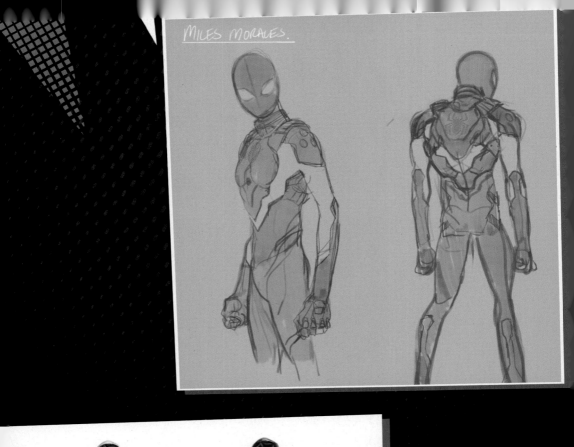

MILES MORALES.

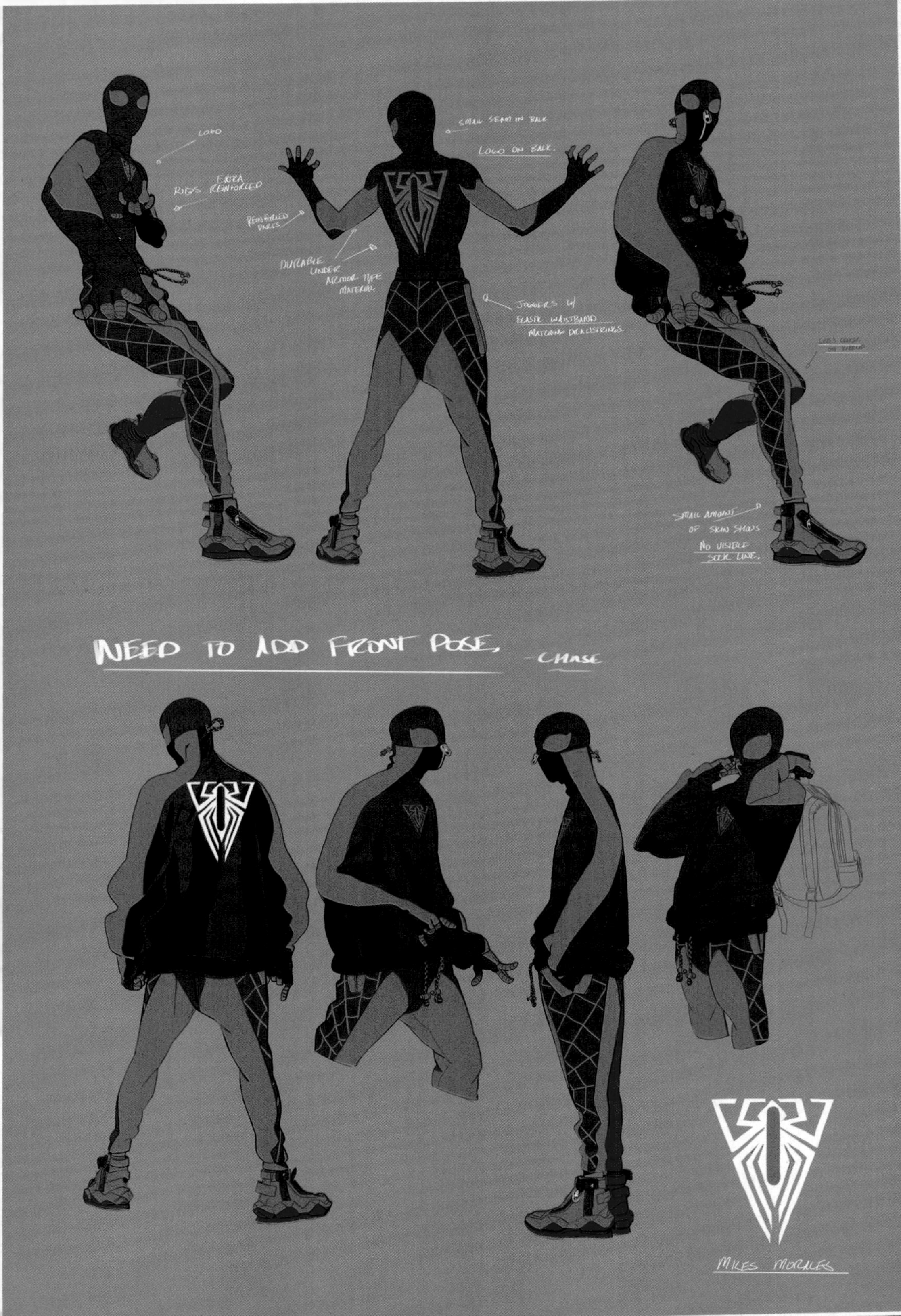

LOGO
EXTRA RIBS REINFORCED
REINFORCED PARTS
DURABLE UNDER ARMOR TYPE MATERIAL
SMALL SEAM IN BACK
LOGO ON BACK.
JOGGERS W/ ELASTIC WAISTBAND MATCHING DRAWSTRINGS
SMALL AMOUNT OF SKIN SHOWS
NO VISIBLE SOCK LINE.
NEED TO ADD FRONT POSE. -CHASE
MILES MORALES

UNDER THE
SWEATER

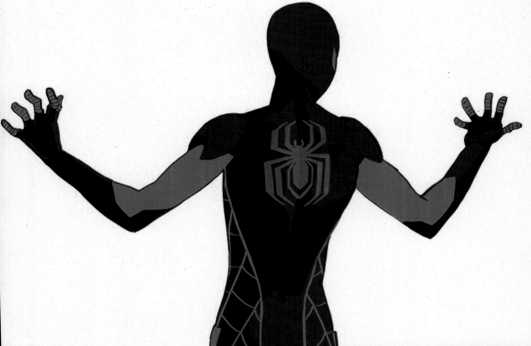

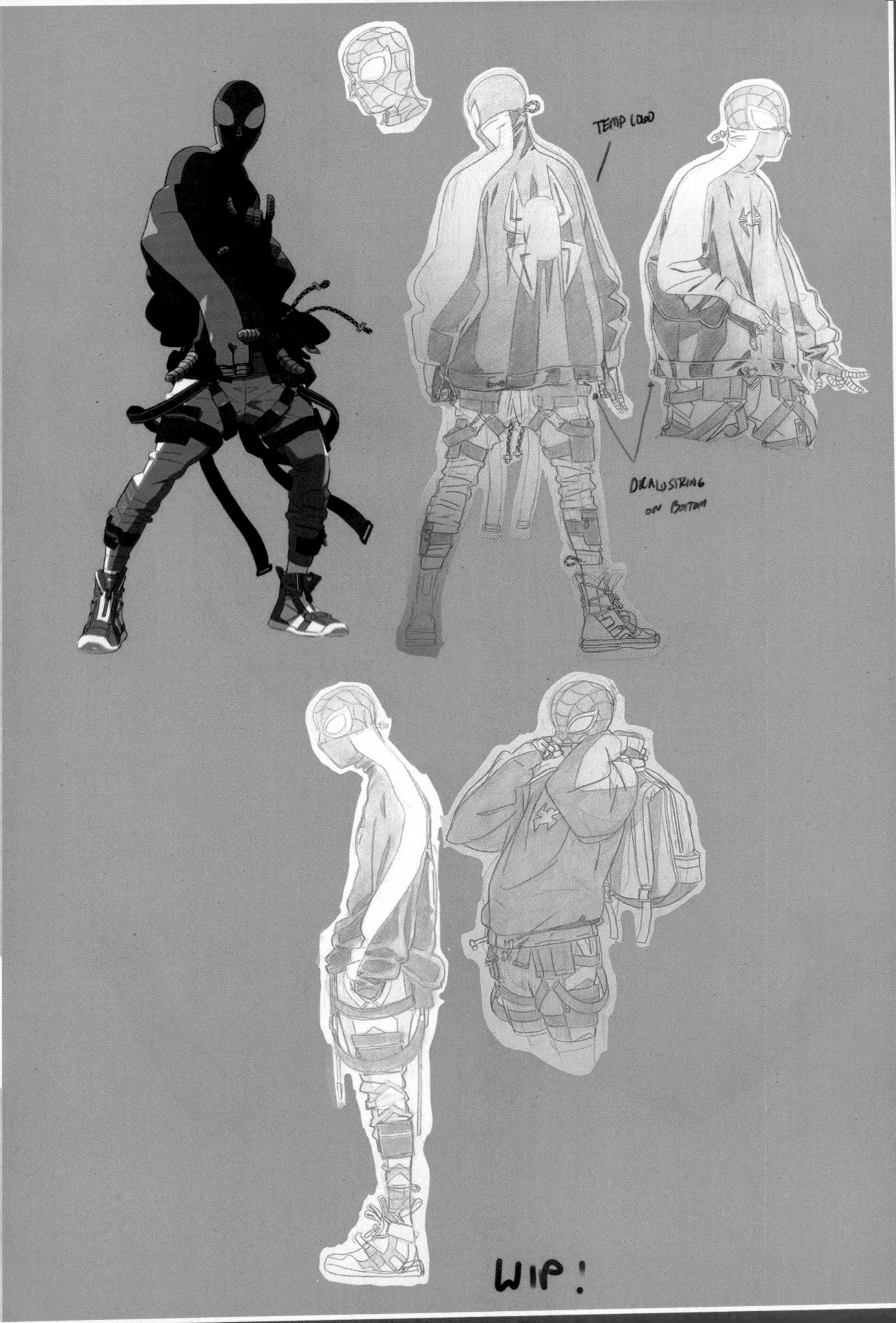
TEMP LOGO
DRAWSTRING ON BOTTOM
WIP!

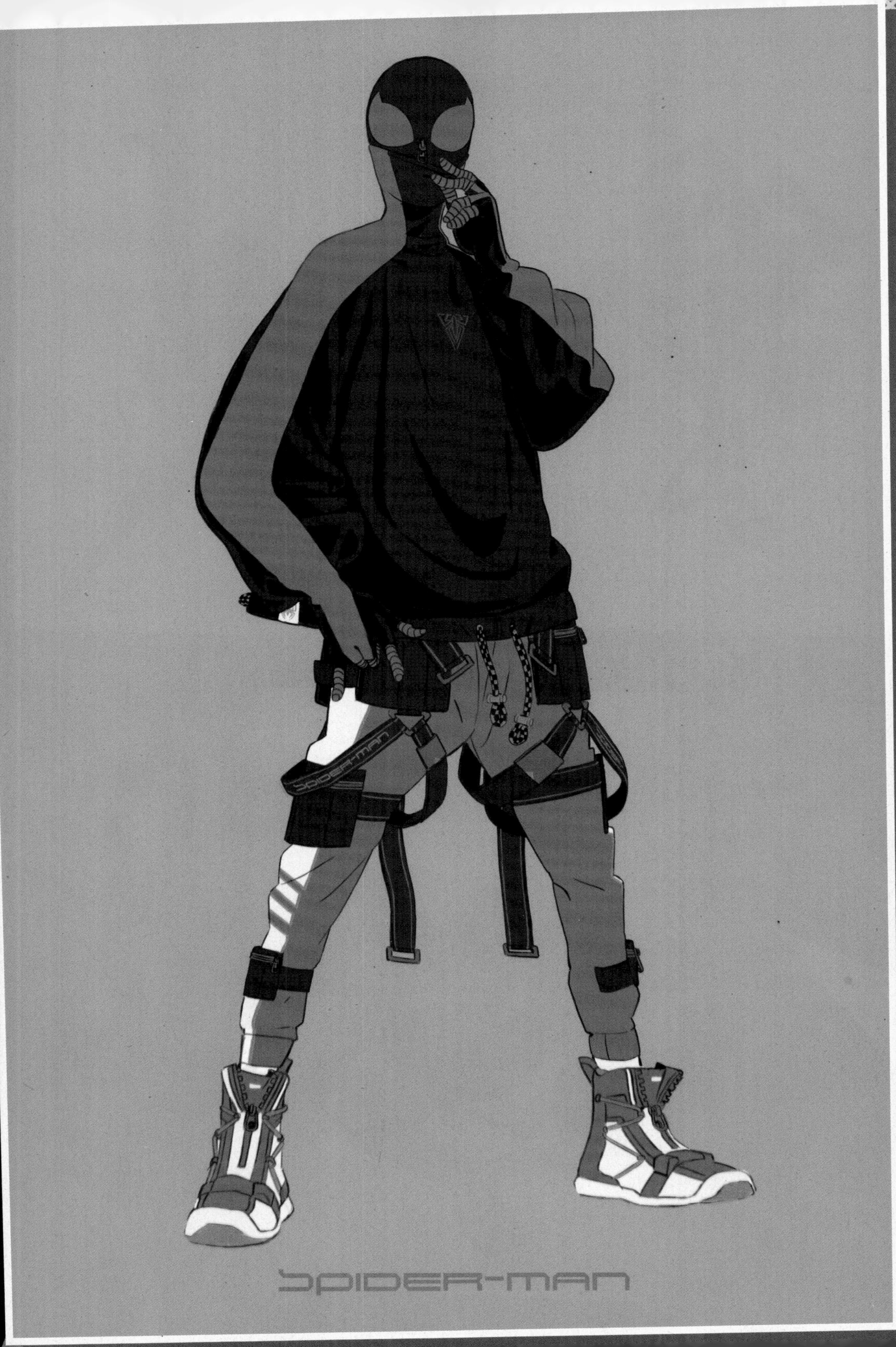
SPIDER-MAN

#30 COVER SKETCHES BY
TAURIN CLARKE

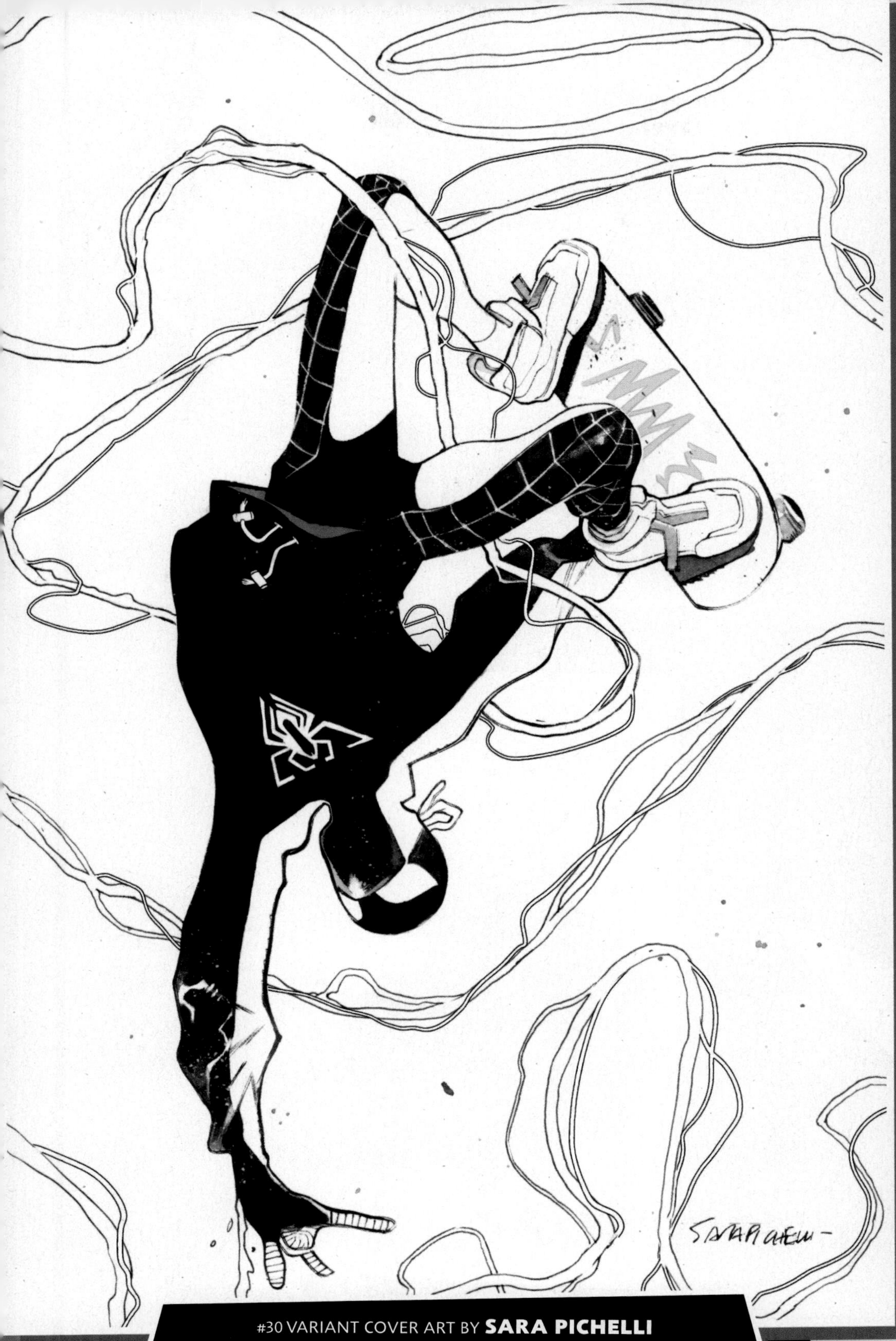

#30 VARIANT COVER ART BY **SARA PICHELLI**

#29 COVER SKETCHES BY
TAURIN CLARKE

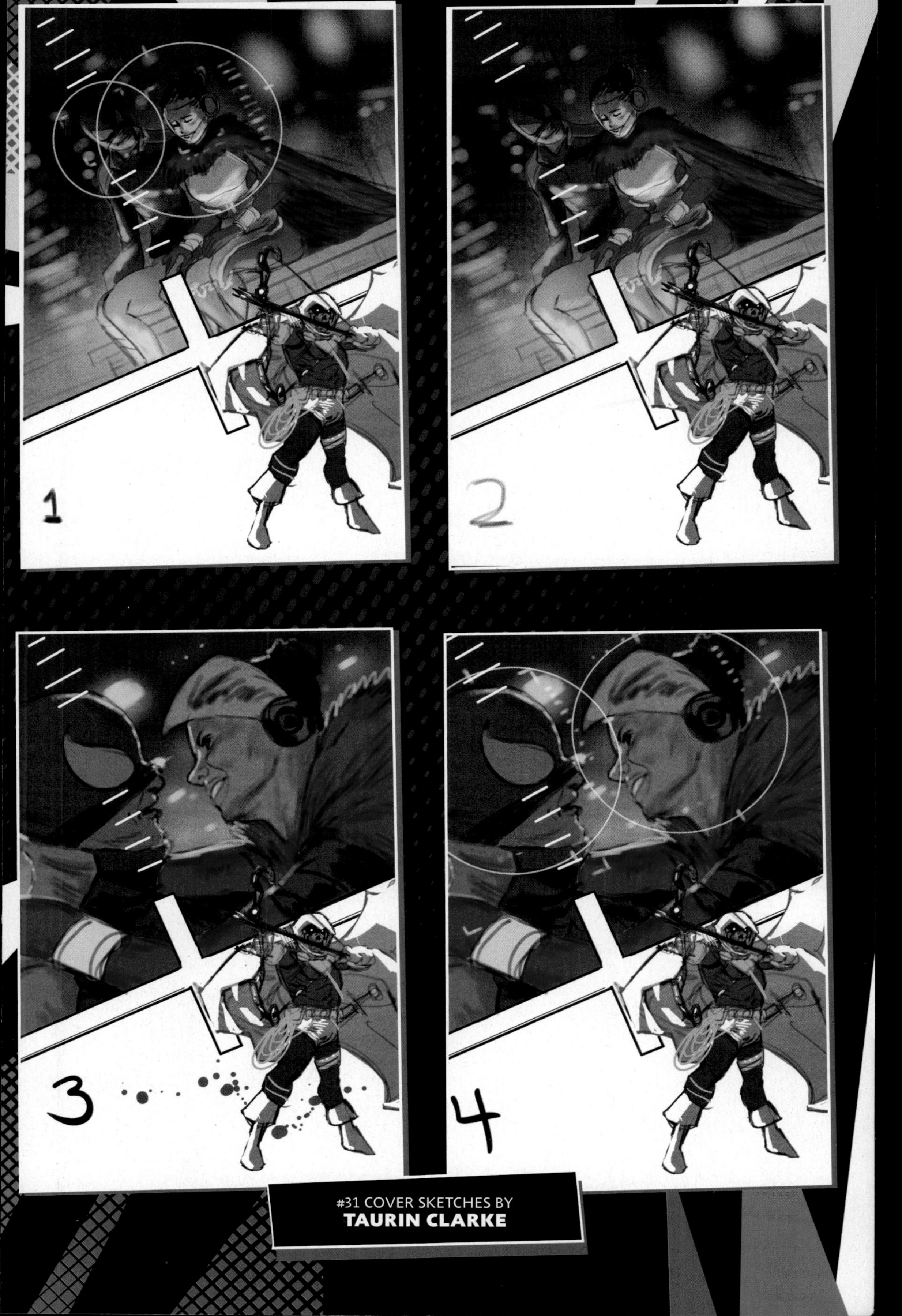
1
2
3
4

#31 COVER SKETCHES BY
TAURIN CLARKE

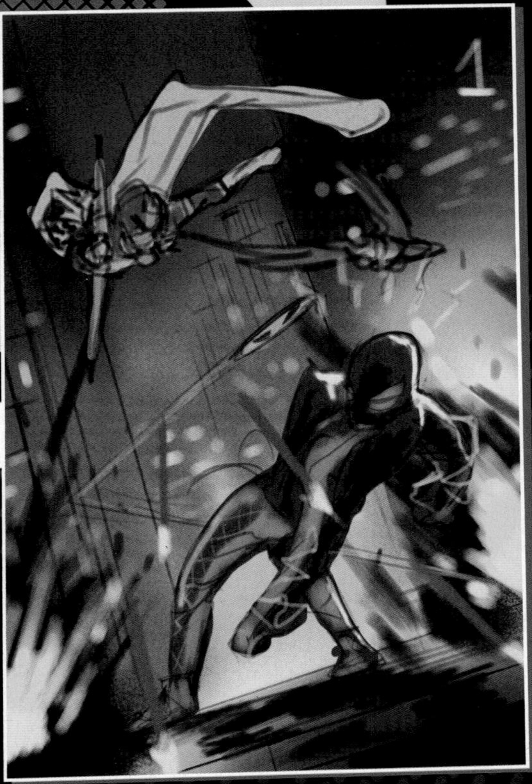
1
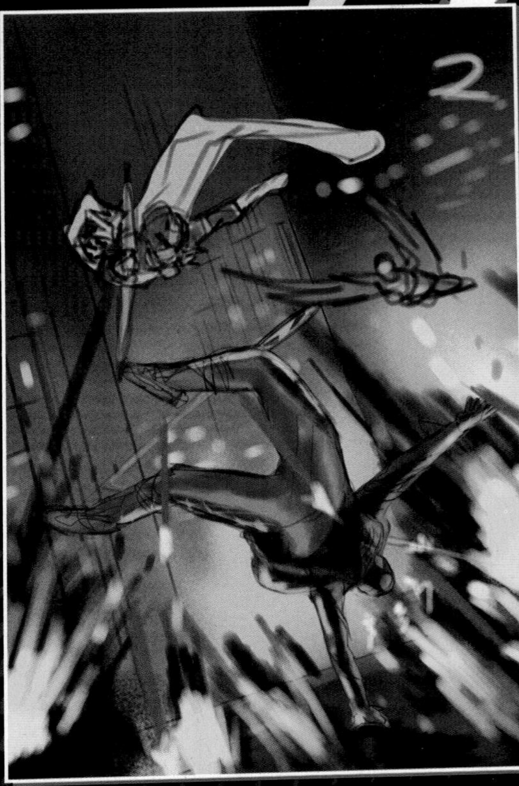
2
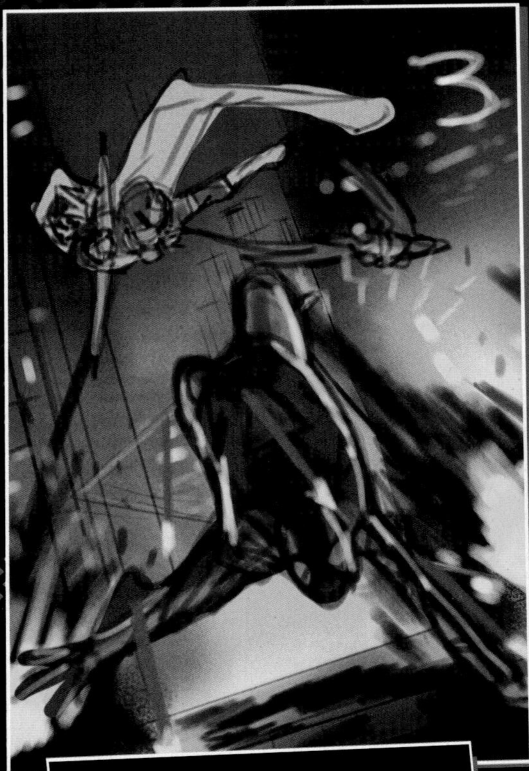
3

#32 COVER SKETCHES BY
TAURIN CLARKE